This book is a systematic introduction to the philosophy of Charles S. Peirce. It focuses on four of Peirce's fundamental conceptions: pragmatism and Peirce's development of it into what he called *pragmaticism;* his theory of signs; his phenomenology; and his theory that continuity is of prime importance for philosophy.

The author argues that at the center of Peirce's philosophical project is a unique form of metaphysical realism, whereby both continuity and evolutionary change are necessary for our understanding of experience. In his final chapter Professor Hausman applies this version of realism to current controversies between antirealists and antiidealists. Peirce's views are compared with those of such present-day figures as Davidson, Putnam, and Rorty.

The book will be of particular interest to philosophers concerned with classical American philosophy and with the relation of pragmatism to current debates on realism, as well as to linguists working in semiotics.

CHARLES S. PEIRCE'S
EVOLUTIONARY PHILOSOPHY

CHARLES S. PEIRCE'S
EVOLUTIONARY
PHILOSOPHY

CARL R. HAUSMAN

The Pennsylvania State University

CAMBRIDGE
UNIVERSITY PRESS

Published by the Press Syndicate of the University of Cambridge
The Pitt Building, Trumpington Street, Cambridge CB2 1RP
40 West 20th Street, New York, NY 10011-4211, USA
10 Stamford Road, Oakleigh, Victoria 3166, Australia

First published in 1993

Printed in the United States of America

Library of Congress Cataloging-in-Publication Data
Hausman, Carl R.
Charles S. Peirce's evolutionary philosophy / Carl R. Hausman.
p.   cm.
Includes index.
ISBN 0-521-41559-4 (hard)
1. Peirce, Charles S. (Charles Sanders), 1839–1914.
B945.P44H38   1993
191 – dc20   92-10648
CIP
A catalog record for this book is available from the British Library

ISBN 0-521-41559-4 hardback

Contents

Preface

This book has two major objectives: first, to offer an introduction for persons beginning the study of Peirce and, second, to address some of the more complex issues and problematic aspects of his thought on the assumption that these issues can be understood in terms of an overarching, coherent philosophical view – what Peirce aimed at as an architectonic. I am not concerned with criticizing Peirce's ideas, although occasionally my comments raise questions that could be pursued in terms of possible criticisms and suggested answers. I refrain from criticism primarily because I do not think this task is appropriate in an interpretive account. In addition, Peirce's way of presenting his thought seems to have been more hypothetical than categorical, continually exhibiting a commitment to fallibilism. Criticism would be proper only if one were intent on moving beyond his thought, perhaps in order to launch one's own hypotheses. There is a sense in which this latter kind of consideration may enter into what I attempt in this book. To some extent my interpretation of Peirce's aims, particularly with respect to his metaphysics, inevitably flows from certain conceptions I have about what he ought to have meant in the context of his broader, long-range perspectives.

The specific interpretations I offer were initiated more than ten years ago while I was conducting seminars on Peirce. After reflecting on the conclusions I had drawn in trying to help students read and discuss Peirce intelligently, I felt the urge to bring my conclusions and the reasons behind them into a single, sustained discussion. This concern was related to my hope to suggest to students a coherent picture of Peirce's complex and sometimes apparently conflicting views. I was, however, also motivated by a long-standing interest in problems of creativity – the meaning and possibility of explaining creative achievement and the place of creative acts in an intelligible universe. When I began studying Peirce seriously after my graduate-school days, I became increasingly aware of a certain kinship between my views and Peirce's understanding of how the universe may be intelligible without one's abandoning the idea that there is real spontaneity and, consequently – because of his interpretation of the effects of spontaneity – creativity in the world. Many of his conceptions of the relations between the conditions of intelligibility and the inexplicable aspects of the world illuminate much of what I found fascinating in my studies of creativity. His central insight concerning this relation is exhibited in his discussion of evolutionary love. Although Peirce discusses the idea of evolutionary love in figurative terms, and only briefly, the conceptions underlying it and its continuity with other aspects of his thought struck me as especially significant. My commitment to this way of approaching Peirce has been a strong stimulus to the writing of this book. I was and am convinced that Peirce deserves to be considered by anyone who is committed to the study of philosophy and all disciplines or "interdisciplines" related to his thought, such as psychology and semiotics (to use in this context the common rather than Peirce's preferred spelling, which was "semeiotic"), as well as theoretical aspects of the natural sciences.

A book of the kind I offer responds in part to the intense, growing interest in Peirce that recently has developed both in the United States and elsewhere. Some of the excitement about Peirce – and the pragmatic movement in general – finds its core in the increasing attention given to the study of issues in epistemology and the philosophy of language from the perspective of semiotics. At the same time, I believe, there is a new, or renewed, concern about metaphysical issues, even if these center on the rejection of metaphysics. Indeed, I think that some of the crucial problems raised in some of the most widely discussed recent developments in philosophy, such as deconstructionism and linguistic turns that have been used in the service of radical relativism, may be clarified if not resolved by many of Peirce's ideas that anticipated these directions in philosophy. In the last chapter, I address this possibility.

Several earlier versions of chapters and parts of chapters were presented as lectures in various contexts, the most important of which was a series of seminars at the University of Mainz, Germany. Indeed, the opportunity to give these lectures and to receive responses from students was vital to my determination to pursue this book. Articles published in *Transactions of the Charles S. Peirce Society* have been integrated with larger contexts of the chapters to which they contribute. These articles also grew out of discussions that occurred in the Peirce seminars to which I referred earlier and in conversations with students and Peirce scholars. However, the organization of the chapters in this book is independent of any chronologically characterized changes in my understanding of Peirce. This point follows from the central organizing principle, which assumes that Peirce's thought was governed by an architectonic that underlay his particular attacks on philosophical issues. There is, then, a linkage binding the different strands of his thought – in particular, fallibilism, pragmatism, semeiotic, phenomenology, antinominalism, anti-Cartesianism, and synechism or his conception of continuity – that were present at least implicitly in his outlook from the beginning of his career. I try to focus aspects of his ideas about these concerns or themes with reference to major organizing topics that were dominant for his thought late in his career, that is, after 1900. These major topics are discussed in the Introduction, which sets forth a summary and overview of the book as a whole.

It may seem remiss to end this preface without heralding the importance of Peirce not only in the history of philosophy but also for the present-day philosophical scene. However, I have always been inclined to the view that what is important "speaks" for itself. If readers do not hear what is spoken, those readers would not be impressed by a "tooting of Peirce's horn." What he said does, I think, speak for itself. Nevertheless, I do not refrain from some fairly explicit suggestions about the relevance of Peirce's philosophy for at least some of the recent developments in twentieth-century philosophy. These suggestions, I hope, show that Peirce's contribution to philosophy was not confined to what is too often assumed by those who have little more than a passing acquaintance with his work. The first of these assumptions is that his philosophical importance lies in his pragmatic conception of meaning, which was a stimulus for William James and the pragmatism that is most widely known. The second assumption (associated with perhaps a slightly more than passing acquaintance) is that Peirce anticipated logical empiricism and some of its self-generated problems. These contributions cannot be denied. Yet there are, I think, other, more fundamental contributions that come to us through his metaphysics – what I call his *evolutionary realism* – that are especially apt for the current scene. I address this point indirectly in the main body of the book and directly in the final chapter. Thus, rather than begin as some other books on Peirce frequently do, and as might be expected here, this book from the outset lets the text speak for itself with respect to its relevance to current thought – more accurately, I let Peirce's text speak for itself to the extent that I can be an instrument for this speech through my exposition.[1]

State College, Pennsylvania

[1] All refrences to writing in *Collected Papers of Charles Sanders Peirce*, volumes I–VI (Cambridge, Mass.: Belknap Press of Harvard University, 1931–5), ed. Charles Hartshorne and Paul Weiss; volumes VII and VIII (Cambridge, Mass.: Belknap Press of Harvard University, 1958), ed. Arthur W. Burks, will appear in the text in parentheses, following the standard form: the volume in Arabic numerals, a period, and the paragraph in the volume cited; using the form *CP* if necessary. References to other sources will be cited in usual note form, by referring to the recent chronological edition, *Writings of Charles S. Peirce: A Chronological Edition*, ed. Max H. Fish, Edward C. Moore, et al. (Bloomington: Indiana University Press, 1982–6), using the form *WOP* followed by page number in Arabic numerals, or by referring to manuscript numbers as they appear in Richard S. Robin's *Annotated Catalogue of the Papers of Charles S. Peirce* (Worcester: University of Massachusetts Press, 1967), using the form MS followed by the number of the manuscript. Page numbers follow the Kentner system.

Acknowledgments

My gratitude for the inspiration and thought that helped make this book an actuality is both deep and extensive. It is impossible to name all those who deserve recognition. The students in the Peirce seminars for which I have been responsible over the past ten years certainly played an important role in helping me see what issues and ideas link Peirce to the interests of the intelligent student who has had little or no background in the study of Peirce. I want to single out several former students who have themselves written on Peirce and who are now Peirce scholars. Each of them has been important to my most recent reflections on Peirce. These are, in chronological order, Douglas Anderson, Edward Petry, Felicia Kruse, and, currently, Janice Staab.

My greatest debt for detailed and substantive critiques of the book in its final stages is to Christopher Hookway. He reacted to all the chapters and offered many helpful suggestions, most of which worked their way into the text. Obviously, however, my treatment of the problems he and I discussed is not his responsibility; I suspect that he would take issue with many of my ways of dealing with them. In addition, I want to express my gratitude to persons who are not Peirce scholars by reputation but who contributed to my approach to, and conclusions about, some of Peirce's most puzzling but significant discussions: Mary Hesse, Carl Vaught, Robert Corrington, Emily Grosholz, Dale Jacquette, and Salim Kemal. I should add that over the years, there have been Peirceans who have responded to some of my work on Peirce and have contributed to my way of thinking about him: Richard Bernstein, Vincent Colapietro, Hermann Deuser, Nathan Houser, Helmut Pape, and Sandra Rosenthal.

I should like to acknowledge my appreciation to the editors of *Transactions of the Charles S. Peirce Society* for agreeing to my use of two articles they published, which appear in revised form as parts of two chapters in the book. I thank the Department of Philosophy of Harvard University for permission to quote from the Peirce papers housed in the Houghton Library. I am also grateful to all the members of the Peirce Project at Indiana University at Indianapolis for their assistance during my studies of the copies of the Peirce papers that they have available. Christian Kloesel and Nathan Houser were very gracious and helpful during that time.

For material support, I thank the National Endowment for the Humanities, from which I received a travel grant to work at the Houghton Library and at the Peirce Project. In addition, I am grateful to The College of the Liberal Arts, the Department of Philosophy, and the Institute for Arts and Humanistic Studies at The Pennsylvania State University – all of which added material support to the NEH grant. Finally, I thank Janice Staab for her copyediting, assistance in indexing, and substantive comments during the last stages of preparation of the book.

Interpretive Orientation

Before turning to the main body of this book, I should like to offer some commentary on the relation of the chapters that follow to other treatments of Peirce's philosophy, particularly in recent publications, and to state briefly how the interpretation assumed here is like and unlike these other views. This commentary should help set the book in context: First, it can serve in place of an appended bibliography – information well presented in some of the most recent books to be mentioned; second, it indicates in a very general way the relation of the following discussion to other works because, with few exceptions, I do not add to my discussion frequent references to points about which I agree or disagree with other writers.

My references to other works are made with the main themes of my own book in mind. Hence it is important to note that, as I have suggested, two overriding conceptions of Peirce's philosophy govern what is said. The first is that Peirce is a metaphysical realist of a unique kind. This thesis plays a prominent role in the chapter on evolutionary realism. The other conception is inseparable from the first; it concerns the way Peirce interwove the idea of spontaneity and radical creativity – the generation of new intelligible components of reality – with his view that what is intelligible must be general, mediated, and founded on continuity. The remarkable outcome of this interweaving of the two ideas is that it integrates continuity with discontinuity – a condition implied by the affirmation of spontaneity. It provides a picture for understanding how moments of what is inexplicable are integrated into intelligible systems.

If we look back at some of the earliest accounts of Peirce's philosophy that helped to stimulate an interest in his work, we should not overlook one strand in interpretation – the "two Peirce theory." Perhaps the key representative of this strand – an approach that provided my own introduction to Peirce – is Thomas Goudge's book *The Thought of C. S. Peirce* (Toronto: University of Toronto Press, 1950). That book serves as an introduction to Peirce, but its thesis that Peirce held two divergent philosophical orientations, a tough-minded empiricism and a speculatively developed metaphysics, is contrary to the architectonic approach I take. An earlier work by Justus Buchler also suggests that there are two "strains" in Peirce's thought, empirical and metaphysical: *Charles Peirce's Empiricism* (New York: Octagon Books, 1966; previously published by Kegan Paul, Trench, Trubner, 1939). Buchler, however, emphasizes the empirical side and regards the metaphysical side as incongruous and secondary.

A third relatively early overall account of Peirce's philosophy is found in Manley Thompson's *The Pragmatic Philosophy of C. S. Peirce* (Chicago: University of Chicago Press, 1953). This book, I think, is noteworthy for its aim to counter the conclusion that Peirce's thought reveals an inner conflict. Thompson's aims in this respect are like mine. Indeed, he places an emphasis on the connections between pragmatism and later developments in Peirce's thought that are crucial to finding an underlying architectonic. Thompson, however, is not concerned with working out the architectonic, and his approach to suggesting a coherent overview is different from mine — which is to take thematic conceptions, connect them, and drive them toward the underlying fusion of evolutionary theory with realism.

Thompson offers what I regard as a transition to works that have a somewhat different approach, that is, works that tend to interpret Peirce's thought not as self-divisive but to some extent as unified. Most of these see unity as a function of a dominant underlying theme. Books of this latter kind appeared about a decade later. One of the first books to illustrate this coherence approach was Murray Murphey's widely acclaimed and respected work on Peirce *The Development of Peirce's Philosophy* (Cambridge, Mass.: Harvard University Press, 1961). Murphey's book treats Peirce through themes, the most fundamental being the changes that occurred in Peirce's conception of logic throughout his career. Although the overall thrust counteracts the idea that there are two opposing Peirces, because differences in Peirce's thought are seen in light of his development, his approach to Peirce does not give weight to what I see as Peirce's envisaged architectonic.

Two books that are consistent with the conviction that there is unity in Peirce's thought, but without basing this unity on an evolving thread, are James K. Feibleman's volume *An Introduction to Peirce's Philosophy* (London: George Allen & Unwin, 1960) and Charles Knight's *Charles Peirce* (New York: Washington Square Press, 1965). Feibleman's book is an attempt to show that there is a system in Peirce's philosophy. Its value lies in the way in which it exhibits the comprehensiveness of Peirce's philosophy by collecting summaries and quotations on diverse areas or topics that are important to his thought. Knight's book is like Feibleman's in offering summary accounts of different topics, although it relies less on quotations and more on exposition. Neither book focuses on one major theme as the core of architectonic conceptions.

W. B. Gallie's *Peirce and Pragmatism* (New York: Dover Publications,

1965) provides an interesting and insightful introduction to Peirce. It is somewhat more thematic than Feibleman's and Knight's books, for its orientation springs from an acceptance of pragmatism as a guiding theme. Gallie achieves this without trying to found Peirce's thought as a whole on the philosophy of continuity and evolution.

Recent books (published since 1980) seem to be somewhat more thematic than Feibleman's and Knight's and even than Murphey's. These books continue the effort to show coherence in what on the surface – as Buchler and Goudge emphasized – suggests ambivalence or a philosopher with differing methods and conclusions. Robert Almeder's work *The Philosophy of Charles S. Peirce: A Critical Introduction* (Totowa, N.J.: Rowman & Littlefield, 1980) has something in common with my own intentions in addressing the issue of whether Peirce's thought has some coherence in terms of a metaphysical commitment to idealism or realism. From the point of view of my conception of Peirce's unique kind of realism, however, Almeder's conclusion strikes me as nodding more toward the idealist side than I do. My impression can perhaps be understood best in terms both of what I say in Chapter 4 about the sense in which percepts, those bits of experience that are interpreted in perceptual judgment, are "external" conditions of experience, and of what I say in that chapter and in Chapter 3, on the semeiotic, about the dynamical object. This however, is not the place to try to explain these points. My purpose is not to offer critiques of other books.

A book that depends emphatically on the thematic perspective is John F. Boler's *Charles Peirce and Scholastic Realism: A Study of Peirce's Relation to John Duns Scotus* (Seattle: University of Washington Press, 1963). The title itself indicates a significant difference from my approach. I do not limit my treatment of Peirce's realism to consideration of scholastic realism. Moreover, Boler's work does not treat the development of Peirce's thought architectonically.

One relatively recent book whose purposes might seem to overlap mine is Joseph Esposito's *Evolutionary Metaphysics: The Development of Peirce's Theory of Categories* (Athens: Ohio University Press, 1980). However, there are three major differences between that book and what follows. His work is devoted to a fair amount of explanation of Peirce's metaphysics in terms of its origins in early formulations of the three categories – categories that are treated in the chapters to follow here primarily in terms of Peirce's phenomenology. The second difference reflects the first: Esposito does not try to work out of Peirce's early pragmatism as it grows into what I call an *evolutionary realism*. The third difference lies in Esposito's interpretation of Peirce, which gives a good deal of weight to objective idealism.

Douglas Anderson's *Creativity and the Philosophy of C. S. Peirce* (Dordrecht: Martinus Nijhoff, 1987) focuses on Peirce's thought in terms of the concept of creativity, which, of course, overlaps and depends on what Peirce has to say about evolution. The spirit of Anderson's book is probably closer to mine than is that of any other I know. However, Anderson does not try to show how pragmatism is founded on a theory of continuity as well as evolution; nor does his book press the case for the unique realism that I see in Peirce.

Several other thematic books seem clearly oriented more specifically than the chapters of this book. These are Nicholas Rescher's *Peirce's Philosophy of Science* (Notre Dame, Ind.: University of Notre Dame Press, 1978), Michael L. Raposa's *Peirce's Philosophy of Religion* (Bloomington: Indiana University Press, 1989), Peter Skagestad's *The Road of Inquiry: Charles Peirce's Pragmatic Realism* (New York: Columbia University Press, 1981), and Vincent Colapietro's *Peirce's Approach to the Self* (Albany: SUNY Press, 1989). I should say that Skagestad's position seems to me to come close, perhaps closest, to mine with respect to Peirce's realism; however, it also seems to me that Skagestad does not integrate his recognition of Peirce's conception of the dynamical object – the condition that is independent of signs (language and concepts) – with the realism he sees in Peirce's statements about the ideal limit of investigation. Nor does he explore the relation of his view of Peirce's realism to Peirce's conception of evolution. Colapietro's work shares something with my approach insofar as it also gives some weight to the importance of Peirce's theory of signs in understanding his view of the self.

Finally, two books should be mentioned for special reasons. Christopher Hookway's *Peirce* (London: Routledge & Kegan Paul, 1985) has been important with regard to many of the points I try to make in discussing Peirce's pragmaticism, as have personal discussions with him. Hookway's book, however, is not intended as an interpretation that focuses on a fundamental theme that threads through architectonic conceptions but is, rather, a general critical account of Peirce's overall philosophy. I know of no other book that treats Peirce's work as a *whole* and succeeds in doing so with such detailed explanations of, and critical commentary on, Peirce's writing, parts of which are quite difficult to interpret. The other book is C. J. Misak's *Truth and the End of Inquiry: A Peircean Account of Truth* (Oxford: Clarendon Press, 1991). This, again, is oriented more toward a thematic approach, but it gives more emphasis than my discussion does to the question of the extent to which Peirce is a scientific realist as distinct from a metaphysical realist of a unique kind.

I have tried to take note of those books on Peirce, most of which are well known, that seem to me to have possible relevance to my aims, but I do not claim to have surveyed all such books. In any case,

I hope those aims are clear and that the pursuit of them will become clear in what follows. I want to introduce Peirce's thought through an account of how his pragmatism must be understood as a fallibilistic foundationalism that affirms a unique realism according to which what is real is a dynamic, evolving extramental condition.

Introduction

Beginning a book on the philosophy of Charles S. Peirce is something like entering a labyrinth with almost as many entrances as passages. What aspect of his thought provides the best entry? Should Peirce's work be considered in chronological order? Should his ideas be traced to antecedents in the history of philosophy? Should his thought be understood as representative of a school or tradition such as empiricism, rationalism, pragmatism, Aristotelianism, or scholasticism? Should he be approached as an antimetaphysician, or should his thought be interpreted more broadly in terms of his metaphysical speculations? Are there certain topics, themes, or theses that are more basic and hence best used as organizing principles in offering an account of his philosophy? These questions reflect the fact that selection, arbitrary or purposeful, is necessary at the outset. The approach to be taken in this book has a purpose. It assumes that there are basic themes in Peirce's thought that can be used as organizing principles. These themes express the two main purposes mentioned in the Preface: to introduce Peirce to readers who have had little or no acquaintance with his ideas and to propose that there is a cohesiveness in his thought that implies an architectonic – an architectonic that has at its core a special kind of realism.

Our entry into Peirce's philosophy, then, will be made through four themes, each serving as the topic of a chapter. These themes were chosen because they are foundational ingredients of his thought as a whole. Thus, they serve the idea that Peirce aimed at the construction of what he called an *architectonic*.[1] Although he did not set forth a systematic account of an architectonic, he did provide a variety of suggestions about the direction in which it would go. The four themes that will move us in that direction are pervasive enough to support their selection as architectonic building blocks. It should be pointed out, also, that the themes will be treated in an order designed to serve the reader who wants to be introduced to Peirce through what may be to some degree familiar and may serve as an initial step in moving to the more fundamental and more complex aspects of Peirce's thought.

[1]Terms mentioned rather than used will be italicized on their first occurrence in the text rather than set in quotation marks throughout.

The first theme is the part of Peirce's philosophy that is probably most widely known: the so-called pragmatic criterion of meaning, which is central to what is called *pragmatism,* but which in his later thought he preferred to call *pragmaticism.* He chose this label in order to distinguish his theory of meaning from what William James called pragmatism. Peirce believed this choice necessary because James had credited Peirce with the invention of pragmatism, and Peirce disagreed with some aspects of James's interpretation of it. Consideration of Peirce's pragmaticism and its connection with semeiotic will be integral to what follows. The second theme with which we shall be concerned is Peirce's theory of signs, or what he called *semeiotic.* The theory of signs follows directly from the first theme; it is the technical development of his theory of meaning and reveals both Peirce's conceptions of knowledge and reality. The third part of Peirce's philosophy consists of his description of the most fundamental features of all experience, which provided one of the ways in which he constructed his theory of categories. The term he used to name this endeavor was *phenomenology,* and sometimes *phaneroscopy.* The final theme concerns Peirce's theory of continuity and is what he called *synechism.* Continuity, he thought, is of prime importance in philosophy. Indeed, all things that are intelligible must be understood as unbroken relations that contain no gaps. He regarded synechism as the basis for his pragmaticism, and as an application of his categories to the world, it is essential to his metaphysics. In particular, it is essential to what I shall characterize as an evolutionary realism. Not only was reality for Peirce permeated by continuity, but it was also constantly evolving. Thus, I adopt the term *evolutionary realism.* Because the term *realism* will recur throughout the book, and because I shall try to press the case that Peirce's metaphysical convictions centered at bottom on a commitment to a unique form of realism, in a moment I shall offer some observations about distinct forms of realism and how they relate to Peirce's thought. Let us begin, then, by indicating the ways these themes are intertwined and by sketching the role they will play throughout the discussion to follow. In this way, we shall have a summary and overview of the main conceptions to be treated in more detail in the main body of the text. After presenting this outline of what is to come, I shall indicate the way in which the approach assumed in treating these themes should be distinguished from other major interpretations of Peirce as they are illustrated in several books that have been published over the past ten years or so.

With the four components of Peirce's philosophy as points of departure, the topics of each chapter will be developed as follows. Chapter 1 focuses on the origins of pragmaticism in two early articles, "The Fixation of Belief" and "How to Make Our Ideas Clear"; Chapter 2 is concerned with the rise of semeiotic out of the early criterion of meaning offered in the second of these articles; the third chapter considers the three phenomenological categories and their relation to semeiotic; Chapter 4 moves from phenomenology and semeiotic to synechism. In the concluding chapter, I consider an application of Peirce's philosophy to an understanding of contemporary issues: Peirce's evolutionary architectonic will be viewed as a response to anti-metaphysical realism as proposed in the much discussed views of Richard Rorty, Donald Davidson, and Hilary Putnam.

My main task is tantamount to attempting to outline the architectonic Peirce had hoped to develop. Needless to say, treatment of the topics that contribute to this envisaged architectonic in the relatively short space of this book must serve primarily as a beginning. I can do little more than offer a sketch.

In proposing the outlines of Peirce's envisaged architectonic, I presuppose a view opposed to the two-Peirce conception found in other interpreters, whether this conception takes the form of dividing Peirce's thought into incompatible empirical and metaphysical concerns or into what seems to me to be a weaker dichotomy of epistemology and metaphysics. As already suggested, my approach to this issue presupposes that however diverse Peirce's various analyses and speculations may be, he, as a logician, worked under what was at least a regulative ideal of an overarching, coherent framework that embraced the many facets of his thought. This framework is the idea of an architectonic that undergirds my interpretation of Peirce's philosophy. The architectonic depends on the idea of continuity and, again as already indicated, a form of realism that distinguishes his most fundamental metaphysical commitment from objective idealism – a perspective that seems to pervade much recent commentary on Peirce's metaphysics.[2]

In order to make this last point defensible, I must give a brief account of my assumptions about realism as distinct from objective idealism. I understand the term realism to apply to at least three ways of understanding the world or of accounting for the way knowledge and experience in general are constrained by what is known or experienced. First, realism may apply to what in the history of philosophy has been called *scholastic realism*. In short, this is the view that there are repeatable conditions that are independent of mental acts and

---

[2]As will be pointed out in Chapter 4, this form of metaphysical commitment might better be labeled in a way that excludes the term *realism,* for the term has associations with a commitment to attaining truth about a fixed, determinate object that is independent of any particular theoretical framework – it is that to which all theories are expected to approximate or be adequate. Peirce's realism transcends this conception of a structured, determinate reality. Yet I use the term *realism* because it conforms to the vocabulary of his historical context and because it seems to me to fit one of the kinds of positions to be outlined in a moment.

that function like rules for the ways particular things behave. This form of realism is emphatically affirmed by Peirce in his later writing, and it will be characterized further when we encounter it in his discussions of pragmatism and pragmaticism. A second view of what constrains thought, which may be regarded as form of realism, is *materialism*. The kind of materialism I have in mind is that which supposes that everything in principle can be understood as identical with or a manifestation of (can be reduced or completely understood with reference to) physical entities and processes. Peirce rejected materialism and his realism should not be thought of as belonging to it. The third application of the term realism is to the view that there are constraining conditions on knowing and experiencing that transcend or are not reducible to mental processes, even if those processes are thought to be independent of particular minds or conscious agents. This is what I believe Peirce was committed to in his architectonic or metaphysical realism. Just what more can be said about the extramental conditions on Peirce's behalf, however, must wait until we have worked through the architectonic themes that are the topics of the chapters of this book. Someone might agree with Peirce in opposing the second form of realism and do so from the vantage point of objective idealism, the view that the constraining condition on all acts of thinking is a transcendent mental reality – an absolute mind that is more fundamental than any particular mental processes. Thus, all reality would embody ideas and sense-qualities; this, of course, conflicts with materialism. This view is easily attributed to Peirce for reasons we shall see later. I shall try to show, however, that as close as Peirce may be to objective idealism, he is closer to the last form of realism I mentioned.

That others have looked on Peirce as an objective idealist is illustrated by Joseph L. Esposito and leading members of the semiotic movement that owes much to Peirce's semeiotic.[3] Esposito notes a commonly quoted statement in which Peirce says of objective idealism that it is "the one intelligible theory of the universe." As I shall point out later, however, to offer this quotation as evidence that Peirce's most fundamental persuasion committed him to objective idealism ignores not only the context of Peirce's statement but also his complaint that Hegel's is a wooden logic and his own insistence that dialectical development does not culminate in the overcoming or even subsumption of either of his first two categories. This is a way of showing that Peirce believed resistance to the full intelligibility of the evolving universe persists into the infinite future. In his valuable and detailed

---

[3]Joseph L. Esposito, *Evolutionary Metaphysics: The Development of Peirce's Theory of Categories* (Athens: Ohio University Press, 1980).

overview of Peirce's philosophy, Christopher Hookway, I think, also underemphasizes Peirce's wish to maintain a form of realism, at least of the kind I am proposing.[4] My reason for suggesting this will be indicated later. The way some interpreters overlook or miss Peirce's leaning toward a kind of metaphysical realism will be considered at greater length in subsequent chapters. With this preliminary comment about my assumption in mind, let me summarize and anticipate the main points to be made in each of the main chapters of the book. My summary is intended to provide an overview the details of which will be filled in as we proceed through each chapter.

The Origins of Pragmaticism

"The Fixation of Belief" and "How to Make Our Ideas Clear," originally appearing in 1877 and 1878 respectively, are probably the best known of all Peirce's essays.[5] For some, they represent the whole of his philosophy. As a pair, they make up an early statement of Peirce's theory of inquiry. Both show Peirce's commitment to the idea that the natural sciences may function as models of the proper way to gain knowledge. In the first article, "the scientific method" is embraced almost, as Peirce puts it, the way one chooses a bride, while other methods of inquiry – tenacity, authority, and apriority – are rejected. In order to see why they are rejected, we should look briefly at the argument as a whole. Some of the reasons that make up this argument lay the basis for those other aspects of Peirce's thought to be treated in this book.

Three points in this early essay deserve to be emphasized because of their importance to the development of Peirce's thought. The first concerns the idea of the roles in inquiry of doubt (which occurs when regularity or habit is disrupted) and belief (which occurs when regularity or habit is established). The purpose of inquiry for Peirce is to settle doubt by replacing it with belief. Unless there were doubt, real felt doubt about some definite incongruity in experience, there would be no inquiry, no active thinking. The process of inquiring is a struggle to overcome the irritation of doubt. Doubt, however, can be settled by means other than thinking. It can be settled by any one of the three methods already mentioned a moment ago. The first method is used when stubborn resistance to doubt is invoked and belief is sustained by tenacity based on prejudice that remains unquestioned and uncriticized. The second method resolves doubt by the fiat of author-

---

[4]Chrisopher Hookway, *Peirce* (London: Routledge & Kegan Paul, 1985). See especially the last chapter.
[5]"The Fixation of Belief" and "How to Make Our Ideas Clear," in *Collected Papers of Charles Sanders Peirce*.

ity. The third method settles doubt by an appeal to untested intuition or self-evidence. None of these methods can be sustained, however, without resistance – resistance imposed on the believer either from brute encounters with something in nature or from social pressures.

The second point to be stressed is that a final community would be reached if inquiry were continued into the infinite future. This is suggested by Peirce's conviction that a basic social impulse would inevitably overcome any beliefs held on the basis of any one of the three methods just mentioned. Each of these methods is exclusive, or dependent on a limited number of inquirers, and each supposes itself to be infallible. In contrast, the method of science, by virtue of its very design, is directed toward the aims of the social impulse – that is, toward the agreement of an expanded, final community rather than a limited number of inquirers who agree with one another at some assigned time. The role of a final community is crucial to the kind of realism that undergirds Peirce's thought from the early – although not the earliest – stages of his career.

Finally, it should be noted that the scientific method presupposes something that is independent of inquiry, some objective condition that would in the long run fulfill the cognitive aims of every inquirer. This condition is reality. Reality is what would be the object of truth, or the opinion of a "final community" arrived at in the long run. This idea is crucial for Peirce's realism. In "The Fixation of Belief," the presupposition of an independent reality – an "external permanency" – is acknowledged as a "fundamental hypothesis" about the object of scientific investigation. Peirce does not try to demonstrate the hypothesis, but he does think that it accounts for the hope of future agreement or a goal that justifies pursuing inquiry.

These three points, then, serve as the basis of Peirce's pragmaticism, which, as I shall try to show, is itself based on a form of evolutionary realism.

The second article, "How to Make Our Ideas Clear," is directly seminal for both pragmaticism and semeiotic. The so-called pragmatic maxim of meaning, which Peirce proposes as a criterion of clarity, is found in this essay.

It appears, then, that the rule for attaining the third grade of clearness of apprehension is as follows: Consider what effects that might conceivably have practical bearings we conceive the object of our conception to have. Then, our conception of these effects is the whole of our conception of the object. (5.402)

Unfortunately, the particular wording of the criterion seems unnecessarily complex, and for some – Brand Blanshard, for instance – it is "a mass of confusion," which is "depressing," because it was offered by a logician.[6] Whether this appraisal is fair need not concern us. The wording of the maxim does permit our determining the kind of expectations suggested in the maxim for ascertaining the meanings of ideas.

It must be emphasized at the outset that the criterion proposed is intended as a way to assess the meanings of general terms. It is questionable whether nongeneral terms can be meaningful. Peirce doubts, for instance, that proper names can be said to have meaning. If they do, that meaning would need to be found in general concepts with which the proper name is associated. It should also be noted that he revises his criterion of meaning in later reflections on what William James and other contemporaries believed Peirce meant. Further, his revisions enable him to clarify the distinction between his view and all forms of nominalism. They point out that meaning must be composed of what is at once general and real. Meaning, as general, depends on what Peirce called *would-be's*, which are patterns according to which occur the outcomes of actions and consequences relevant to the idea in question. Would-be's are conditions that function much like rules, by leading to certain kinds of consequences that would be encountered if the general, or rule, were applied to the world. Thus, according to the maxim, the meaning of "hard" is determined by tests such as attempting to scratch it and finding that it will not be scratched by many other substances. Meaning is to be understood as disclosed in dispositional conditions, in habits, according to which the meaning or would-be could be expected to be exemplified if the concept that articulates the meaning were put to the test.

Peirce's formulation of the rule for attaining clarity in this early work does not obviously indicate that the criterion has to do with general terms and with would-be's. Indeed, Peirce interprets the question of testing in a more nominalistic way than he does later. In addressing the question whether a diamond that never will be tested for hardness is really hard or soft, he says in 1878 that the issue would be settled with reference to our modes of speech. When he returns to this point in the later discussions of pragmaticism, however, he acknowledges that he had been too quick in regarding the issue as only a matter of language. This acknowledgment is the occasion for explaining what he should have meant, namely, that "nomenclature involves classification; and classification is true or false, and the generals to which it refers are either reals in the one case, or figments in the other" (5.453). The seeds for this point and accordingly, for the refinements Peirce proposes later in order to emphasize the reference of the maxim to generals, can be seen in the original quotation if we focus on the

---

[6]Brand Blanshard, *Reason and Analysis* (La Salle, Ill.: Open Court, 1962), p. 194.

expression *might conceivably*. This expression suggests a criterion that does not require a concept to have actual, practical bearings. Instead, it refers to possibility, to what *would* occur if the idea of hardness *were* tested. If the original maxim is reformulated in terms of Peirce's aim in his fully developed pragmaticism, the realism already affirmed in "The Fixation of Belief" will be obvious. In the comment on the truth value of classification and its reference to generals, which for Peirce are reals, he stresses the point that meaning has to do not with what *did* happen, but with what investigation *would* lead to. Let me quote a relatively long passage from a 1905 paper.

Pragmaticism makes the ultimate intellectual purport of what you please to consist in conceived conditional resolutions, . . . and therefore, the conditional propositions, with their hypothetical antecedents, in which such resolutions consist, being of the ultimate nature of meaning, must be capable of being true, that is, of expressing whatever there be which is such as the proposition expresses, independently of being thought to be so in any judgment, or being represented to be so in any other symbol of any man or men. But that amounts to saying that possibility is sometimes of a real kind. (5.453)

The realism toward which Peirce was led in his expansion of pragmaticism, then, was, as he sometimes seemed proud to announce, a realism of a rather extreme sort. He characterizes this form of realism sometimes as scholastic and sometimes as Platonic. It seems to me that the term *Platonic* is appropriate insofar as he thought that generals are real, independent, dynamic, ordering conditions that are not exhausted by, but are effective with respect to, sequences in which particular empirical consequences are encountered.

Semeiotic and Pragmaticism

There is an obvious connection between pragmaticism and Peirce's semeiotic. The pragmaticist's maxim is a criterion of meaning, and the essential vehicle of meaning is the sign. Further, concepts that have meaning are referential to the meanings they have. If, then, a concept has meaning, it must be a sign that has an object. This object, in part, consists of the consequences referred to by the sign. Peirce refines his account of the relationship between a concept or sign and its meaning in his analysis of the sign situation – that is, the process in which signs function in rendering experience intelligible. Meaning, then, is a relationship among three components: sign, interpreter, and object. Let me again quote from a fragment written in 1897.

A sign, or *representamen*, is something which stands to somebody for something in some respect or capacity. It addresses somebody, that is, it creates in the mind of that person an equivalent sign, or perhaps a more developed sign. That sign which it creates I call the *interpretant* of the first sign. The sign stands for something, its *object*. It stands for that object, not in all respects, but in reference to a sort of idea, which I have sometimes called the *ground* of the representamen. "Idea" is here to be understood in a sort of Platonic sense, very familiar in everyday talk. (2.228)

Although the quotation comes from a rather late stage of Peirce's thought, the basis for this conception of the sign situation can be found in a manuscript, "On A New List of Categories" (1.545–567), written even earlier (1867) than the two articles that served to introduce his pragmaticism.

In any case, what needs emphasizing is that signs are not simply dyadic relations in which something called a sign stands for an object. For a sign to be meaningful it must function in a triadic relation in which sign and object interact with interpretation. This implies that signs function in ongoing processes of interpretation; however, their semeiotic meaning is never exhausted by any finite context of interpretation. Every sign is caught up in an interpretive web. At the same time, however, interpretation is itself grounded in something that prevents interpretation from being arbitrary. One reason for the resistance to arbitrariness has been overlooked by some commentators who believe themselves to be adopting Peirce's theory of signs. The reason lies in what Peirce says about the way a sign stands for something *in some respect*. The respect is the *ground* of the sign or representamen. It is "a sort of Platonic Idea." As has been suggested in connection with Peirce's explanation of pragmaticism, the respect or ground is a general, which is to be a dispositional condition for the meaning of the sign. Thus, meaning is grounded in a real, a condition that functions in part independently of any particular sign and any particular interpretation. The real that functions this way is the intelligible side of the object, and it links sign and object through the mediation of an interpretant; that is, it is the object as immediate, or as represented for the interpreter. But because it functions in partial independence from the interpretive side, the ground of the sign relation has an objective side, or an aspect of otherness. For Peirce this is the basis for the object functioning as what he calls *dynamical*. This aspect of the object functions as an external constraint, or as the object insofar as it manifests resistances encountered in the process of interpretation. The function of grounds in relation to the objects of signs can be clarified to some extent by a brief consideration of Peirce's phenomenology.

The Phenomenological Categories and Semeiotic

Peirce's discussions of phenomenology serve not only as descriptions of his categories but also as descriptions of the most pervasive factors in experience that frame the fundamental basis for his metaphysics. Peirce thought of his phenomenology as concerned with a "short list" as distinct from a "long list" of categories. The latter set of categories concerns forms of judgment and modes of thought as they delineate classes or kinds of predication that organize phenomena. The former concerns the broadest categories or aspects of all phenomena. Peirce identifies three such categories, which, he insists, are inextricably interwoven and present to consciousness, no matter what the particular phenomenon. They cannot be isolated from one another in any given instance. Any one of them, however, may be more dominant in any given phenomenon; and the first and second categories, the autonomous, qualitative aspect of phenomena and the brute compulsiveness of phenomena, may be distinguished in terms of an abstractive process of what Peirce calls *prescinding*. By means of this kind of abstraction, the first category can be considered as distinct from the second and third and the second as distinct from the third, the general and mediating aspect of phenomena. The third cannot be prescinded from the others. It is the richest in the sense that when it is considered as characteristic of a phenomenon, it presupposes and is describable in terms of, although not reducible to, the other two categories.

Peirce's phenomenological analysis is opposed to atomism of the sort found in British empiricism. The analysis is not undertaken as if there were discrete bits of sense-data that serve as building blocks for our ideas. Sense-data are products of analysis. Instead, Peirce's phenomenology begins in the midst of things, within a total experiential situation in which phenomena are given as complex wholes. Initially, what can be discriminated as the indecomposable elements or categories of these wholes are considered without respect to whether they are real or unreal. It is in this loose sense that the attitude governing the analysis is phenomenological. This attitude is provisional, however. Peirce does not sustain his metaphysical neutrality. Rather, he also regards the categories of phenomenology as modes of being. Let us briefly consider Peirce's exposition of the categories.

The first category, called *Firstness*, is the category of quality. Every phenomenon has a qualitative aspect, or an immediate presence that offers the phenomenon as sheer possibility. Firstness also is monadic in the sense that it is that aspect of a phenomenon which gives it its presence such as it is regardless of anything else. In this respect it has no relation to any other phenomenon. Because of this absence of relation beyond itself, the qualitative character of a phenomenon does not have any specific, identifiable character as a particular quality. Peirce's first category might be likened to the idea of Kant's manifold of sense ready to be structured and made intelligible. Illustration of this category, then, poses a problem, because once any instance is named, it is no longer immediate. Once specific identification occurs, or once characterization begins, we have another category functioning. Perhaps the least misleading way to suggest an illustration is to call attention to feeling as present in the way an aura surrounds something. We orient ourselves toward things in the world so that there is a feeling tone that pervades all discriminated objects of experience.

The second category may be regarded as the category of facticity. It is that aspect of phenomena encountered as resistance. Qualities as such do not resist. But as embodied, they do. Thus, whatever is encountered is experienced as fact, as something that to some extent resists or reacts against our will. The need to acknowledge *Secondness* can be seen by noting that when one thing, the first, is related to a second thing, there is a degree of opposition in the contrast between the two relata. Further, resistance is manifest when phenomena are attended to as something other than the consciousness doing the attending. Because of the resistance encountered in phenomena independently of being interpreted, Peirce refers to Secondness as something brute. Secondness is illustrated each moment when we encounter resistance to our will and each time we discriminate differences among things; yet Secondness is prior to the intelligibility of these discriminations.

The idea that phenomena are brute with respect to their Secondness calls attention to Peirce's view that the first two categories are not in themselves categories of intelligibility. These first two aspects of all phenomena do not make phenomena intelligible. Intelligibility requires mediation, a relation of one thing to another by means of a third. Insofar as phenomena are intelligible, they are components in mediating relations. Mediating relations exemplify the third category, or *Thirdness*. Thus, Thirdness is triadic, whereas Firstness, as mentioned, is monadic and Secondness is dyadic.

Thirdness is also characterizable as the general aspect of phenomena. It is that aspect of what we encounter that exhibits persistence through repeatable exemplifications. Because characterization requires reference to what can be identified in more than one instance or example, the repeatable aspects of phenomena make it possible to characterize things. As a condition of characterizing aspects of phenomena, Thirdness is the counterpart of cognitive attention (although cognitive attention itself instances Thirdness). Further, what appears to cognition includes a hypothetical element, a feature by virtue of which dispositions – or conditions of application to future data – serve as the habits that make up the world, insofar as the world is intelligible. Thirdness, then, is the category of law as such, of the lawfulness of phenomena, which prompts us to predict things and events on the basis of tendencies observed in phenomena. The Thirdness of phenomena invites prediction, even though no specific prediction can be actually and completely fulfilled. Because Thirdness is the hypothetical, repeatable aspect of phenomena, it is the counterpart and exemplar of thought, of what is cognitive in experience. Cognition depends on connections among things. As lawfulness, Thirdness is that aspect that gives things their tendency to be connected with other things. Thirdness is exhibited in what Peirce calls *generals*, which are like scholastic universals that have a dynamic function – a point to be emphasized later.

Consideration of the category of Thirdness must now be extended to the question of the relation of the phenomenological categories to semeiotic. One way to approach this is to consider two ways in which Peirce illustrates Thirdness. Let me stress the fact that unlike the first and second categories, illustration of this third category is straightforward. This is to be expected, because Thirdness is not prescinded away from the object of cognition, as the others must be in order to be described. As pointed out, Thirdness is the category of intelligibility, which means for Peirce that it is present in phenomena insofar as they are related to one thing through another. On the basis of mediating connections, phenomena can be given predicates, which are identifiable through general terms that express the repeatable mediating connections among phenomena. Thus, Thirdness is exemplified in triadic relations. One example that Peirce found particularly helpful in explaining the nature of a genuine, mediated, triadic relation is that of the activity of giving. In such an activity, there are three relata, the giver, the thing given, and the receiver. The relation of giving cannot be reduced to any pair in this relation, because giving does not consist in an agent surrendering something and then another agent taking that thing. Such laying down and picking up could occur if the first agent lost rather than gave something to someone else. The meaning of genuine giving requires all three relata that are continuous in relation to one another by virtue of the whole triadic relation called *giving*.

A second example is of particular importance for showing the relation of the categories to semeiotic. A genuine instance of Thirdness is found in the sign situation. Here again there are three relata interacting in interdependence: the sign, the object, and interpreter or interpretant. Meaning can only take place when all three components are functioning and affecting one another. Thus, to return to the early conception of how to ascertain meaning, we can see that the category of Thirdness was implicit in what Peirce said as he refined his maxim. Conceivable effects are the meaning of a term just to the extent that they are in the process of being embodied according to rules, the conditions operative in generals – in dispositions to behave in certain ways. Likewise, the meaning of a genuine sign is a law or habit of embodiment.

It is worth noting that, for Peirce, all genuine triadic relations involve meaning, because a genuine triad cannot be broken into two dyads, and the third component of the triad constitutes that triad as a meaningful whole. To put it another way, a genuine triad is genuine because thought or meaning binds together the relata of the triad.

Still further connections between phenomenology and semeiotic can be seen in one of Peirce's classifications of signs. Each class that he discriminates can be correlated with one of the categories. The three kinds of signs in the classification of importance here are: symbol, index, and icon. Beginning with iconic signs, we can see that they instance Firstness in that they function as signs by virtue of an immediate or unmediated relation to their objects. The first of Peirce's subdivision of icons, the immediate relation between icon and object, is illustrated in pictures that signify what they picture through resemblance. Qualities present in the picture are present in the object of the picture. This is not to say that the qualities that iconically connect a picture with its object count as nothing but instances of Firstness. To characterize these things is already to take them beyond the status of pure immediacy. Icons, however, are those kinds of signs that are closest to being adequate illustrations of Firstness. They are monadic in being signs in terms of a qualitative aspect, and this qualitative aspect is just what it is apart from any other thing.

The second kind of sign is the index. An indexical sign stands in dyadic relation to its object. A bullet hole, for instance, is an index of a bullet. A demonstrative pronoun is an index of what it denotes. Although a dyadic relation is not mediated by a third relatum, it is not reducible to its relata — the hole and the bullet, or pronoun and what is denoted, in isolation from one another. Indexical relations are references. It is with respect to its indexicality that a sign refers to its object. As dyadic, the relation exemplifies two things standing in an unmediated relation. The relation is not general, although it may contribute to general relations that are themselves thirds. Further, because there is a contrast between the two relata in the dyad, the index and its object, an index manifests a kind of resistance and is correlated semeiotically with Secondness.

Symbols are instances of Thirdness par excellence. They are genuinely intelligible signs. Their intelligibility is the outcome of their being interpreted, as illustrated by the examples of giving and meaning. Both giving and meaning are intelligible triadic relations with respect to the role of interpretation. A symbol is a sign interpreted with respect to the way it refers to an object. Interpretation, then, is added to the monadic and dyadic relations of iconic and indexical signs to form the full, triadic sign relation. This triadic relation implies that icons and indexes as such are not intelligible until they are a given place in a system of interpretation. It was only by prescission from the symbols that constitute our systems of interpretation that I have characterized icons and indexes as if they could function meaningfully in isolation from symbolic functions. But such prescinding is not necessary for symbols. A symbol presents its meaning as a rule of interpretation. In fact, the interpretation of a symbol is an activity of finding rules for the way the symbol refers to its object. The rule that is found is a general; as such, it is an instance of Thirdness. At the same time, the rule is an interpretation that turns into a further symbol – as should be expected of genuine sign situations that are components of interpretive webs, and as should be expected of instances of Thirdness that are components of the web of habits or regularities that make up the intelligible world.

The last point about the way symbols or generals, regarded as instances of Thirdness, are integral to systems leads to our fourth topic: the move from phenomenology and semeiotic to metaphysics.

Foundations in Synechism

We have already seen that Peirce committed himself, early in his career, to a general kind of metaphysics that is something like a form of scholastic realism. Peirce's conception of generals as reals was not, as indicated earlier, a commitment to the reality of universals in the sense in which universals are construed as static, completely determinate identities. For Peirce, generals are dynamic; they are tendencies that grow. A general should not be thought of apart from a telos. With respect to being a habit, a third or general is what it is by virtue of its influence on its future instances. A general is developmental, leading toward a more and more determinate realization of what had been unrealized. Generals can grow – first, individually, by changing identity or by being modified as rules can be modified, and, second, as complexes of intelligible identities or rules that contribute their intelligibilities to an evolving system of generals.

The idea of evolving generals is, I think, one of the most important dimensions of Peirce's metaphysics and even of his philosophy as a whole. The idea seems to me to be key to the architectonic he had hoped to construct. How this is so must be considered in terms of what he says about spontaneity and determinism as well as the way he characterizes synechism. But let us first look at his conception of synechism.

It was said earlier that synechism was the basis for pragmaticism. Thus, Peirce says that the proof of pragmaticism "would essentially involve the establishment of the truth of synechism" (5.415 [written in 1905]). Elsewhere, he indicates what he means by *synechism*. The term refers to "that tendency of philosophical thought which insists upon the idea of continuity as of prime importance in philosophy and, in particular, upon the necessity of hypotheses involving true continuity" (6.169).[7] However, the idea of *continuity* underwent changes throughout Peirce's career. Earlier, he regarded continua as infinitely divisible, and in other contexts, he wrote of a continuum as that which contains its own limit. His latest accounts of it seem to emphasize the point that what is continuous should not be understood in terms of divisibility into parts. Rather, a continuum is what can never be filled by parts. Thus he says, "A continuum, where it *is* continuous and unbroken, contains no definite parts; that its parts are created in the act of defining them and the precise definition of them breaks the continuity" (6.168). Immediately after defining "synechism," he says that "a true continuum is something whose possibilities of determination no multitude of individuals can exhaust" (6.170). The point is that Peirce insisted that there be no break in the connections among whatever is intelligible.

If continuity is the ground of synechism and the truth of synechism is the proof of pragmaticism, then continuity must be essential to understanding pragmaticism. How it is essential can be seen in what pragmaticism must presuppose about explaining phenomena. Let me quote Peirce again.

In short, synechism amounts to the principle that inexplicabilities are not to be considered as possible explanations; that whatever is supposed to be ultimate is supposed to be inexplicable; that continuity is the absence of ultimate parts in that which is divisible; and that the form under which alone anything can be understood is the form of generality, which is the same thing as continuity. (6.173)

Thus, if pragmaticism requires that understanding be founded on generals, and generals are continua, then the basis of synechism, continuity, is essential to the proof of pragmaticism.

The link between continuity and generals calls attention again to the essential place of Peirce's realism as a basis for pragmaticism. But it also suggests the cohesiveness of the different parts of Peirce's philosophy – semeiotic and phenomenology, as well as synechism and pragmaticism. For the idea of continuity, as this is seen in the role generals play in determining pragmaticistic meaning, is crucial to the idea of semeiosis, or the process of sign interpretation. And the idea of continuity also can be seen as an ingredient in the phenomenolog-

[7]From an 1902 article in *Baldwin's Dictionary of Philosophy and Psychology,* vol. 2 (New York: Macmillan, 1902).

ical category of Thirdness sustained by the mediation and regularities that are threaded through experience and which give us the sense that experience is headed somewhere and that we find prediction to be bound up with intelligible experience. There are, of course, many complexities that deserve exploration. There is one issue in particular, however, that must be broached if this sketch is to represent what I hope is an adequate overview of Peirce's philosophy as a whole. This issue concerns the relation of synechism to Peirce's view that semeioses and Thirdness are evolutionary.

The difficulty in bringing these two essential parts of Peirce's philosophy together can be seen when we notice that he hypothesizes that spontaneity is a real ingredient in the world. He even refers to the condition of spontaneity as an agency. He makes this point in his dispute with necessitarians – his chief quarrel being with mechanistic or efficient causal determinists, though his argument applies to any view that construes all events as predictable in principle. Referring to the evidence he has selected to support his argument, he says, "From these broad and ubiquitous facts we may fairly infer, by the most unexceptional logic, that there is probably in nature some agency by which the complexity and diversity of things can be increased" (6.58). Moreover, in his discussion of cosmic evolution, Peirce proposes the idea of *agape,* which is the operative principle of what he calls "evolutionary love." Agape is a kind of love that is open to the variations, even the deviations, of laws and the agencies of laws. Peirce thus rejects the idea that there was a set of laws, all fixed or determined at some alleged beginning of the world, and covering all details of things and events now and in the future. Such a determinist's view could only explain diversity by supposing that all details of diversity and irregularity, as we find them in the world and expect them to be present in the future, had been present in the laws from the beginning. Peirce thinks this view farfetched, believing that a more reasonable view is that unpredictable deviations from laws, and the growth and diversity observable all around us, are and will be a real part of the universe. Thus, he affirms cosmic evolution.

For Peirce, then, developmental teleology prevails at all levels and all stages of evolution. A personality, to cite one of Peirce's own examples, is subject to change in terms of this sort of teleology. Thus, Peirce says that a personality is a coordination of ideas – or, as we can infer, a coordination of generals or habits. And such a coordination is a teleological harmony in which there is purposive pursuit of ends. But the purposes functioning here not only are not predeterminate ends, they also are, or may be, ends generated by the personality itself. Thus, a telos can be sui generis. There is novelty in the world, and we can expect there to be novelty in the future.

This insistence on the novelty of the world is consistent with what Peirce says in other places. He differentiates himself from Hegel by pointing out his own conviction that freshness (under the category of Firstness) and resistance (under the category of Secondness) will not be overcome in some final end. The universe will always have some irregularity – will inevitably bear the mark of freshness and brute fact. Now, if spontaneity is real and if unpredictable novelty is essential to evolutionary growth, it might be objected that the principle of continuity cannot be sustained. At least, this seems to be so if the intelligible world is continuous throughout and if continuity permits no breaks. However, there are, I think, two ways to reconcile spontaneity with continuity in Peirce's thought. One way is to take him strictly, or at his word, when he says that synechism insists that continuity is of prime importance. This is not to say that it is present everywhere, universally, without breaks. It is, instead, to say that continuity is of primary importance, presumably insofar as the universe is intelligible. Furthermore, this limit on universal continuity can be seen in Peirce's insistence that there are continuities, not one all-pervasive continuum, that suggest there must be gaps or discontinuities between one continuity and another.

The second way of approaching the problem of reconciling spontaneity with synechism is, I think, particularly interesting and challenging. I shall conclude this introduction with some of the suggestions for responding to this challenge – suggestions that anticipate what will be developed further in the fourth chapter.

What is needed is a close examination of what constitutes continuity. It was noticed earlier that for Peirce, what is continuous is not something properly thought of as divisible – even infinitely divisible. Rather, a continuum is what cannot be filled. Its possibilities are inexhaustible. Infinitesimals, which may be said to constitute a continuum, the parts of which are inexhaustible, are possible positive contributions to the continuum.

If we keep in mind that Peirce identified intelligibility with generals and thus with continuities of possible future instances, it can be said that a continuum is inevitably open to the growth of intelligibility. The instances of a continuum are fundamentally infinitesimals. But infinitesimals are the possible individuals that may persist in enhancing the continuum – or, in terms of equating continuity with intelligibility, infinitesimals are the possibilities of intelligibility. Every continuum, every general, is open to the possibility of more intelligibility. The architectonic that could be constructed on the basis of this notion of continuity, and the view that there is spontaneity in the world would include the conception of the growth of intelligibility into the infinite future at the same time that instances of spontaneity served as the nodes from which new intelligibility originates. Growing intelligibility means that the universe becomes increasingly lawful; yet this very lawfulness is evolving because moments of spontaneity also fill an inexhaustible universe.

My proposal concerning the ways in which pragmaticism, semeiotic, and the phenomenological categories can be brought together as components of an architectonic founded on synechism has been shown to depend on an interpretation of continuity. The task of expanding this interpretation will be central to the fourth chapter of this book.

Conclusion

Let me summarize the main points of my sketch of Peirce's architectonic. One way to bring together the building blocks of the architectonic is to focus on semeiosis, or the sign process, and evolutionary synechism. What Peirce says about the evolution of the cosmos is a counterpart to what he says about the development of the interpretation of signs. Instances of what is sui generis in the world, that is, the instances of spontaneity in nature and in human personality, are correlative to instances of what is sui generis in sign interpretation, that is, in instances of spontaneity within the interpretation and invention of signs. This means that the basis of pragmaticism is a reality that not only is objective or independent of opinions but that is also a complex of dynamic habits of the world. Phenomenology is the proper discipline to initiate a description of this world of dynamic habits. The category of Firstness approaches most directly the feel of such a world. The category of Secondness approaches most forcefully the constraints of the world. And the category of Thirdness approaches most fully its intelligibility. An appropriate projection of this phenomenological beginning is the study of metaphysics, that is, of synechism, or the principle of continuity.

The project just mentioned is, of course, a gigantic task. What was suggested in the sketch offered here, however, can be a kind of stepping-off place for specific applications of Peirce's philosophy. One application is to some of the problems associated with understanding metaphorical meaning. Within the main text, I shall suggest what can be learned from seeing how Peirce's notion of agape, or the principle of evolutionary love, which for him functions as a responsible agent of evolution, can be applied to some of the problems of creativity. Specifically, the idea of agape is helpful in understanding the puzzling way human creators act responsibly to generate something new that being new could not have been predetermined by the creator. The fourth chapter will focus on this idea so as to take it one step farther as a crucial component of Peirce's envisaged architectonic.

Two overriding conceptions of Peirce's philosophy govern what will be said. The first is that Peirce was a metaphysical realist of a unique kind. This is indicated by the term that will play a prominent role in the fourth chapter: *evolutionary realism*. The other conception is inseparable from the first; it concerns the way Peirce interwove the idea of spontaneity and radical creativity, which is the generation of new intelligible components of reality, with his view that what is intelligible must be general, mediated, and founded on continuity. The remarkable outcome of this interweaving of the two ideas is that it integrates continuity with discontinuity – a condition implied by the affirmation of spontaneity.

1

The Origins of Pragmaticism

The 1877 and 1878 articles "The Fixation of Belief" and "How to Make Our Ideas Clear" are generally thought to initiate pragmatism, which Peirce would later call *pragmaticism*. Both are parts of a series of six papers intended for a book called "Illustrations of the Logic of Science." They represent Peirce's concern with proposing a theory of inquiry based on his conception of experimental science.[1] At the time they were written, Peirce regarded it as his mission to incorporate the logic of experimental methods into philosophy. An explicit expression of this aim can be found in his later writing where he aligns himself with "those few fellow-students of philosophy, who deplore the present state of that study, and who are intent upon rescuing it therefrom and bringing it to a condition like that of the natural sciences" (5.413). Thus, Peirce's discussion of the way beliefs may be fixed and of the proper criterion for clarifying ideas is a means to this longer-range goal. The consequences of realizing this goal imply the reinterpretation of traditional philosophical issues. Most of the issues so important to Peirce throughout his career will be seen to emerge within the context of his concerns in the 1877 and 1878 articles.

Before considering these articles, let me make two preliminary observations. The first is that I bypass four earlier essays, "On a New List of Categories," "Questions Concerning Certain Faculties Claimed for Man," "Some Consequences of Four Incapacities," and "Grounds of Validity of the Laws of Logic." Some key points in three of these will be taken up later in connection with semeiotic and with further consideration of Peirce's view of inquiry. My purpose in this chapter is to initiate my interpretation of Peirce through pragmaticism.

The second preliminary remark concerns Peirce's description of inquiry in "The Fixation of Belief" as a process of struggle to pass from a state of doubting to a state of belief. The passage is a struggle among, and eventual survival of, successful beliefs, and it seems to exemplify the influence of the Darwinian conception of biological evolution on late nineteenth-century thought. That there was such influence on Peirce is made explicit by a reference near the beginning of the article

---

[1]"The Fixation of Belief" and "How to Make Our Ideas Clear" were the first two of six articles originally published in *Popular Science Monthly* in 1877 and 1878, respectively.

to Darwin's application of statistical method to biology. In "The Fixation of Belief," however, the focus is on the logic of inquiry rather than a theory of evolution. The extent to which Peirce accepted Darwinian thought is most appropriately considered in relation to his later efforts to propose a general hypothesis concerning cosmic evolution.

Belief and the Logic of Inquiry

As already indicated, the logic in question in this relatively early article is conceived as the methodology Peirce believed to be essential to the natural sciences — empirical as distinct from the formal sciences, such as mathematics. In such sciences, Peirce believed, reasoning moves from what is known to what is not yet known. Specifically, Peirce wanted to show the connection between this empirical logic and the way the mind works, for it is by reasoning well that inquiry, or thought in general, can best reach its aim.

Peirce's own account of inferential thought assumes four conditions of inquiry. The first is that inquiry presupposes a fundamental guiding principle. The principle is needed because we sometimes experience doubt and, when we do, our minds are prompted to pass from doubt to belief. (Examination of the characteristics of doubt and belief will be undertaken later.) Thus, we need a principle to guide us. Moving from doubt to belief is essential, because the formation of belief, or the settlement of opinion, which is the resolution of doubt, is the goal of any specific inquiry. The way we ought to resolve doubt, using our principle, is connected to the second condition of inquiry, which is the expectation that the settlement of belief is best achieved by good reasoning, that is, the reasoning that necessarily reaches true conclusions. The third condition is the use of the scientific method, which is the proper method of good reasoning. The final condition is a fundamental hypothesis that there must be a reality that serves as the justification for pursuing inquiry. Peirce insists that scientific method depends on this hypothesis. Let us consider how Peirce's discussion brings these four conditions into focus.

Peirce calls attention to the role of habits of mind or of reasoning, or what he calls "guiding principles," in determining whether we reason well or poorly. For instance, the guiding principle "that what is true of one piece of copper is true of another" governs the inference that if we "observe that a rotating disk of copper quickly comes to rest when placed between the poles of a magnet," this "will happen with every piece of copper" (5.367). It is habits of mind such as this guiding principle that constrain us to give conclusions to premises. If we follow good habits of inference, we reach true conclusions, independently of idiosyncrasies of our particular feelings and impulses. "The habit is good or otherwise, according as it produces true conclusions from true premises or not; and an inference is regarded as valid or not, without reference to the truth or falsity of its conclusion specially, but according as the habit which determines it is such as to produce true conclusions in general or not" (5.367). Peirce's concern here, of course, is with ampliative reasoning in which premises and conclusions are understood in terms of empirical evidence and generalization rather than with deductively derived conclusions.

Peirce's point is that good reasoning, that is, good inferring, depends on our following a good habit of mind. A habit of mind is good if it generally leads from true premises to true conclusions. Such a habit is to be the basis for valid inferences, and these lead to conclusions that are true or false regardless of one's impulse to accept or reject them. When a habit of mind that determines inferences is formulated as a proposition, it is called a *guiding principle* of inference. Of the guiding principles that govern reasoning, some are essential to all reasoning; they are not limited to a particular object of research such as is the principle of rotating copper disks. These more fundamental guiding principles have to do with what is taken for granted in asking why a particular conclusion follows from particular premises in some particular instance of reasoning. In other words, some principles concern the basis of reasoning itself.

This point can be seen in light of the suggestion that a guiding principle seems to be an instance of the principle of induction – by which I mean the principle that what has been repeated in the past will be repeated in the future. This principle, of course, has traditionally posed a problem for philosophers, because there seems to be no conclusive way in which to prove that the future will resemble the past. Peirce does not intend to attack this problem here. However, what he does say about the assumption that it is possible to pass from doubt to belief according to rules is based on his conviction that inductive inference is integral to thought. Further, unless the kind of expectations of resolving doubt that function in guiding principles were justifiable, we would live in a continuing state of doubt with no predispositions to engage the world in specific ways. Our lives would be chaotic.

What is of particular importance for our study of Peirce, however, is that one of the fundamental guiding principles assumed when we ask "why a certain conclusion is thought to follow from certain premises" (5.369) is "that there are such states of mind as doubt and belief – that a passage from one to the other is possible, the object of thought remaining the same, and that this transition is subject to some rules by which all minds are alike bound" (5.369). It might be objected that Peirce's characterization of the principle of doubt and belief as an assumption is not a guiding principle, because his examples of guiding principles seem to be rules or habits of inference. However, we should notice first that he says that guiding principles may be formulated as propositions that determine inferences. This suggests that they are rules for distinguishing classes of inferences. Second, we should notice that Peirce also says that "any fact may serve as a guiding principle." Although Peirce does not here explain what he means by the term *fact*, it is not likely in this relatively early article that he means by it something existent that is not, without interpretation, intelligible. I assume that he means by fact something that is to some degree intelligible so that a fact is propositional and asserts a purported truth. After saying that any fact may serve as a guiding principle, he distinguishes between those facts that are essential and those that are relevant to distinct "objects of research." It is among the former that he includes the doubt–belief principle. This principle of doubt and belief, then, expresses what must be necessary for there to be a process of reaching the basic aim of inquiry – an aim that Peirce refers to later.

The passage to belief, as a rule, is not easy, however. It includes some degree of struggle, differing beliefs being tried and discarded until a satisfactory one is found. Thus, inquiry, or thought in general, is an activity that, if not quite described by Peirce as dialectical, at least manifests the interplay of opposition and resolution. Further, inquiry has only one aim: the settlement of opinion, which is to say, the formulation of a belief that takes the place of doubt. It is important in this connection to notice that Peirce makes explicit that he does not refer to true opinion as only that which needs to replace doubt, but rather to opinion that is thought to be true. Thus, he adds, "We may fancy that this is not enough for us, and that we seek, not merely an opinion, but a true opinion. But put this fancy to the test, and it proves groundless." We are entirely satisfied "as soon as a firm belief is reached," a belief that "we *think* to be true" (5.375). What Peirce says here might be understood to place Peirce's view close to the broader interpretation of "pragmatism" found in William James, at least to the extent that inquiry apparently is to be justified by what satisfies an individual subject, or by what seems only to meet the test of being satisfactory, or showing a strong inclination to accept a conclusion. Furthermore, the description of the aim of inquiry as firm belief, belief that we *"think* to be true" – that is, distinguished from true opinion – may seem to conflict with Peirce's earlier description of good habits as producing true conclusions. However, even though Peirce does, in his early career, sometimes seem to align himself with what James later identified and set forth as pragmatism, consideration of the context of these remarks and the way Peirce leads the discussion that follows indicates that he does not intend to make truth subjective. Nor does he intend to propose that the conclusion of inquiry is merely the function of what accidentally satisfies an inquirer, or that it is accepted by an inquirer *only* because the inquirer comes to feel strongly about a belief. A reconciliation of Peirce's statement that inquiry stops when a belief is reached, whether or not the belief is a true conclusion, with his statement that good reasoning leads to true conclusions independently of individual idiosyncrasies, not only highlights one of the issues with which Peirce struggled but also shows the extent to which Peirce leaned toward a form of realism – a point to be developed in a moment.

It should be added that some interpreters of Peirce have said that there is an inherent tension in his thought between two seemingly opposed commitments. One commitment is based on the conviction that when we are honest about what and how we think, when we are not playing games with thought – by feigning doubt or by proposing assumptions that are purely abstract conjectures in order to prove a philosophical point – then we recognize and acknowledge only assumptions and conclusions that relate directly and specifically to our preparedness to act. The commitment is seemingly opposed to the assumption that there is something real, something independent of the need that any particular person or group of persons has to believe and act. This independent reality constrains both the form and the content of our thoughts. A tension of the sort suggested by the apparently opposed commitments is present in the issue just raised concerning what is required of conclusions that satisfy inquiry. And, it seems to me, this kind of tension contributes to the very structure of the architectonic at which Peirce aimed. But if tension is integral to an architectonic, and an architectonic is a system, then the opposition that runs through Peirce's thought is not a contradiction. There is a way of reconciling the two poles, both of which are vital to Peirce's aims, that does not extinguish either of them or the tension between them but that does give the poles places in a larger framework.

One piece of evidence that Peirce did not prefer the subjective pole of the opposition can be found in a footnote to the passage in which he says that we are satisfied when we reach a belief that we *think* to be true. He says in this note that truth is of the character of a proposition, and a proposition that would, *"with sufficient experience and reflection,"* lead to satisfaction (5.375, note 2). Thus, the satisfaction that concludes inquiry is not in the form of an immediate gratification but rather is the result of critical assessment. Further, the role of critical assessment is, as we shall see, explicit in Peirce's insistence on using the scientific method to settle opinion rather than the other three rejected methods, mentioned in the Introduction and to be explained further later. The point of preferring the scientific method is that it requires that any one inquirer or any particular group of inquirers have a vision that looks beyond itself toward a larger community, a community that is to be satisfied in the long run. We shall see that Peirce later makes clear that this "to be" is a "would-be."

Another way to see how Peirce avoids adopting a subjectivist view of satisfying inquiry is by noting that Peirce's purpose in "The Fixation of Belief" is to show that good reasoning is necessary to reach an adequate resolution of doubt. No temporary settlement of opinion is fully adequate; it is inevitably followed by further doubt. What is needed is a kind of reasoning that is designed to lead to beliefs that are not temporary. Such reasoning is good reasoning. Good reasoning, then, is required in order that thinking will be led to true conclusions, conclusions that can be sustained or that have sufficient stability to resist whimsical or idiosyncratic needs. The alleviation of doubt that is fully satisfactory comes from firm beliefs that function in the long run and in a community that has a status independent of any particular group at any fixed time. Peirce argues that the surest way to arrive at such conclusions, or to practice good reasoning, depends on following the kinds of procedures found in the scientific method. Let us then return to the way Peirce develops his argument.

Closer consideration of the characteristics of doubt and belief, which, Peirce says, begin and end inquiry, should help show why Peirce does not view inquiry as aimed at personal or particular satisfactions. Examination of the characteristics of doubt and belief also is necessary to a proper understanding of the leading principle of logic, that is, the principle presupposed by all inquiry.

Let us begin by considering what doubt is. In doing this, we are forced to recognize that the characteristics of doubt and belief are interdependent. To say what doubt is depends on seeing what belief is, and vice versa. As already observed, doubt is the initiating condition of inquiry. It occurs when there is a loss or a breakdown in our system of beliefs. But what is belief? The term *belief* can be understood in at least two senses: psychological and logical or ontological. According to the first sense, a belief is a subjective or behavioral process. According to the second, it is, or is interpretable as, a proposition, or as an ontological referent. In this latter sense, it is a regularity in thinking, a disposition to envisage regularities in consequences that follow from the thought and that are objective in relation to psychological acts. Thus, in this logical-ontological sense, belief is a type of process that is not reduced to actual mental states or events, but is an objective condition that mental, habitual acts exemplify. Peirce's discussion suggests that he conceives belief in both a psychological-behavioral and a logical-ontological sense. As we shall see in a moment, the ontological sense is based on the connection between the idea that a belief is psychological as a kind of behavior with the idea that a belief is a regularity.

Following a definition of belief formulated by the psychologist Alexander Bain – which Peirce tells us was urged by Nicholas St. John Green during the meetings of the Metaphysical Society to which he belonged in the 1870s – belief is defined as "that upon which a man is prepared to act." Peirce adds that, "From this definition, pragmatism is scarce more than a corollary; so that I am disposed to think of him [Nicholas St. John Green] as the grandfather of pragmatism" (5.12). According to this conception, belief is a disposition to act in a certain way with respect to the envisaged consequences of holding the belief. Believing something is being prepared to act on the conviction that the belief concerns certain results and that, if one were to act in a certain way, these results would be experienced. To use one of Peirce's own examples, to believe that a diamond is hard is to anticipate that if one tried to scratch it, it would not be scratched by many other substances.

If beliefs are dispositions to certain kinds of conduct and to expect their accompanying consequences, then beliefs can be thought of as habits. They are repeatable ways of acting, much like rules (including leading principles). One of Peirce's ways of identifying objects that persist or endure from one perceptual or conceptual act of attention to another is to call the terms used to refer to such objects as *general terms* and the objects themselves of these terms as *generals*. The term *object* as used here does not refer to individual things but to the referent of an expression that, as enduring from moment to moment, is conceived as a property or quality. Thus, generals are what are referred to by expressions that indicate repeatability of the referent. Generals may be thought of as what, in terminology stemming most directly from Aristotle, are called *universals*. They are attributes, and an attribute is that to which a general term such as *hardness* or *soluble* refers. As was said in the Introduction, however, generals for Peirce are not static or abstract objects of attention; they are dynamic. When we turn later to one of the dimensions of Peirce's realism, we shall see further the sense in which generals must be distinguished from one common conception of universals, that is, if universals are regarded as fixed, definite forms of repeatable instances of phenomena. In any case, what is important at the moment is to see that an object of a belief is general and, as such, may be thought of as a rule or pattern by which aspects of things are related to one another. Hardness refers to a pattern of instances of testing, one kind of test being the attempt to scratch a thing called *hard*. The tests are related to one another so that the term hardness can be applied by a rule of regular behavior (testing by attempting to scratch). Generals are the objects of beliefs, which are habits. Generals, however, can evolve. They are dynamic and changeable, and belief is fallible.

This conception of belief suggests how characterizing belief as the end of any given inquiry is inseparable from characterizing doubt, which initiates inquiry. Just as belief can be understood in two senses, so can doubt. As psychological, doubt may be a subjective feeling of uncertainty or it may be the experience of blocked behavior. As logical or ontological, it may be a falsified proposition, a lack of necessity in an argument, or it may be an anomaly, an incoherence, an irregularity or deviation noticed in nature. Peirce's description of doubt in the present context leans toward its behavioral sense rather than the logical or ontological. However, if we anticipate later stages of his thought, we can see that doubt can be understood in the logical-ontological sense. Thus the breaks in regularity that occur where there is psychological doubt may be continuous with breaks in regularity in biological and physical processes.

In his discussions in "The Fixation of Belief," Peirce explains that doubt arises when a complex of habits or beliefs is shaken. Doubt is thus characterized negatively, in a way that suggests an important point on which Peirce insists in various contexts throughout his career. If doubt is genuine, it is not a state of mind that is assumed for the sake of coming to some preconceived conclusion or presumed first principle. As mentioned earlier, the kind of doubt Peirce points to is not make-believe; it is not adopted for methodological purposes, as Peirce thinks it was by Descartes. We shall see when we consider some of the antecedents of pragmatism that Peirce was strongly opposed to the Cartesian philosophical position that, as he put it, feigns doubt in order to establish an indubitable foundation. The kind of doubt that begins inquiry and that is directed toward gaining knowledge in the sense either of developing new beliefs, or of reestablishing beliefs needing additional support, must be a doubt that is definite and conditioned by some encountered constraints or resistances to our ways of acting – that is, some interruption of the habits or beliefs that guide our expectations. Only such doubt is genuine. Thus, Peirce says, "Some philosophers have imagined that to start an inquiry it was only necessary to utter a question whether orally or by setting it down upon paper, and have even recommended us to begin our studies with questioning everything! . . . There must be a real and living doubt, and without this all discussion is idle" (5.376).

It is appropriate at this point to digress briefly in order to touch on an issue raised by an indirectly related comment Peirce makes later in discussing progress in scientific thought. He says that one must be willing to abandon the whole aggregate of one's beliefs: "There is no room for doubt. But the scientific spirit requires a man to be at all times ready to dump his whole cartload of beliefs, the moment experience is against them" (1.55). This principle goes hand in hand with his fallibilism – a part of Peirce's philosophy that will be considered only in passing when it is relevant to the contexts of the discussion. Fallibilism, however, is characteristic of his general hypothetical approach to all issues that turn on ampliative or synthetic knowledge.[2] One may be prompted to ask whether Peirce's fallibilism and readiness to abandon all beliefs are not inconsistent with his rejection of Cartesian doubt. Brief consideration of this question may sharpen what Peirce has to say about doubt in the early articles on cognition. There are two points to notice in Peirce's statement about a readiness to jettison belief.

First, Peirce recommends not that we doubt everything we possibly can, or even any particular thing, but rather that we be ready to reject any or all beliefs under a specific kind of circumstance, namely, at that moment, at that individual point in time, when experience conflicts with belief. I assume that this means that he is not recommending that the scientist make a systematic effort to doubt. Presumably something specific must negate experience in order to justify rejection of belief.

The second point is that jettisoning beliefs is not doubting them but taking a step toward replacing them. To doubt is to hold in abeyance with a readiness to accept what is doubted if doubt is assuaged. This is in particular exemplified by the form of doubting that Cartesianism proposes. However, there is a dimension of Peirce's fallibilism that seems to be shared with Cartesian doubting. The readiness to disbelieve is a generalized disposition, which is not unlike the general resolve to doubt whatever does not withstand the challenges of reasoning. Furthermore, a readiness or disposition is not an event or interruption in the regularities by which much of our experience occurs, and Peirce is opposed to Cartesian doubt insofar as it is not provoked by some surprise or encountered resistance. Why, then, is he willing to accept a disposition to react to such resistance before it is actual? There is an answer that seems plausible to me in the context of the larger view toward which Peirce aims and which is not approached as closely in the cognition papers as it is in the later manuscript concerning scientific thought. The recommendation that the scientist be ready to reject one's cartload of beliefs may be a proposal

[2]The fallibilistic dimension of Peirce's philosophy is not singled out and discussed in its own right not because it is unimportant but primarily because it is so pervasive that it appears in various forms within each of the major architectonic conceptions on which this book is organized. Thus, Peirce's resistance to absolutistic commitments appears in his semeiotic in the role of indexical signs and what he says about the objects of signs, in his phenomonology that makes fallibilistic conditions internal to the categories, and in his hypothetical suggestions about evolution and metaphysical realism.

that scientific thinking tends to establish a metaphysical disposition, a habit of expectation that is exemplified not only in human attitudes, when they are scientific, but also in anticipation of the habits of nature. As we shall see later in connection with Peirce's conception of evolution, there is reason to generalize this disposition to the natural processes. Spontaneity, the possibility of actual chance occurrences and departures from regularities or laws that contribute to evolution, is sustained and serves as an infinitely projected condition of the universe. The readiness to jettison the whole cartload of one's beliefs, then, may be regarded as an expression of what may be called a *metaphysical skepticism* or a *metaphysical ingredient* in thought as it relates in a continuum (to be discussed later) to nature, which is the object of scientific investigation. This highly speculative suggestion, I think, is not inconsistent with the whole of Peirce's philosophy. However, the reasons for attributing such a view to Peirce must be offered later.[3] It is necessary now to return to the specific issue from which we departed in this digression.

Because genuine doubt is conditioned by interruptions of habits, it is felt as a sensation of irritation, a dissatisfaction and a consequent compulsion to find a resolution. "But this is not all which distinguishes doubt from belief. There is a practical difference. Our beliefs guide our desires and shape our actions. . . . The feeling of believing is a more or less sure indication of there being established in our nature some habit which will determine our actions. Doubt never has such an effect" (5.371). As he put it in a later paper, "A man in doubt usually tries to imagine how he shall, or should, act when and if he finds himself in the imagined situation. He supposes himself to have an end in view, and two different and inconsistent lines of action offer themselves." Thus, the practical effect of doubt is the loss of a predisposition or habit. And the resolution of this loss is the establishment of belief or habit.

Relief from the irritation experienced when one doubts, then, is the mark of the resolution at which inquiry aims. Peirce's reference to what an inquirer feels as a sign of belief, however, returns us to the question of the subjectivity of the goal of inquiry. Peirce resists a sub-

---

[3]Perhaps a simpler way of accounting for Peirce's readiness to abandon all one's belief is to say, as was suggested by Christopher Hookway in correspondence, that Peirce means to formulate the converse of his anti-Cartesianism. If we should not pretend to doubt, neither should we refuse to doubt when surprised. I suspect that this is a version of the first part of my point that Peirce assumes a fundamental epistemological disposition or readiness to modify beliefs when departures from belief occur. My extension of this point to a metaphysical disposition is based on the idea that Peirce commits himself to a presupposition about nature and in turn about reality when he suggests that the world is ready to surprise us. I am not convinced that epistemological and metaphysical commitments are clearly distinguishable.

jectivist answer. Thus, Peirce addresses us with the rhetorical question, "If the settlement of opinion is the sole object of inquiry, and if belief is of the nature of habit, why should we not attain the desired end, by taking as answer to a question any we may fancy, and constantly reiterating it to ourselves, dwelling on all which may conduce to belief, and learning to turn with contempt and hatred from anything that might disturb it?" (5.377). His answer to this question can be found in his explanation of the inadequacy of the first of three methods that have been used in the history of thought in order to settle opinion.

The first of these methods is called "the method of tenacity." This method is inadequate because it "will be unable to hold its ground in practice." And why should it fail to hold its ground? Because, Peirce says, "the social impulse is against it. The man who adopts it will find that other men think differently from him, and it will be apt to occur to him, in some saner moment, that their opinions are quite as good as his own, and this will shake his confidence in his belief." This shaking of confidence "arises from an impulse too strong in man to be suppressed, without danger of destroying the human species. Unless we make ourselves hermits, we shall necessarily influence each other's opinion; so that the problem becomes how to fix belief, not in the individual merely, but in the community" (5.378).

The social impulse is also the basis of Peirce's rejection of the second possible method of settling opinion, "the method of authority," the method of institutions that act as tenacious individuals for a whole community. Peirce observes, "For the mass of mankind, then, there is perhaps no better method than this" (5.380). "But no institution can undertake to regulate opinions upon every subject." Sooner or later, some individuals "will be found who are raised above that condition." These men possess "a wider sort of social feeling." They see the variations in doctrines in different countries and times, "and they cannot help seeing that it is the mere accident of their having been taught as they have, and of their having been surrounded with the manners and associations they have, that has caused them to believe as they do and not far differently" (5.381).

The recognition of the limitations of the method of authority leads to the third possible way of settling opinion, the a priori method, which Peirce understands as adopting propositions on the ground that they are "agreeable to reason." According to this method, beliefs are settled by being regarded as propositions guaranteed by the light of reason – propositions that all "reasonable" human beings accept. The light of reason, which seems to have been thought of as a natural inclination, is presumed to guide thought independently of individual and institutional perspectives. Although, as Peirce says, it is "more respectable from the point of view of reason," this method is fundamentally dependent on the fashions of the ways humans think at a given time and place. He attempts to justify this conclusion in a long footnote in which he describes the way some of the major philosophers in the past have followed this method.

Let me point out here that this characterization of the third method may be seen in relation to the second method for making our ideas clear, which is to be considered when we turn to the second article in the series on the logic of inquiry. The second method of gaining clarity is based on definitional consistency. We might ask, Why is this kind of criterion, one that conceives of the a priori method as a method of self-consistency, not assigned to the third method for fixing belief? The answer, I think, can be seen if we recognize that in discussing the methods for resolving doubt, Peirce is concerned with empirical knowledge, or beliefs that bear on action. Thus, a method that would be essentially a demand for self-consistency would still need to be applied to experiential consequences – it would be tied to experimental results, at least in a loose sense of experiment in the context of commonsense attempts to settle opinion. The application of a self-consistent method would need to invoke natural inclination, "the light of reason," or, to use another term of Peirce, "taste," in order to determine the appropriateness of the application. This same point can be applied to the methods of tenacity and authority, which sustain self-consistency until compelling contingencies challenge them.

What is important, however, is that the a priori method, or method of agreeableness to reason, breaks down, as do the first and the second, because of the power of the social impulse. What is accepted as agreeable to reason is "always more or less a matter of fashion, and accordingly metaphysicians have never come to any fixed agreement, but the pendulum has swung backward and forward between a more material and a more spiritual philosophy, from the earliest times to the latest" (5.383). Inevitably, some persons will resist the acceptance of beliefs that are dependent on the particular conditions of an individual or particular group of individuals who claim to be following the light of reason. "To satisfy our doubts, therefore, it is necessary that a method should be found by which our beliefs may be determined by nothing human, but by some external permanency – by something upon which our thinking has no effect" (5.384). Before commenting on this proposal for a fourth method of inquiry, it is appropriate to take up a criticism of Peirce's appeal to an external permanency and a social impulse – a criticism crucial to understanding Peirce's rejection of the first three methods of settling opinion.

The question has been raised whether Peirce's invoking of the social impulse is merely an unjustified psychological assumption. Indeed, as Christopher Hookway puts it, when Peirce introduces his appeal to the social impulse, he may be accused of being inconsistent with his stand against psychologism, or the method of reducing logical issues to matters of psychological conditions.[4] In any case, it is appropriate to ask, What evidence is there for saying that there is a social impulse?

This question presupposes that the introduction of the role of a social impulse is a generalization based on an observation that human beings are inclined toward finding agreement with the widest possible community; thus, the question presupposes that, for Peirce, wherever disagreement is found, even if that occurs between one whole society and another, we are inclined to seek to resolve the disagreement. After all, the leading principle that refers to states of doubt demanding to be resolved applies, because any disagreement or resistance experienced by an individual, a whole society governed by an authority, or a group guided by what they believe is agreeable to reason is the condition of doubt — that is, the occasion of dislodging accepted beliefs. Hookway defends Peirce on the ground that "anyone who accepted the realist hypothesis [that there is an external permanency to which beliefs must conform] would be subject to the 'social impulse.' "[5] This defense suggests that Peirce's position is circular: The social impulse leads to a belief in independent reality, while this belief leads to our having a social impulse. As Hookway points out, this circularity is necessary in light of Peirce's aim of identifying the presuppositions of the logical question. What remains to be shown is that the hypothesis of realism justifies the pursuit of inquiry, which is an expression of the social impulse.

In any case, it is likely that Peirce introduces the idea of a social impulse in light of an empirical generalization found in Darwin's discussion of social feeling in animals and humans. If the Darwinian discussion were the only basis for Peirce's claim, however, Peirce would seem to be inconsistent with his rejection of psychological reductions of validity criteria. Suppose that humans lacked the social impulse. Would the methods of tenacity, authority, and a priority be adequate? I think Peirce would answer no. They would still fail because there are contingencies or resistances to our thinking that are not limited to our impulses. I think Peirce assumes that his appeal to a social impulse is more than a generalization based on observation. There are

[4]Christopher Hookway, *Peirce* (London: Routledge & Kegan Paul, 1985), p. 48.
[5]Ibid.

other considerations that account for Peirce's introduction of the social impulse.

One indication that Peirce does not intend that his appeal be limited to an empirical generalization is that he says at an earlier stage of
his career that justification in philosophy is not dependent on any
single chain of reasoning. In an earlier article, "Some Consequences
of Four Incapacities," he says that philosophical argument is like a
cable that has many strands, none of which is itself demonstrative or
conclusive but each one of which contributes to a conclusion. Thus,
he says that the reasoning of philosophy "should not form a chain
which is no stronger than its weakest link, but a cable whose fibers
may be ever so slender, provided they are sufficiently numerous and
intimately connected" (5.265). Thus, it may be suggested that another
fiber that supports the idea of a social impulse is the assumption that
a social impulse serves as a principle concerning what must be the case
(a necessary condition) for human nature if full satisfaction in the
resolution of doubt is to be attained. The function of the social impulse, then, can be understood as a logical principle that is supposed
on the basis of something like a transcendental deduction. That is, it
is an argument the conclusion of which is a presupposition said to be
necessary for something that is generally accepted. Thus, we generally accept the idea that we try to resolve conflict. However, this would
not make sense if there were not a social impulse.

A somewhat weaker way to make the point is to say that Peirce
introduced the idea of a social impulse as a recommendation, as a
hypothesis that concerns what people ought to do and that also may
account for what is observed at least on some occasions where people
differ with each other – on which occasions they attempt to reconcile
their differences. In the present context, the presupposition is that
we should act on the conviction that there is a social concern, or a
requirement that finite contexts of human thought and action are limited and ought to be transcended; for doubt demands to be settled in
as stable a way as possible, in the long run.

Another, more speculative reason for the social impulse, which is
consistent with later aspects of Peirce's thought that may have been
anticipated in this early essay, is that the social impulse can be regarded as having an ontological basis. Ingredient in the universe is a
teleological tendency that drives all process toward increased order.
This, of course, supposes the hypothesis of evolution to be discussed
later. Suffice it to say here that the social impulse is fundamentally a
tendency, a habit or disposition to act, to move away from fragmen-
tation and conflict toward lawfulness and consistency. In the 1870s,
however, Peirce's concern was to show that a proper method that can

assure us of good reasoning is needed – indeed, is inevitable – if inquiry is to exemplify such a process. Let us, then, return to his discussion of the methods.

On the assumption that the first three methods for resolving doubt fail, what method might succeed? Peirce's answer follows from the recognition that the other methods fail because they are dependent on the limitations of finite human demands. A method is needed "by which our beliefs may be determined by nothing human, but by some external permanency – by something upon which our thinking has no effect" (5.384). The method must be based on something that functions as a condition for beliefs and that is independent of all particular beliefs. But the independent condition cannot be some source to which one individual or a group of individuals claims to have special access. If this were the basis of the method, we would have once again a version of the first or second method, that of tenacity or authority. Rather, "our external permanency . . . must be something which affects, or might affect, every man." And the method appropriate to this condition "must be such that the ultimate conclusion of every man shall be the same. Such is the method of science" (5.384). The only satisfactory resolution of doubt, then, must be a belief reached in the long run, an ultimate conclusion, which is justified by its reference to the reality presupposed by science.

Peirce's commitment to a form of scientific realism is, then, clearly established. This is made explicit in his reformulation of the point that there is a need for a method by which beliefs are determined by an external permanency. Science provides that method because it assumes the "fundamental hypothesis" that "there are Real things, whose characters are entirely independent of our opinions about them; those Reals affect our senses according to regular laws" (5.384). The hypothesis of external permanency is needed to assure us that our method for settling opinions is aimed at ultimate conclusions that could be agreed to by all humans; only a method based on this condition could lead to a fixing of beliefs that is final in principle – or a settlement that could be final in the long run. Because the realist hypothesis is a fundamental commitment of science, science must be the proper method of good reasoning, which is reasoning that, leading from true premises to true conclusions, is the most appropriate method for resolving doubt. But what justifies the realist hypothesis?

An adequate answer to the question of justifying the realist hypothesis depends, among other things, on what Peirce means by *reality*. This further question is central to the aim of this book, and it will be addressed directly in this and subsequent chapters – the last chapter in particular. At the stage of Peirce's thought with which we are now concerned, Peirce is fairly far removed from giving an approximation

to a definitive answer. Suffice it to say here that reality for Peirce is a
condition that is independent of what any particular individual or
group of investigators thinks. Further, when he wrote "The Fixation
of Belief," Peirce avoids offering reasons for the realist hypothesis in
the sense of stating demonstrative proofs. "Investigation," he says,
"cannot be regarded as proving that there are Real things" (5.384).
Peirce discusses the problem of justification by treating the adoption
of the method that presupposes that the realist hypothesis and the
method of science are interdependent. This treatment of the issue, as
observed earlier, suggests that we can build up our reasons in the way
fibers brought together can make up a cable. Thus, Peirce presents
several suggestions that are intended to make up the cable supporting
his claim about the need for the realist hypothesis. First, he says that
there is a harmony between the method of science and "the conception on which it is based," which is the realist hypothesis itself. By
harmony, I assume that Peirce refers to the idea in science of the need
for independent tests that are subject to public inspection and of the
need for the possibility of falsification in the future. This expectation
of science at least suggests that there is reason to accept the realist
hypothesis. The hypothesis is in harmony with the expectations of
independent, public tests. Peirce also points out that our practice in
science and our general interactions with everyday experience show
that we at least act as if there were something independent of our
perspectives.

I shall go no further in considering Peirce's particular reasons to
support his thesis. But I do want to emphasize that when Peirce says
that the realist conception and the method of science are in harmony,
he means, it seems to me, that the scientific method is committed to
adjusting its hypotheses and conclusions in light of counterevidence,
of the constraints of experience or, specifically in scientific practice,
of the constraints of experimental evidence. Like the recognition that
doubt and the impulse to overcome it implies that there is some unifying or resolving belief, the admission of the relevance of constraints
on beliefs is in harmony with the idea that there is something independent of inquirers.

It should also be noted that Peirce concludes his discussion of the
need for adopting the scientific method as the most adequate way to
fix beliefs with an intriguing suggestion. He not only admits that he
does not provide demonstration as part of his argument, but he also
lets us know that he intends his argument as a recommendation. He
says, with a certain rhetorical flourish, that the method one uses should
be chosen in the way one chooses a bride in marriage. "The genius of
a man's logical method should be loved and revered as his bride,
whom he has chosen from all the world" (5.387). If this were the only

justification for adopting the scientific method, then this fourth method would be no more secure logically than the others. There are two ways, however, in which Peirce offers more support for the fourth method. As we have seen, the scientific method is the one method that promises resolutions of doubt in the long run. In addition, however, we should emphasize the point that Peirce's arguments in philosophy are proposed as a complex of distinct reasons. No one reason or set of reasons need be conclusive, yet the force of the group should be sufficient to make the conclusion likely.

In any case, in the final analysis, then, it seems to me that Peirce recognizes that in trying to justify his theory of inquiry, which is to justify his conception of science, we face an ultimate presupposition. We face the problem of justifying an unconditioned condition. If so, then we should not expect to find higher-order or more fundamental conditions that are said to justify the condition in question. We must face the consequence that our acceptance of this condition can only be justified by pointing out that the alternatives to the condition we affirm break down as support for our most vital purposes. In other words, only the scientific method, regarded as following the presupposition that there is an independent reality that constrains inquiry, can fulfill our aspirations to reach a final agreement among all human thinkers. Even if this hoped-for final agreement could only be reached in the long run, even if none of us nor any limited group of inquirers could ever reach this final opinion, the idea of the final agreement serves at least as a regulative ideal. It is an ideal that justifies our continuing inquiry, our readiness to be shown our error, and our determination to pursue investigation that converges on final agreement.

The pursuit of this ideal, once again, is an outflow of what Peirce calls the social impulse. This impulse for him is of most fundamental importance. Let me emphasize this still once more by turning to Peirce's own words, words that were offered in a sequel to the series of papers that we are considering:

> It seems to me that we are driven to this, that logicality inexorably requires that our interests shall *not* be limited. They must not stop at our own fate, but must embrace the whole community. The community, again, must not be limited, but must extend to all races of beings with whom we can come into immediate or mediate intellectual relation. It must reach, however vaguely, beyond this geological epoch, beyond all bounds. He who would not sacrifice his own soul to save the whole world, is, as it seems to me, illogical in all his inferences, collectively. Logic is rooted in the social principle. (2.654)

The depth of Peirce's commitment to a self-transcending drive is even more remarkable than his rhetorical commitment of marriage to the scientific method.

The Pragmatic Maxim

The idea that a belief is a habit, a disposition or rule of action, suggests an entry into Peirce's discussion of the pragmatic maxim in "How to Make Our Ideas Clear," the second article in the series we are considering. As was pointed out, a belief is either a self-conscious or a nonconscious preparedness to act in a certain way. This preparedness is present as a disposition. If the belief is conscious, then it is conditioned by an envisagement of patterns of future consequences. If the belief is held without one's being explicitly aware of it, it is conditioned simply by the order into which future consequences fall. For example, we may be consciously aware of believing that fire burns. Thus, as conscious of this, we envisage being burned if we get too close to the flame. We also hold this belief when we are not conscious of doing so. Thus, the belief is present as a habit or disposition to keep our hands away from the flame.

The maxim of clarity, later called the *pragmatic maxim,* presented in this second article follows directly from Peirce's characterization of belief. The maxim, quoted in the Introduction, refers meaning to expectations of consequences. In fact, meaning is equated with conceivable consequences, which is another way of formulating the thesis that beliefs are equated with dispositions to act in certain ways and thereby to be governed by expectations of envisaged consequences. Peirce himself shows the connection between the two articles: "The principles set forth in the first part of this essay lead, at once, to a method of reaching a clearness of thought of higher grade than the 'distinctness' of the logicians [whom he has been criticizing]" (5.394). Peirce explains his view by suggesting how establishing beliefs and experiencing doubts can be compared with moments in a continuous process such as music, a comparison to be considered in a moment. He then goes on to offer his main thesis:

The essence of belief is the establishment of a habit; and different beliefs are distinguished by the different modes of action to which they give rise. If beliefs do not differ in this respect, if they appease the same doubt by producing the same rule of action, then no mere differences in the manner of consciousness of them can make them different beliefs, any more than playing a tune in different keys is playing different tunes. (5.398)

It will be helpful to dwell for a moment on the significance of Peirce's analogy between beliefs and musical melodies. He assumes that the pattern of tones in different keys remains the same tune or melody. And he regards the order of tones that make up the tune as analogous to the mode of action to which a belief refers. It may be asked, then, what is the analogue that a belief has in relation to a different key in which a single tune may be played? Presumably, the analogue is the "manner of consciousness," which is a context that may be different for the same belief or mode of action. In the case of music, different keys determine different actual tones or sounds. But the pattern that these actual tones take may remain the same from one key to the next. The difference in actual tones is then analogous to the difference in the manner of consciousness in which a belief is held. Thus, if we look again at the ways in which consequences affect what satisfies doubt, Peirce's analogy confirms the point made in our consideration of the first article in this series, the point that Peirce understands the resolution of doubt to be determined not by the special contexts in which beliefs are held – that is, by personal or particular subjective conditions – but, rather, by an objective rule, a pattern that is not limited to specific, actual circumstances, just as a tune is not limited to specific, actual tones or sounds appropriate to specific keys but is determined by the order, the pattern, the mode or rule of action in accordance with which the notes occur.

It might be objected that a melody played in different keys may have a different effect, if the change of key occurs, for instance, in the development of a single composition. But I think Peirce's answer would be that in such cases the effect is that of something other than the melody itself; the difference in effect is a function of a larger whole, the movement or sonata, for instance, just as the meanings or effects of different beliefs may occur in larger contexts of discourse that have their own holistic meanings. Peirce's point, I am suggesting, is that whatever is meaningful is the order or pattern of our experiences, or the mode in which the action occurs. Although there are variables that may be noticed, they do not constitute that meaning. However meaning is determined, it must be an identity that is repeatable and to some extent invariant.

It seems to me that in his second article on how to clarify meaning we can detect a reformulation of the view affirmed in "The Fixation of Belief." This is what might be called a shift that, although Peirce does not make the point explicit, also reveals his tendency to insist on objective reference and on a form of realism. The discussion in the second article centers on something referred to by the term *idea*, which, in the statement of the maxim, takes the place of *belief*. One reason for this change in terms, I believe, is that Peirce is treating his topic in the context of certain issues in the history of philosophy. He is primarily concerned with the criteria of clarity assumed or argued for by philosophers in the Cartesian tradition. But another reason concerns something that underlies Peirce's immediate purposes. He wants to formulate a conception of meaning that should be understood as objective or as not confined to subjective aspects of belief as it might be understood in the psychological sense. Thus, the term *idea* suggests a step away from assumed self-conscious states toward the object of belief. It should be clear that my point is not to propose that Peirce changed his position in turning to the second article, but to emphasize again that his thought is directed toward not only intersubjective expectations but toward a realism, toward something independent of subjective conditions, as the basis of the agreement of opinions in the long run. The term *idea*, more directly than belief, suggests that meaning has to do with rules and the instances or consequences that exemplify those rules. Let us then examine the rule for making ideas clear.

We should notice first that just as there are methods to be rejected in the discussion of how to fix belief, so there are methods or criteria for gaining clearness that are not sufficient in the search for an adequate standard or grade of clearness. The first two methods for making ideas clear are rejected by Peirce primarily because they depend on contingencies. The first method, called by Descartes, *clearness,* depends on acquaintance. The second method of gaining clarity is by achieving distinctness, and this depends on apprehension of what is found in a definition. In either case, neither way guarantees that an inquirer is not merely entertaining what only seems to be clear and distinct – something that is either apparently familiar or is only abstract and not made relevant to empirical knowledge. What, then, is the proper method or criterion? What is the proper method for Peirce's "third grade of clearness"?

Two preliminary explanatory comments should be made about Peirce's purposes in proposing a criterion for making our ideas clear. First, it is important to recognize that the criterion with which we are concerned is not itself a criterion of truth. Although there is a relation between determining clear meaning and determining truth, what is at issue is how to decide what the meaning of a term is, regardless of whether the term is applied in a proposition or a judgment that it is subject to truth or falsity. This distinction is important in light of Peirce's insistence that his conception of the pragmatic maxim differs from that of William James and, perhaps more important, from the way the word "pragmatism" "begins to be met with occasionally in the literary journals, where it gets abused" (5.414). James developed pragmatism as a general theory for assessing the truth of ideas as well as a theory of meaning.

A second important consideration is that Peirce's maxim is intended to apply to general terms, to terms that cover recurrent and repeatable data – for example, general terms such as *hardness, force, transubstantiation.* Thus, the meanings that may be given to particularizing or nongeneral terms – terms that cover one thing or a finite set of data – are not at issue. It is even questionable, Peirce points out, whether such terms as proper names have meanings. This restriction of the maxim to general terms is something Peirce takes pains to emphasize later, when reflecting on what others were making of the idea of pragmatism. However, the point is evident in "How to Make Our Ideas Clear." After all, the discussion of modes of action and rules that characterize dispositions shows that Peirce's concern is with general conditions of experience. And, as pointed out in the Introduction, certain key words in the statement of the maxim show this as well. Let us turn to the maxim. In doing so, I shall discuss it in terms of the reinterpretation of it that Peirce offered in his later writing.

The maxim is the rule that in order to be clear about meaning we should "consider what effects, that might conceivably have practical bearings, we conceive the object of our conception to have. Then, our conception of these effects is the whole of our conception of the object" (5.402). Let us examine this formula by concentrating first on what the maxim says about concepts, objects, and practical bearings that have consequent effects. If we ask about the meaning of a concept, we are told to consider the object of that concept – that is, to consider what the concept is about, what its reference is. What are we to look for in considering the object or referent? Peirce recommends that we consider the practical bearings of the object of the conception – that is, consider the effects it has that make a difference in our expectations. The effects follow from "practical bearings," or actions, that would be performed on the basis of believing the idea. The envisaged actions and their effects express a disposition to expect these effects, effects that make a difference to our expectation. Just as a belief is a habit or disposition to action in a certain way, so the meaning of the idea that makes the belief intelligible is about a series of conditional actions with specifiable effects.

What kinds of effects follow from conditional action? It seems that in the 1878 paper, Peirce refers to sense-experience in using the word *effects*, because in the previous paragraph he claims that we cannot have an idea that relates "to anything but conceived sensible effects." We seem to be advised to equate the conception of the object with the conception of sense-experiences. Any direct or immediate object of the idea seems to be collapsed into or equated with the practical, sensible effects. In later commentary, however, Peirce also suggests a less constricted conception of effects in emphasizing that the meaning he requires is general – in contrast to sense-experiences that are discrete and individual – and is tied to concepts or what is conceivable, and that meaning concerns possibilities. I shall return to this point in a moment.

Peirce's main concern in this article is to show that if we believe ourselves to have two different concepts and we find that the object of one of these concepts has the same effects as the other, then the two concepts are the same. As Peirce puts it, if we "fancy that we have" a different concept, we deceive ourselves. If we return to the analogy of belief and musical tunes, we may conclude that a deception about having two different beliefs that have the same effects has its analogue in music – if we were to believe that a melody played in two different keys constitutes two different melodies. As I suggested earlier, presumably the difference in the actual notes played would be analogous to the manner of consciousness or subjective, contingent conditions according to which the concept is experienced. Responses of this kind might be interesting in their own right to a psychologist or rhetorician, but they do not constitute the melody itself as different.

Nor are such differences of response part of the meaning of the concept. When the maxim is applied, as Peirce in fact applies it, to the question of how to interpret the doctrine of transubstantiation, we can see why the Protestant and the Catholic differ in their answers. Each holds the doctrine with different manners of consciousness. Each affirms the significance of the wine under different subjective conditions proper to certain religious convictions and under the assumption that these special circumstances give the proper meaning to the doctrine. Nevertheless, Peirce insists, the meaning of the term *wine* – the object of the concept of wine – remains the same, for it consists wholly in the effects it has, which are identified as its qualities, or as what we consider its experienced properties: its color, taste, disposition to evaporate at a certain rate, and so forth.

At this point, one might persist in trying to subjectivize Peirce's maxim by emphasizing what we have noted as Peirce's seeming reduction of envisaged consequences to actual sense-experiences that sentient subjects consider and expect to encounter when acting on these expectations. In response, we must recall that in the previous paper Peirce assigned the settling of opinions to long-run intersubjective consequences. Accordingly, his reference to the effects that comprise meanings can be interpreted as intersubjective and as part of a public domain of experience. That there is also a reality that is independent of all such experience, something answering to the realist hypothesis of science, remains to be discussed further when Peirce applies his maxim to the concept of the real.

Peirce's application of the maxim to the meaning of the term *hard* brings out a key issue that worried Peirce later in his reflections on the maxim. It is this application that is of particular importance to the main direction of our study of Peirce's philosophy. In accord with the description of the maxim in terms of the effects of the objects of concepts, we can apply it by noting that the object of the concept of hardness is a quality. The quality of hardness has certain practical bearings or effects that distinguish it from other qualities. Peirce identifies these effects by describing the way a thing that is hard behaves under certain conditions. Thus, he answers the question of "what we mean by calling a thing *hard*" by saying that "evidently that it will not be scratched by many other substances. The whole conception of this quality, as of every other, then, lies in its conceived effects. There is absolutely no difference between a hard thing and a soft thing so long as they are not brought to the test" (5.403). Experienced consequences, encountered in testing when we act in accord with our expectations when the term *hard* is attributed to the diamond, then, exhaust the meaning of the term *hard*. But the equation of what it is to be hard with the effects of trying to scratch the thing thought to be hard raises a question at once addressed by Peirce.

Suppose, then, that a diamond could be crystallized in the midst of a cushion of soft cotton, and should remain there until it was finally burned up. Would it be false to say that diamond was soft? This seems a foolish question, and would be so, in fact, except in the realm of logic. . . . We may, in the present case, modify our question, and ask what prevents us from saying that all hard bodies remain perfectly soft until they are touched, when their hardness increases with the pressure until they are scratched. . . . there would be no *falsity* in such modes of speech. They would involve a modification of our present usage of speech with regard to the words hard and soft, but not of their meanings. (5.403)

This answer seems to lean in the direction of what, since Peirce, has come to be known as a form of positivism, or at least of linguistic conventionalism, which rejects all questions and their answers as meaningless, if they do not refer us to actual, definite sense-experiences or to linguistic conventions alone. Thus, any question that does not permit a definite answer in terms of actual tests, as is the case of the question about the untested diamond, is meaningless with respect to anything real or independent of the way we learn or resolve to use words. The same inclination is explicit in Peirce's discussion of another example, the meaning of the general idea of force. The idea is traced to changes of motion in a continuous path and by degrees. After explaining how accelerations, which are the effects of the object of the idea of force, can be calculated, he says, "Whether we ought to say that a force *is* an acceleration, or that it *causes* an acceleration, is a mere question of propriety of language, which has no more to do with our real meaning than the difference between" a French idiom and its English equivalent (5.404).

At a later stage in his career (see MS 289), Peirce admits that his 1878 answer to the question of whether meaning is nothing but the actual effects of tests and is a matter of language alone might be interpreted as affirming a "positivist" framework. At one point he referred to it as too nominalistic. His reflections on this and the extent to which he subjects himself to self-criticism appear in extended footnotes to the 1878 statement of the maxim published in the *Collected Papers*. The footnotes have been added by Peirce in (apparently) 1893, 1903, and 1906, when he was developing what he then called pragmaticism. He also refers to the maxim in "What Pragmatism Is," published in the *Monist* in 1905, using a form of dialogue in which a questioner points out that Peirce objects to his apparent equation of the test of a conception with its practical effects. His answer in the dialogue provides us with a firm account of what he meant by the term *pragmaticism* and why he adopted this term in order to distinguish his view from more popular interpretations of pragmatism. Consideration of his answer brings us directly to the topic of pragmaticism and the realist hypothesis to which we shall return after a few more observations about Peirce's purposes in "How to Make Our Ideas Clear."

What remains to be understood is that Peirce is intent on dispelling notions and presumed arguments in which philosophers make claims about entities or powers underlying and causing the effects that are referred to by general concepts. They make claims that cannot be supported by ideas for which meanings can be given. Thus, in commenting on his illustration of the application of the maxim to the idea of force, he says that authors have spoken of force as a " 'mysterious entity,' which seems to be only a way of confessing that the author despairs of ever getting a clear notion of what the word means!" (5.404). He wants to show that general terms like force do not refer to powers underlying the effects conceived to be implied by the term.

One can see how Peirce's vigorous demand that meaningfulness be identified with effects, which are consequences the relevance of which is dependent on our language, invites the interpretation of what James attributed to him as pragmatism, and the interpretation of the main outlook of his philosophy, as antimetaphysical and either as psychological in its view of consequences or as strictly and positivistically bound to experimental science. And one might expect to find this same orientation in his discussion of the application of the maxim to the conception of reality. But such expectations are not satisfied. One reason they are not is that they are expressions of overlooking the possibility that Peirce's antimetaphysical position is not a stand against metaphysics as such but against some of the speculative metaphysics that he opposed – in particular, Cartesianism and, in a qualified way, Hegelianism, as well as theologically driven philosophies. Expectations that Peirce is psychologically or positivistically oriented, however, are not satisfied. This again reveals his attempts to introduce some form of realism into his philosophy of inquiry. His discussion of how to make the conception of reality clear leads directly into the major points that distinguish his pragmatism as pragmaticism.

Peirce presents his illustration of the conception of reality according to his maxim by building on the way the conception should be treated in terms of the first two grades of clearness. According to the first grade, the conception is familiar, as it is to "every child" who "uses it with perfect confidence." But familiarity does not make definition easy, and definition is the appropriate domain of the second grade of clearness. The definition offered contrasts reality with its opposite, fiction. The outcome is that *the real* is defined "as that whose characters are independent of what anybody may think them to be" (5.405). However adequate this definition may be, Peirce says, it does not make the idea of reality "perfectly clear." His maxim is invoked as a way of providing this clarity. Reality is first equated with ("consists in") the "peculiar sensible effects which things partaking of it produce." These effects can only be the beliefs that real things cause, because all sensible effects that are produced by real things become beliefs. Are the real things, then, independent of the beliefs they cause, or are the real things other beliefs that cause the beliefs of the moment?

The former alternative is suggested by what seems to be a circularity in Peirce's definition. Reality is certain effects. These are the effects that are caused by what is real. But what is real comprises those effects that are caused by what is real, or what is caused by what is real is what is caused by what is real. Again, reality is the effects that are equated with beliefs that are caused by real things. But the real things that cause beliefs in real things must be those effects or beliefs that are caused by real things. Real things are real things, and these are beliefs. I think this way of characterizing reality reflects Peirce's struggle to move from a reduction of presumed external reality, which has no practical bearing, into a form of realism that does justice both to the vital, experiential direction in which he wished philosophy to go and to the objectivism that he saw science presupposing in the form of the hypothesis of realism. This struggle is worked out further in the final statement of the application of the maxim to the conception of reality. At this point, it will be seen, the issue turns on whether there is some object that both causes and is independent of all beliefs, or whether, instead, the beliefs or ideas, finally, are only about either more beliefs or about some final beliefs – what Peirce suggests is a final opinion. But if a final opinion were reached, what is it about? Something independent of, or something dependent on, the final opinion?

The final statement of the application of Peirce's maxim to the idea of reality is a product of his development of the point that the effects that are caused by reality are certain sorts of beliefs. In order to distinguish which beliefs are caused by real things, we must distinguish true from false beliefs, because true rather than false beliefs are beliefs about what is real. But as seen in "The Fixation of Belief," true beliefs are those that are settled in the long run – are settled by the experiential or scientific method that is capable of self-correction until there is a convergence on a final opinion (5.406). We have no beliefs that are known to be true. Only the beliefs that are integral to a system that constitutes the final opinion of investigators could be known to be true. Consequently, Peirce's maxim of clarity tells us that the idea of reality is the idea of the object of the final opinion: "The opinion which is fated to be ultimately agreed to by all who investigate, is what we mean by the truth, and the object represented in this opinion is the real" (5.407). But is this object independent of the opinion? Peirce's answer is not conclusive.

But it may be said that this view is directly opposed to the abstract definition which we have given of reality, inasmuch as it makes the characters of the real depend on what is ultimately thought about them. But the answer to this is that, on the one hand, reality is independent, not necessarily of thought in general, but only of what you or I or any finite number of men may think about it; and that, on the other hand, though the object of the final opinion depends on what that opinion is, yet what that opinion is does not depend on what you or I or any man thinks. (5.408)

It seems clear that Peirce has not made up his mind exactly to what extent or in what way there may be something real independent of all thought, or thought in general, insofar as there is thought that is not merely a collection rather than a system of opinions. He certainly does not say that realities are necessarily independent of thought in general. Notice that he says that reality is independent "not necessarily" of thought in general. Thus, it is possible that the object, reality, is independent of thought. Peirce's expression, "not necessarily independent of thought in general," is overlooked by those who want to push him into the corner of some form of idealism, and is another example of why Peirce's tendency to move toward a fundamental realism is slighted.[6] To be sure, his approach to the issue raises problems. On the one hand, if reality is indeed independent of thought in general, then Peirce assumes some form of realism – or at least a Kantian view; he does not tell us what this reality is, insofar as it is independent of thought. This might seem to commit him to accep-

<hr />

[6]Although Christopher Hookway does not definitively force Peirce into an idealism, in considering Peirce's ideas about the relation of thought to reality, for instance, he takes Peirce's proposal that matter is effete mind without qualification (ibid., 262). I infer that he apparently does not think that Peirce's "not necessarily" was intended to set him off from the idealist's position.

tance of a thing-in-itself, the character of which remains unknowable and inconceivable. On the other hand, if reality is not independent, he is an idealist for whom what is real is indistinguishable from thought in general.

Peirce's leaning toward realism is less ambivalent in his later reflections on the application of his maxim to ideas that are not brought to actual tests. And even though the issue of the independence of the object of the final opinion is not settled, Peirce emphatically affirms a form of realism, which he sees as a foundation for pragmaticism. It has been suggested already that the long footnotes that Peirce appended to his discussion of the application of this maxim highlight the qualifications that move pragmatism into pragmaticism. In response to the criticism that the maxim is "skeptical and materialistic," he confirms the intersubjective requirements of his view as seen in the earlier of the two articles. He says, "We must certainly guard ourselves against understanding this rule in too individualistic a sense" (5.402, note 2). It is relevant not to the consequences for one person but in general to the results of what people do: Their "fruit is, therefore, collective; it is the achievement of the whole people." And in expanding this point, he shows that his thinking has led him to avoid asserting, even as an actualizable hope, the idea that inquiry – about both meaning and true belief – can be settled at some fixed time in the future. "What is it, then, that the whole people is about, what is this civilization that is the outcome of history, but is never completed? We cannot expect to attain a complete conception of it." Peirce even introduces a religious element into his explanation of his intentions. "We may say that it is the process whereby man . . . becomes gradually more and more imbued with the Spirit of God." And, suggesting the importance of the idea of continuity, which is essential to his synechism and evolutionary realism, he says, "When we come to study the great principle of continuity and see how all is fluid and every point directly partakes of the being of every other, it will appear that individualism and falsity are one and the same." But what is of most immediate importance to the question of whether Peirce wished to affirm a realism rather than risk a subjectivist interpretation of his criterion of clarity is his explanation in the footnote to the passage in which the maxim is described. Here he emphasizes that in the statement of the rule of clearness, "one finds, 'conceivably,' 'conceive,' 'conception,' 'conception,' 'conception.' " He then comments on the use of these terms:

This employment five times over of derivatives of *concipere* must then have had a purpose. In point of fact it had two. One was to show that I was speaking of meaning in no other sense than that of *intellectual purport*. The other was to avoid all danger of being understood as attempting to explain a concept by percepts, images, schemata, or by anything but concepts. I did not, therefore, mean to say that acts, which are more strictly singular than anything, could constitute the purport, or adequate proper interpretation, of any symbol. (5.402, note 3)

Peirce suggests that, given his emphasis on *conceive* and *concept* and terms with associated meanings, his original statement is sufficient to make his earlier self-criticism mistaken. His point is that the original statement of the maxim implies that meaning is not exhausted by any finite number of actual effects encountered in tests appropriate to general terms. Thus, he says, "Pragmaticism makes thinking to consist in . . . symbols whose purport lies in conditional general resolutions to act." Meanings of general terms are themselves general. They express rules that conditionally apply to actual consequences.

This point can be seen also in Peirce's later, pragmaticist's reinterpretation of the example of the untested diamond. In a 1905 article, Peirce explains why his pragmaticism is "the scholastic doctrine of realism," which, Peirce says, he defended in 1871.[7] In the work of 1871 to which he refers – and which, it should be noted, is earlier than "The Fixation of Belief" and "How to Make Our Ideas Clear" – Peirce explains his understanding of realism. It is committed to the kind of view already seen in the discussion of how opinion is settled.

All human thought and opinion contain an arbitrary, accidental element, dependent on the limitations in circumstances, power, and bent of the individual; an element of error, in short. But human opinion universally tends in the long run to a definite form, which is the truth. . . . The individual may not live to reach the truth, there is a residuum of error in every individual's opinions. No matter, it remains that there is a definite opinion in which the mind of man is, on the whole and in the long run, tending. (8.12)

Again, Peirce's conception of scientific realism shows his conviction that reality correlates with final agreement. Peirce's view of general meaning, or, in traditional terminology, universals, is important as well, however. In the 1871 review, he prefers the realist interpretation according to which, given its usual definition, "there are real objects that are general, among the number being the modes of determination of existent singulars, if, indeed, these be not the only such objects." In other words, there are rules that function independently of particular thoughts, that guide thought – resolutions to act in certain ways – and that are conditions of the regularities according to which events and things are repeatable.

If Peirce affirms this, then we can see that his position is consistent

[7]Peirce refers to the review of *The Works of George Berkeley, D.D., formerly Bishop of Cloyne: including many of his Writings hitherto unpublished* (Oxford: Clarendon Press, 1871), ed. Alexander Campbell Fraser, in *North American Review* 113 (October 1871), pp. 449–72. Also in *CP* 8.7–38 and *WOP*, vol. II, pp. 462–87.

when he engages in his critical commentary on his 1878 interpretation of the meaning of the term *hard* when applied to an untested diamond. He explains that he "endeavored to gloze over" the point that there are real possibilities – general modes of determination of existent particulars – because in 1878 he considers the point "unsuited to the exoteric public addressed; or perhaps the writer wavered in his own mind" (5.453). He repeats that calling an untested diamond hard or not "would be merely a question of nomenclature." "No doubt this is true, except for the abominable falsehood in the word MERELY, implying that symbols are unreal. Nomenclature involves classification; and classification is true or false, and the generals to which it refers are either reals in the one case, or figments in the other." If diamonds, whether or not they are tested, are classified as hard, our classification is either true or false; so if they are truly hard, then they are reals and their being hard is real. Peirce's next bit of explanation is particularly important.

> For if the reader will turn to the original maxim of pragmaticism . . . he will see that the question is, not what *did* happen, but whether it would have been well to engage in any line of conduct whose successful issue depended upon whether that diamond *would* resist an attempt to scratch it, or whether all other logical means of determining how it ought to be classed *would* lead to the conclusion which, . . . would be "the belief which alone could be the result of investigation carried *sufficiently far*." (5.453)

But if the hardness of the untested diamond is a matter of what would occur if a certain action were taken and certain tests were performed, although this action need not in fact occur, then general meanings consist of conditionals. Thus in the first article in a series published in the *Monist* in 1905, he insists that what is now being called his "pragmatism" is a "theory that a *conception,* that is, the rational purport of a word or other expression, lies exclusively in its conceivable bearing upon the conduct of life" (5.412).[8] The point here is that he uses the words *conception* and *conceivable* (as distinct from *conceived*), which directs us to the dispositional function of the meanings of terms – to their possible consequences. This point is reinforced in a paper unpublished in his lifetime:

> My pragmatism, having nothing to do with qualities of feeling, permits me to hold that the predication of such a quality [as hard and soft] is just what it seems, and has nothing to do with anything else. . . . Those qualities have no intrinsic significations beyond themselves. Intellectual concepts, however – the only sign-burdens that are properly denominated "concepts" – essentially carry some implication concerning the general behaviour either of some conscious being or of some inanimate object, and so convey more, not merely than any feeling, but more, too, than any existential fact, namely, the "would-

---

[8]*Monist* 15 (1905), pp. 161–81.

acts," "would-dos" of habitual behaviour; and no agglomeration of actual happenings can ever completely fill the meaning of a "would-be." (5.467)

Again, in the second of the *Monist* articles, he says, "Pragmaticism makes the ultimate intellectual purport of what you please to consist in conceived conditional resolutions, ... and therefore, the conditional propositions, with their hypothetical antecedents, in which such resolutions consist, being of the ultimate nature of meaning, must be capable of being true." This is not to say that they must be true but only that they are capable of being true – testing the diamond and not being able to scratch it might actually occur; but so might testing and finding that the thing tested can be scratched, in which case, doubt might arise as to whether the substance is a diamond or even whether diamonds are after all hard. He sums up his point by saying that the claim that conditional propositions must be capable of being true "amounts to saying that possibility is sometimes of a real kind" (5.453). Thus, if something is not false or not known to be false, it is possible. We do not know that it is false to say that the diamond is hard (will not be scratched); it remains untested. Hence, it is possible that the diamond is hard (will not be scratched). And this possibility is not merely abstract, for it applies to a kind of thing that has been experienced (in the past) and that *could* occur again.

With these kinds of considerations in mind, Peirce explicitly acknowledges the way he thinks it necessary to qualify his answer to the question about the diamond that he gave in 1878.

The question is, was that diamond *really* hard? It is certain that no discernible *actual* fact determined it to be so. But is its hardness not, nevertheless, a *real* fact? To say, as the article of January 1878 seems to intend, that it is just as an arbitrary "usage of speech" chooses to arrange its thoughts, is as much as to decide against the reality of the property, since the real is that which is such as it is regardless of how it is, at any time, thought to be. Remember that this diamond's condition is not an isolated fact. There is no such thing; and an isolated fact could hardly be real. (5.457)

Peirce explains his point about facts' not being isolated by enumerating many of the properties of diamonds – such as being a mass of pure carbon, having certain shape when not cut or trimmed, being highly refractive, and having a certain specific gravity – and adds, "From some of these properties hardness is believed to be inseparable" (5.457).

One of the main reasons to look at Peirce's reconsideration of "How to Make Our Ideas Clear" is to see what Peirce intended when he proposed his maxim, and how what he intended is what he now calls pragmaticism. It should be noticed, then, that Peirce does not regard himself as having changed his mind in a fundamental way since the time the earlier paper was written. At most, he believes that he "perhaps wavered." Further, if he did waver, it was not because he changed his fundamental position from a nominalism or some form of subjectivism but because he wanted to emphasize his point (for an "exoteric" audience) that there are no occult entities or powers that are meanings corresponding to our ideas. That his basic insistence on a form of realism is not at issue is seen in the way he explains his general intent in stating the maxim, as shown by the terminology emphasizing conceivable, possible consequences. It also may be emphasized again that he defended realism before as well as after his discussion in the early so-called pragmatism papers. As he says in an unpublished paper of 1905, "For pragmaticism could hardly have entered a head that was not already convinced that there are real generals" (5.503). This is not to say that Peirce affirmed some form of realism from his earliest writing – he did indicate a preference for nominalism in his very earliest writings. And this preference may have affected his formulations of his views later, after he had swung toward a form of realism.

Before pursuing the point that Peirce sides with realism in his conception of pragmaticism, let me make clear that my comments on the distinction between pragmaticism and pragmatism are intended to emphasize that Peirce seems to have believed himself to have leaned toward the realist status of meanings of general terms in the 1878 paper and regrets having expressed himself in a more nominalistic way, or in a way that regards meanings as reducible to actual experiences – and to linguistic habits alone. It should not be inferred, however, that Peirce's later thinking about pragmaticism did not develop beyond its early beginnings in the 1878 pragmatic maxim. The view of evolution – to be discussed in the fourth chapter – that became integral to his view of reality was not formulated until the 1890s. And his view of the role of self-control and the aim of investigation as concrete reasonableness, or the determination of experiences and natural processes through the actualization of intelligible laws remains to be worked out after these early papers.

In any case, it should be clear that Peirce's pragmaticism is committed to a realism. In fact, he even goes so far as to align himself not only with scholastic realism, of which he reminds us in his reflections, but also with Platonism. In a paper of 1906, in an explanation of why he is not a nominalist, he says, "Every realist must, as such, admit that a general is a term and therefore a sign. If in addition, he holds that it is an absolute exemplar, this Platonism passes quite beyond the question of nominalism and realism" (5.470). But he does not claim that there are Platonic Forms in the sense that they are individual static principles of intelligibility that have existence. His counterparts to Platonic Forms in this sense are what he calls *would-be's* that serve in the capacity of dynamic universals. Peirce's would-be's or generals are possibilities that function as rules and are real because they have objectivity in relation to the thoughts that are about them. Would-be's are dispositional properties that have some independence of any particular thought.

Pragmaticism as a Realism or an Objective Idealism

The question of whether there is an object of thought in general – rather than the thoughts of individuals or particular communities – that also has an independent status, even for the convergence of thought at the end of all inquiry in the final opinion, is, however, still open, as suggested earlier. The answer is linked to two alternative questions. Did Peirce intend to propose that inquiry will *in fact* terminate sometime in the future in some final, fixed opinion? Or did he intend to propose that the goal of inquiry must be assigned to a point in an infinite long run or to a point regarded as an ideal end that inquiry will in fact never reach? If we affirm the former, then Peirce's theory of inquiry is based on a metaphysical claim that is committed to a closed teleology, a view that sees purposive processes pervading the universe such that those processes are required to reach some closure when thought is somehow completed and perfected. If we accept the latter alternative, that the goal of inquiry is in the infinite future or is an ideal, then it seems that the theory of inquiry is based on a regulative ideal. Accordingly, the goal of inquiry is a convergence toward which we cannot help directing thought (given the social impulse that drives us to overcome difference), but, more important, the goal is something toward which we *ought* to direct thought (to satisfy the impulse to overcome difference). The former alternative, according to which we will reach completed knowledge as an actual goal of inquiry, puts Peirce much closer to some form of objective idealism. The latter alternative puts him closer to a Kantianism. Which of these two alternatives fits Peirce's architectonic best, or whether there is a third option, remains to be determined in the discussion of his metaphysics of evolutionary realism. Before leaving Peirce's pragmaticism, however, several additional considerations that he regards as integral to the view must be mentioned.

The additional points that fill out Peirce's conception of pragmaticism are found in several unpublished discussions as well as the commentaries he offered in the articles published in the *Monist*. The first point is a reiteration of Peirce's conception of himself as insisting on attending to the model of experimentalism in philosophy. He opens the first *Monist* article by praising the experimentalist for not accepting claims about "deeper reality" than the laws connecting possible objects of experience (5.411–12). But, as already indicated, it does not follow that he is committed to a positivism. The point is that the tests of ideas lie in possibilities. In the present context, Peirce makes this point by saying that the experimentalist is properly concerned with *kinds* of experiments, with conceivable results. It follows that if an idea implies a prediction about future consequences, the prediction should not be construed as specifying particular data. Rather, it should be understood as anticipating kinds of things that happen in general. If our idea of an earthquake implies predictions about tremors and crevices, the details of these results are left open. The prediction need not conceive exactly where and when a crevice will occur. Likewise, the idea of the diamond that never will be tested need not imply specific or actual tests. What is crucial is that there are generalities, relevant and effective in the future, that are predicted, regularities foreseen that would be exemplified under certain conditions, conditions that are in part established by a purpose articulated in a plan of action. "The unity of essence of the experiment lies in its purpose and plan, the ingredients [conditions in the context of any specific experiment] passed over in the enumeration" (5.424). Also, "When an experimentalist speaks of a *phenomenon*, . . . he does not mean any particular event that did happen to somebody in the dead past, but what *surely will* happen to everybody in the living future who shall fulfill certain conditions" (5.425). Most important, "The pragmaticist maxim says nothing of single experiments or of single experimental phenomena . . . but only speaks of *general kinds* of experimental phenomena. Its adherent does not shrink from speaking of general objects as real, since whatever is true represents a real" (5.426). This is essentially that to which Peirce wants pragmaticism to be committed.

Peirce's discussion of the sense in which he is an experimentalist brings to the fore three conceptions associated with pragmaticism that are fundamental ingredients in the envisaged architectonic. These are the affirmation of a *realism* – the reality of general objects – that I have emphasized, the role of the *future* as the ground or foundation of what can be known, and a teleological condition present in *purport* or purposive action following from a plan. Given what has been said about Peirce's commitment to realism, we may pass at once to the second two points. Peirce says, "The rational meaning of every proposition lies in the future. How so? The meaning of a proposition is itself a proposition. Indeed, it is no other than the very proposition of which it is the meaning: it is the translation of it." And the meaning that results is "that form in which the proposition becomes applicable to human conduct . . . that form which is most directly applicable to self-control under every situation, and to every purpose." Meaning, then, concerns the future, and it concerns conduct, or controlled, purposive action in the future. "This is why he [the pragmaticist] locates the meaning in future time; for future conduct is the only conduct that is subject to self-control" (5.427).

The conception of the condition of the future as a ground should also be obvious in light of what we have seen in the function of the final opinion that serves as the goal of inquiry. This goal offers the only basis for fully true belief or for any particular true beliefs that inquiry may determine at an assignable time and place. It is in this sense that he thinks of himself as a "fallibilist," a position that follows from the self-correcting procedures of the scientific method – presupposing both a willingness and an expectation to revise thinking when resistances and constraints are encountered that challenge the habits of beliefs. Thus, Peirce avoids being labeled a "foundationalist" in what I take to be the sense that is often rejected by many if not most contemporary philosophers – that is, in the sense of requiring one's thought to be founded on an ultimate, immutable ground. Such a ground, Peirce thinks, is assumed on the one hand by Cartesianism with its demand for first principles and by British empiricism with its insistence that sense-impressions are discrete foundational experiences on which knowledge is built. Indeed, like other pragmatists, Peirce may be regarded as ahead of the present fashion of condemning this form of foundationalism. However, Peirce's commitment to the objectivism of a future reality that is independent of at least particular, individual, and social conditions for beliefs is a commitment that rejects a relativism that seems so easy to fall into, once foundationalism is renounced. Thus, Peirce does not swing to the extreme of rejecting foundations in favor of absolute contingency as the root of knowledge. His fallibilism is not so extreme. It might be said that he swings to a regulatory foundationalism of the future or, more accurately, a fallibilistic, evolutionary foundationalism – a point of view that I hope will be clearer after we address his evolutionary realism.

The third conception associated with pragmaticism, *purport,* is integral to the content of the future that grounds meaning and truth. If future conduct is predicted as the meaning of a proposition, then some control is required, and purport must inform belief. Thus, in answering a hypothetical questioner about the possibility that the pragmaticist makes doing the "Be-all and the End-all of life," Peirce emphasizes the generality of pragmatistic purport and the consequent commitment it has to an end, a "Be-all and End-all of life" that is a summum bonum, a highest good, that is not action but is "that process of evolution whereby the existent comes more and more to embody those generals which were just now said to be *destined,* which is what we strive to express in calling them *reasonable*. In its higher stages, evolution takes place more and more largely through self-control, and this gives the pragmaticist a sort of justification for making the rational purport to general" (5.433). The link between this conception of pragmaticism and Peirce's metaphysics of evolution is obvious.

A second general consideration associated with Peirce's pragmaticism that needs to be highlighted concerns what he calls his "Critical Common-sensism." This view is treated in the second of the *Monist* articles. He says, "Two doctrines that were defended by the writer about nine years before the formulation of pragmaticism may be treated as consequences of the latter belief [expressed by the pragmatic maxim]" (5.439). One of these is scholastic realism, upon which I have already remarked. The other is critical commonsensism, which he proceeds to explain by discussing six "distinctive characters" by which it is "marked." Of importance here are the first four that indicate aspects of pragmaticism only hinted at in what we have seen. The first three all center on the function of acritical – that is, uncriticized – and some uncriticizable beliefs with which thinking must begin.

It is significant that although Peirce affirms fallibilism and insists that genuine doubt must begin inquiry, he does not hold the view that science and philosophy begin in the midst of a chaotic condition, or radical doubting of all beliefs. After all, this would be to exercise feigned doubt, or some version of Cartesian methodological doubt. Instead, Peirce thinks that inquiry begins in the midst of a mass of accepted beliefs – beliefs that are taken to be indubitable – and inferences (5.440). These are beliefs and inferences of which we may or may not be conscious, and of which we may be only partly conscious. But when reasoning takes place, just to that extent, consciousness of belief and inferential processes is essential. Reasoning is deliberate and controlled. "There are, however, cases in which we are conscious that a belief has been determined by another belief, but are not conscious that it proceeds on any general principle. . . . Such a process should be called, not a reasoning, but an *acritical inference*" (5.441). Further, "It will be found to follow that there are, besides perceptual judgments, original (i.e., indubitable because uncriticized) beliefs of a general and recurrent kind, as well as indubitable acritical inferences" (5.442.). The mass of indubitable beliefs change ever so slightly over time. Yet they are sufficiently stable to be thought of as instinctual. There are two points that are of importance here. The acknowledgment of acritical beliefs and inferences as conditions within which doubt arises and remains to be settled by inquiry highlights Peirce's rejection of the assumption that we can ever clear ourselves of conviction, no matter how committed we might be to doubting everything in order to reach rock-solid foundations. At the same time, the acritical base from which we start thinking is not a foundation, because it, or parts of it, are subject to change. The change may occur without our conscious effort or reflection. But of most importance is the change that may occur through conscious, deliberate control – the self-control of reasoning.

The fourth character of critical commonsensism is "the most distinctive." It is the "insistence that the acritically indubitable is invariably vague" (4.446). Peirce's analysis of vagueness serves as a basis not only for his understanding of generality, which is so important to characterizing reality, but it also may be seen in connection with synechism and Peirce's conception of the continuity that runs throughout an evolutionary universe. The latter topic, of course, must be considered later. The way Peirce's comments about vagueness relate to the meaning of "generality" is direct: Vagueness and generality are species of indeterminacy. A thought is indeterminate if it is undecidable whether a character or its negation belongs to its object. A thought that is vague is indeterminate and requires further thought to interpret or determine its application to its object. Peirce's example in this context is, "A man whom I could mention seems to be a little conceited" (5.447). There is nothing in the statement that justifies its application to a man in view, or to any other particular man. Only the utterer can determine this. Peirce adds that anything is vague "in so far as the principle of contradiction does not apply to it" (5.448). A thought is also general if it is indeterminate and "extends to the interpreter the privilege of carrying its determination further" (5.447). Peirce cites the example, "Man is mortal." "To the question, What man? the reply is that the proposition explicitly leaves it to you to apply its assertion to what man or men you will" (5.447). "Anything is general in so far as the principle of excluded middle does not apply to it" (5.447). The relevance of the two kinds of indeterminacy for the metaphysics of evolution will be suggested later. At the moment, we should recognize that the generals that Peirce refers to as constituting the meanings of concepts are real with respect to their indeterminacy as general – permitting application – rather than with respect to their vagueness. In other words, what is general offers a rule of application. What is vague offers no such rule. Further understanding of how generals function with respect to being indeterminate for interpretation and also with respect to making thought more determinate for interpretation, that is, refining it with respect to vagueness, awaits the treatment of Peirce's theory of categories.

One final comment should be made before we turn to the next major topic, Peirce's semeiotic. In the previous *Monist* article, Peirce proposes to state in a third article a proof that the doctrine of pragmatism is true (5.415). The third article is entitled "Prolegomena to an Apology for Pragmatism" (4.530–72). What should be noted is that Peirce refers to this as a prolegomena and an "Introduction to the defense"

(4.534). Presumably, he does not set forth his discussion in this article as the defense or "proof" itself. The main part of it is devoted to an explanation of part of his logic, the existential graphs. The sense in which this serves as an apology will not be examined. Suffice it to say that the discussion of the graphs is intended to show how Peirce views meaning to be found in conduct — to show "what nature is truly common to all significations of concepts; whereupon a comparison will show whether that nature be or be not the very ilk that Pragmaticism (by the definition of it) avers that it is" (4.534, note 1). The discussion moves into semeiotic, because Peirce's account of what is common in all significations or exactly what kind of sign an existential graph is requires discussing the kinds of signs there are. It is worth noting, too, that this article prepares the way for what Peirce promises in still the next paper, in which the "utility of this diagrammatization of thought in the truth of Pragmatism shall be made to appear." The paper does not appear. In any case, if we are to build on Peirce's pragmaticism in order to reach the architectonic, or to see pragmaticism as the kernel from which the architectonic follows, then we must turn to the theory of signs and the categories that provide its framework.

2

Pragmaticism and Semeiotic

The following discussion of Peirce's pragmaticism and semeiotic will focus on five main topics. First, it will be helpful to sketch the way in which pragmaticism implies semeiotic. Second, the anticipation of semeiotic in the early series of articles, "Certain Faculties Claimed for Man" and "Some Consequences of Four Incapacities," will be considered in order to indicate the way in which Peirce's development of his anti-Cartesianism and his departure from Kant served as a basis for his semeiotic. Third, we shall see how the keys to pragmaticism point us toward Peirce's conception of the three conditions of sign action, or what Peirce refers to by the term semeiosis. These conditions will then be discussed. Fourth, it will be found that one of the conditions of semeiosis, the object, is presemeiotic, or preinterpreted, and at the same time semeiotic. A distinction Peirce makes between two kinds of object, the immediate and the dynamical, will then be considered briefly. Finally, Peirce's classification of signs will be outlined.

Thoughts Are Signs

The implications of pragmaticism for semeiotic should be clear. Pragmaticism is a theory of meaning. The meanings of general concepts or terms, it will be recalled, are dispositions, habits, or laws that can be formulated in linguistic expressions. Insofar as these meanings are indeterminate with respect not only to vagueness but also to generality, they remain to be interpreted with respect to the particular consequences that follow from acting in accord with them. They must be interpreted with reference to the patterns of consequences that they represent. The concept of hardness represents a mode of experiencing the results of tests such as scratching, a high degree of resistance to pressure, and other consequences. As representations, then, general terms are signs. They are signs that stand for rules for the purpose of delineating meanings. Further, if meaning consists of ever-widening connected consequences, then the pragmaticist's maxim concerns a dynamic system of references – a growing web of consequences and their interpretations, which not only are referred to but which themselves also refer to further interpretations. The pragmaticist maxim is a maxim that must imply a system of signs.

An explicit (although brief) explication of semeiotic as it relates to pragmaticism appears in Peirce's "A Survey of Pragmatism," written in about 1906. It will be helpful to notice what Peirce says here about signs before we turn to other papers in which he sets forth his semeiotic, because the discussion in the 1906 paper is explicitly made integral to pragmatism. (In this context, I shall use the term *pragmatism*, rather than *pragmaticism*, following Peirce's own usage in the paper under consideration.) Furthermore, his discussion of signs contains in condensed form the substance of his semeiotic. In "A Survey of Pragmatism," Peirce initiates his account of the link between pragmatism and semeiotic with the assertion that "The next moment of the argument for pragmatism is the view that every thought is a sign" (5.470.) This identification of thoughts as signs appears elsewhere, indeed, very early in Peirce's career, in the seminal essays of the late 1860s. In the present context, however, the classification of thoughts as signs explicitly affirms the point as essential to pragmatism. Thinking, then, is sign development, or a process of sign interpretation, and the entire process is called *semeiosis* (which Peirce sometimes spells "semiosis").

Consistent with his aim of distancing himself from the popular version of the scope of the pragmatic maxim – and as we have seen in connection with his reflections on the maxim – he claims that the idea that every thought is a sign is not a form of nominalism. In this context, what he means is that his conception of thoughts as signs should be understood as extending to real referents of thoughts that are not individual existent things that are unknowable in themselves. He insists that, on the contrary, what he sometimes calls *reals* are generals rather than individuals.

A thought, then, is a general concept. Further, there are repeatable patterns that are objects of thoughts as well as themselves thoughts. Thus, when he says that his view that thoughts are signs is not a nominalism, he goes on to explain that he is proposing a form of realism – a realism of "a somewhat extreme stripe" (5.470). Thus, here and in other places, as we have seen, Peirce associates pragmaticism as a theory of thought-signs with a realism, which can be understood with reference to a form of Platonism. A general, or the object of a general term, is a real condition of intelligibility that is not exhausted by a set of sensible consequences.

This realism, as has been pointed out, is not a Platonism that regards generals as abstract forms that are set apart from empirical consequences. As we might expect from Peirce's attachment to experimental inquiry, signs make a difference in empirical as well as intellectual consequences. Thoughts or signs are active and dynamic. They act on one another. At the same time, generals are dynamic rules or patterns that are conditions of activities, or the way conditions and consequences in nature are ordered. And they are dynamic not only because they are conditions of actions but also because they evolve.

It should be noted that Peirce does not say that all signs are thoughts. Signs are themselves generals that have their functions in nature, or in what thought is about. Thus, signs are effective in nature as well as in thought. And their effective role in nature exhibits a dimension of semeiosis that underlies the thought–sign equation. Let us then focus on the semeiosis implied by this equation. Before doing so, however, let me point out that it remains to be discussed whether what thought is about — that is, whether the effective actualization of patterns of consequences — is itself interpretable as nothing but thought.

In their effective capacity, thought-signs or generals function dyadically, that is, as relations in which there are two things or events, one acting on the other. The object of the sign acts on the sign, as a bullet acts so that it leaves a hole that can be interpreted as a sign of the bullet. Yet if signs were only dyads, they would not have risen to a level of experience for which thought is intelligible or meaningful, because it has not yet been interpreted. Smoke is a sign of fire in the sense that it is a result of fire and can thus be thought of as an indication of fire. However, smoke is not a thought-sign unless it is interpreted. Until a third thing is introduced into the relation — something that mediates between the two things by interpreting one as the sign of another — no genuine sign can be said to function. What makes a sign genuine is its being part of a triad that cannot be broken or analyzed into sets of dyads. Consequently, the presence of an interpretant, which is one member of the triad, is essential to the genuineness of the sign situation and to the sign that functions in that situation. This point is borne out in a paper of about 1902: "The triadic relation is *genuine*, that is its three members are bound together by it in a way that does not consist in any complexus of dyadic relations. That is the reason the Interpretant, or Third, cannot stand in a mere dyadic relation to the Object" (2.274). Things that are not genuine signs, however, may function in a way that may lead to their becoming signs. They are not genuine signs if they are not yet subject to the conscious control of inquiry. An experience or thing in nature that stands only in a dyadic relation, a relation in which there is not a third thing or event mediating between it and something else, is something that is not functioning as a genuine sign — as an interpreted sign. However, if a thing or an experience is to be or become intelligible, then it must be interpreted or be interpretable, and this is to be triadic, or capable of becoming triadic. In short, in their fullest or genuine function, signs must be participants in triadic actions that relate sign, object, and interpretant. It should be noted that I use Peirce's term *interpretant* rather than *interpretation,* which Peirce also uses. "Interpretant" is broader, covering all intelligible outcomes that relate one thing to another, and neutral with respect to whether an individual mental process, a human intelligence, does the interpreting. Interpretants need not be existent minds, mental acts, or individual events of any kind. Thus, Peirce says, it is not necessary that the interpretant should actually exist. A being *in futuro* will suffice (2.92). My point is that Peirce wants to generalize the condition necessary for the triadic, mediating action that constitutes semeiotic processes. This distinction between interpretant and interpretation will be considered further later.

The idea of being triadic must be spelled out. The larger framework required for understanding this connection will lead us to other works in which Peirce defines and classifies signs. However, in anticipation of this classification, it will be helpful to consider an earlier stage of Peirce's thought that precedes his early pragmatism of "The Fixation of Belief" and "How to Make Our Ideas Clear." We shall turn back to the development of his anti-Cartesianism found in the very early 1868 papers, "Questions Concerning Certain Faculties Claimed for Man" and "Some Consequences of Four Incapacities."

The Anti-Cartesian Basis of Pragmaticism and Semeiotic

The main points in the two papers on human faculties that bear on this study concern especially Peirce's insistence on the continuity of thought. The way in which thought is said to be continuous is the basis of the function of thoughts as signs. Continuity and the semeiotic character of thought also have a bearing on the presence of spontaneity and, in turn, the condition of evolution. In these two early papers, however, Peirce's purpose is not to address these points directly. Instead, they must be seen as implied by what he says. His main concern is to establish logic as a science that is independent of psychologism (the view that logic is dependent on psychology), the Kantian conception of things-in-themselves, and the commitments of Cartesian presuppositions, which Peirce thinks are contrary to the principle of continuity. Let us look briefly at the first of the two papers in order to see the main issues that Peirce attacks. We can then concentrate at somewhat greater length on the second and better-known paper, which treats the consequences of the errors in the Cartesian conception of human faculties that Peirce points out in the first paper and elaborates on in the second.

The overall purpose of "Questions Concerning Certain Faculties" is epistemological: to determine the possibility and the limits of knowledge. To accomplish this task, Peirce discusses seven questions, which he treats in scholastic fashion insofar as he subjects them to discussion of affirmative and negative answers to each. In attacking the first question, he rejects the crucial Cartesian notion of cognitive intuition, a rejection that is central to the development of his semeiotic. Thus, Peirce regards intuitions as noninferential experiences, as we shall see in a moment. This is not to say, however, that he denies that we have intuitions. Throughout, he objects not to the fact that there are intuitions but to the possibility of their being known to be intuitions without recourse to inference. Further, in a footnote, he distinguishes two kinds of intuitions. One kind of intuition occurs when we have knowledge of the present as present. This kind is mentioned in both the note and the main text; and it is not rejected (5.213, note 1, and 5.214). If Peirce had reflected on what he only identifies here, however, the term *knowledge*, which is used in identifying intuition of the present as present, would, I think, be replaced with the expression *consciousness of.* I believe this is his meaning; otherwise, an intuition consisting of knowledge of the present as present would be an inference. Such experience is important for the analysis, to be discussed later, of how propositions are formed and categories presupposed, which he offers earlier in "On A New List of Categories." It is also important for the phenomenology that he developed later in his career. However, the kind of intuition that he does reject is alleged cognition that is not determined by a previous cognition of the same object. Peirce associates the condition of there being an object that is the same for more than one cognition with his denial that there can be a Kantian transcendental object – an object in itself, which has a direct or unmediated affect on thought without being in itself knowable. We have seen that Peirce struggled with the idea of such an object. In the paper under consideration and its sequel, he explicitly argues against it. The problems generated by this rejection when it is seen in the light of Peirce's realism have been indicated and will be considered further. In any case, it is clear here that Peirce insists that we have no way intuitively of distinguishing an intuition from a cognition determined by other cognitions. Such a distinction depends on inference, relating one instance of experience to another or to a transcendental object – the latter being rejected. Whatever is asserted as knowledge must be part of a system. Cognitions cannot be insulated. They must function through connections. They must lead somewhere. It is obvious that this conception of cognition is the basis for Peirce's identification of thought with signs. There is an interpretative component in every cognition.

Peirce's principle of the interdependence of all instances of knowledge applies not only to attention to things regarded in the world within which consciousness occurs, but also to attention to consciousness itself. Thus, in treating the second question, he denies that we have cognitively valid intuitive self-consciousness or knowledge of our private selves. Self-consciousness develops after birth when we become aware of erroneous judgment and ignorance, which requires inference, because recognition of limitation where expectations are thwarted consists of recognizing relations. And one relation holds between the phenomenon that was not expected and something that expected or anticipated it. Thus, one *supposes* a self, a self that is fallible.

For our present purpose, we may pass over the third and fourth questions. These concern the distinction between subjective cognition and nonsubjective cognitions and the possibility of introspection that marks off internal from external facts. The key point in "Questions" that bears on semeiotic is Peirce's answer to the fifth question concerning whether we can think without signs. And it is here that he develops the allusion to signs or representations that are essential to the origin of cognition as it is analyzed in the earlier paper, "On a New List of Categories." Thus, the first of the cognition papers that we are considering lays the groundwork suggested in the earlier paper in which both Peirce's semeiotic and his categories are initiated.

Thought, then, consists of signs. Every thought must be interpreted by another thought, because each thought itself is what it is in a moment and cannot by itself exist at different moments. If it were absolutely isolated, however, it would not persist and function cognitively; so it must be sustained through time by another thought, which in turn is sustained by still another thought. Each thought depends on addressing itself to the mind at another time. It should be noted that with the introduction of temporal conditions for the relation of one thought to another, Peirce presupposes a principle of continuity. At this stage, Peirce does not focus attention on the principle. As we shall see later, his accounts of his view about continuity show that his thinking about it evolved. In this early paper, however, the need for understanding continuity is made obvious. More attention to the problems that give rise to the need for assuming continuity is added in the discussion of the seventh question. Before turning to the seventh question, it should be mentioned that the sixth question concerns the possibility that we can conceive what is incognizable – which Peirce views as self-contradictory – and serves as the basis for denying that there can be a thing-in-itself that is unrelated to thought. What is self-contradictory is the supposed conception of what is not and cannot be conceived or related to thought. If a thing is not related to thought, then it cannot be conceived. If it is conceived, then it must be related to thought.

The seventh question addresses directly the point that there cannot be a first cognition or a cognition that is not determined by a previous cognition. (A Cartesian supposes that there must be a beginning to thought in some first premise.) The discussion offers support for the question of the impossibility of intuitively knowing whether we have an intuition, and it adds to the argument offered in answering the first question, whether underived cognitions are genuine cognitions. As we have seen, Peirce already has insisted that thoughts are temporally related. No thought can occur and be meaningful in an instant. A first cognition, or undetermined cognition, would be an intuition, which would need to take place in isolation. Furthermore, as Peirce puts it, we cannot know by a first cognition whether it is indeed a cognition. We cannot use a first cognition or intuition to decide whether it itself or another determination of conscious experience is an intuition and cognitively meaningful. We could only know this by inference, as shown in his answer to the first of the seven questions concerning human faculties. If there were a first cognition, it would have to be known as such by means of a process of relating it to other cognitions; its cognitive value would depend on inference, and on the process of relating it, which is temporal. However, Peirce points out, we face the problem of understanding how instances of cognition can be related to one another in time. How do intervals join? As a suggestion for answering this question, Peirce formulates an analogy between an inverted triangle dipped in water and the temporal relations among instances of cognition. Each line on the triangle established by the surface of the water represents an instance of consciousness functioning cognitively. The longer lines present at the larger part of the triangle are analogous to a more lively state of consciousness, whereas the shorter lines formed at the narrower part of the triangle, the lines closer to the apex, are analogous to less lively states of consciousness that are more remote in time.

Suppose an inverted triangle . . . to be gradually dipped in water. At any date or instant, the surface of the water makes a horizontal line across that triangle. This line represents a cognition. At a subsequent date, there is a sectional line so made, higher upon the triangle. This represents another cognition of the same object determined by the former, and having livelier consciousness. (5.263)

How is any present line connected with the previous one? In what does the interval between them consist? Peirce proposes that these intervals are infinitesimal, because there is no moment at which there is no activity whatsoever. There are no gaps. Between any two lines there are other lines.

To say, then, that if there be a state of cognition by which all subsequent cognitions of a certain object are not determined, there must subsequently be some cognition of that object not determined by previous cognitions of the same object, is to say that when that triangle is dipped into the water there must be a sectional line made by the surface of the water lower than which no surface line had been made in that way. But draw the horizontal line where you will, as many horizontal lines as you please can be assigned at finite distances below it and below one another. For any such section is at some distance above the apex, otherwise it is not a line. Let this distance be a. Then there have been similar sections at the distances $1/2a$, $1/4a$, $1/16a$, above the apex, and so on as you please. So that it is not true that there must be a first. . . . The point here insisted on is not this or that logical solution of the difficulty, but merely that cognition arises by a *process* of beginning, as any other change comes into place. (5.263)

As already pointed out, Peirce does not pursue the conception of continuity assumed here. However, it is clear that he does insist on the idea that there is no absolute beginning of thought. If there were, then there would be no interval between this thought and a past thought. There is inevitably some smaller interval of time prior to any alleged first act of thought. There is always some distance between any given line and the apex, or object with which thought is concerned. Further, there is continuity of thought, which is to say that in cognitive experience, which is distinct from unconnected moments of feeling and brute intrusions in experience that come with surprises, there are no gaps within time and memory that are active in consciousness. Conscious thought emerges from a continuum. The importance of this conception of thought will be emphasized in the discussion of the categories as well as in the account of continuity that Peirce includes in what he says about synechism.

Before moving to the second paper in the sequence, a question should be raised concerning the significance of the triangle and its apex just prior to its being dipped. In considering the relation of one thought to another that the first is in process of determining, Peirce says, "the apex of the triangle represents the object external to the mind which determines both these cognitions. The state of the triangle before it reaches the water, represents a state of cognition which contains nothing which determines these subsequent cognitions" (ibid.). The triangle as a whole thus seems to be insulated, autonomous, with respect to any process of cognition. The triangle represents a cognition that as yet is undetermining with respect to future cognitions; thus, it must be a possibility for knowledge – a mental condition that has not yet acted or has not been acted on. Presumably, Peirce's account of the place of such a mental state in a more general epistemology must be seen in light of the mass of provisionally indubitable beliefs with which philosophy begins. It also remains to be worked out in terms of the categories that he proposes later. And in that context, the mental state not yet enacted is, I think, an aspect of his first category, which, as will be explained later, is a category of possibility.

The undipped apex is an external object, which suggests that it is an object that transcends any mind or finite system of minds that might know it. However, this object cannot be incognizable, in light of the denial of the possibility of conceptions of incognizable objects. Indeed, that an object should be incognizable, as we have noticed, has been said to be self-contradictory. And the cognizability of external objects is confirmed in the analogy, for the apex of the triangle that represents the object is integral to the triangle; and so the object would be integral to mind or thought in general, which is represented by the triangle as a whole, insofar as minds contribute to thought in general or to cognition. Thus, it is not clear how to account for the triangle before it touches the water.

One suggestion is that when Peirce says that the apex is an external object, he means that the apex is a limit that the series of conscious thoughts would approach if the triangle (the mind) were dipped (became activated). The analogy would be faulty on this account, however, because the direction required by the image by which conscious thoughts relate to the apex moves thought away from the apex. The more recent cognitions are those farther removed from the apex. Instead, we might regard the apex as what Peirce in his semeiotic calls the *suppositum* or initiating object of interpretation. The apex would then be a limit, but it would be a limit that is not approached directly; instead it is a limit to which thought could only return if the entire triangle were submersed and the whole of thought consumed the cognition, including the *suppositum* or object of thought in general. This possibility will be raised later when we consider what Peirce has to say about the aim of inquiry in papers he wrote a decade later.

As is suggested by the title, "Some Consequences of Four Incapacities," which is the sequel to the paper on which we have been focusing, identifies four incapacities or limits on what the mind can accomplish cognitively. These are drawn from the seven questions addressed in the former paper that we have just considered. Thus, on the basis of the denials in the former paper, Peirce insists that we have (1) no power of introspection, (2) no power of intuition, (3) no power of thinking without signs, and (4) no conception of the absolutely incognizable.[1] He discusses the consequences of each of these limits. Our

---

[1] Peirce does not systematically discuss consequences of each of the answers to the seven questions posed in the earlier article, although he seems to suggest that he will do so at the beginning of his second article. Instead, he merges the main points of all his answers, presumably thinking that the four points he does discuss cover the incapacities insofar as they are all related to the fundamental question about the power to have cognitive intuitions and to have any experience that is cognitive without its having relations to other experiences that are cognitive.

main concern is with the third, that thought requires signs, which introduces one of the most explicit early accounts of the conditions of sign processes:

Now a sign has, as such, three references: first, it is a sign *to* some thought which interprets it; second, it is a sign *for* some object to which in that thought it is equivalent; third, it is a sign, *in* some respect or quality, which brings it into connection with its object. Let us ask what the three correlates are to which a thought-sign refers. (5.283)

In answering his question about the three correlates to which a sign refers, Peirce lays the basis for the more fully developed semeiotic that we shall consider in a moment. It should be helpful to highlight three ideas that are presented in Peirce's discussion. The idea of the eventfulness and temporality of thought-signs is emphasized. Thoughts "flow freely" following the "law of mental association," each thought suggesting something to a following thought, and the former is a sign of the latter. And because "there is no intuition or cognition not determined by previous cognitions, it follows that the striking in of a new experience is never an instantaneous affair, but is an *event* occupying time, and coming to pass by a continuous process" (5.284). Thoughts grow and die out gradually. Peirce here anticipates his 1892 paper, "The Law of Mind," which plays an important role in showing how Peirce came to grips with the idea of continuity and its integral place in his synechism.

The second idea to be highlighted has to do with the objects of signs: "The next question is: For what does the thought-sign stand — what does it name — what is its *suppositum*? The outward thing, undoubtedly, when a real outward thing is thought of. But still, as the thought is determined by a previous thought of the same object, it only refers to the thing through denoting this previous thought" (5.285). Peirce here cites the example of an individual man who has a proper name. Abraham Lincoln, to cite an example not used by Peirce, is the *suppositum*, or what I have called "the initiating object," for a sign process. This individual, Peirce proposes, is referred to by some character or class to which he belongs — the class of presidents of the United States. One then first thinks of Abraham Lincoln as a president. And this thought may be followed by other interpretations of this president as male, and human. However, being human refers to Abraham Lincoln through the previous thought, president, so that Lincoln is thought of as a president who is a human being. "And so in every case the subsequent thought denotes what was thought in the previous thought" (5.285). Thus, a sign stands for its object "in the respect which is thought; that is to say, this respect is the immediate object of consciousness in the thought, or, in other words, it is the thought itself, or at least what the thought is thought to be in the subsequent thought to which it is a sign" (5.286). Peirce's account here lends credence to interpreting his semeiotic as idealistic, or as pansemeiotic. There is, however, another dimension of the objects of signs that Peirce suggests and insists on elsewhere, that is, the object as real and independent of the object as represented, or as a sign. This is the dynamical object, which we shall consider later.

The third idea introduced by Peirce in his discussion of the consequences of his thought-sign principle that deserves to be brought to our attention concerns the properties of things that are capable of functioning as signs. "Since a sign is not identical with the thing signified, but differs from the latter in some respects, it must plainly have some characteristics which belong to it in itself, and have nothing to do with its representative function" (5.287). For instance, inscriptions of words are signs in part because of the shapes of the inscriptions. Smoke may be a sign because it has a relation to fire. He then offers a description of these independent characters, providing the groundwork for one of the classifications of signs developed in his mature semeiotic. Here his description concerns what he calls *the material condition* of signs, conditions that are the basis for the way a thing functions as a sign, or the kind of sign it is. For instance, an image in a mirror may be a sign of the thing reflected because of the colors and shapes of the image. This condition is the basis of iconic meaning. Or, to cite another example, smoke may be a sign of fire because its properties make up an effect of an existent cause, fire. This condition is the basis of indexical signs. The classification of signs as both icons and indexes along with signs as symbols will be considered in a moment. Let us now proceed to the semeiotic as it appeared later in a more developed form.

Signs and Their Conditions

In approaching the larger framework for understanding Peirce's semeiotic in its developed form, let us begin with definitions, or what perhaps should be more loosely called *descriptions*. There are various passages in which Peirce describes signs and the conditions under which they function. For the most part, they refer to the triad sign, object, and interpretant. For instance, to return to the manuscript of about 1902, he says:

A *Sign*, or *Representamen*, is a First which stands in such a genuine triadic relation to a Second, called its *Object*, as to be capable of determining a Third, called its *Interpretant*, to assume the same triadic relation to its Object in which it stands itself to the same Object. (2.274)

And, in a long manuscript that contains an extended discussion of semeiosis, he says:

Grant, then, that every thought is a sign. Now the essential nature of a sign is that it mediates between its Object, which is supposed to determine it and to be, in some sense, the cause of it, and its Meaning. . . . the object and the interpretant being the two correlates of every sign. . . . the object is the antecedent, the interpretant the consequent of the sign. (MS. 318, pp. 328–32)

Peirce's point may be illustrated by the example of the thought of Abraham Lincoln. The thought of him as a president stands in a triadic relation, for it is one of three components necessary for the relation to be meaningful. The components are (1) its object, what is named; (2) itself; and (3) another thought-interpretant that the sign (2) determines. The interpretant that the sign determines is the thought, human being, which stands for Abraham Lincoln just as the interpretant-thought of being a president does. The interpretant, being human, may be further developed into another interpretant, the thought of being male, and in turn this may be further developed by the thought of being a believer in the abolition of slavery. Thus, the first interpretant and the further interpretants assume triadic relation to the object of the determining interpretant as did the first.

There are four main points that I should like to highlight in these descriptions of signs. First, Peirce says that a sign is determined by its object. Thus, there must be an independent factor in the process of interpreting signs. This is not to say that interpretation contributes nothing. It should be clear that Peirce is not a naive realist. However, it is to say that there are external resistances, some independent condition constraining interpretation. The sign is determined by "something *other than itself*." Accordingly, Peirce also insists that a sign itself cannot give one acquaintance with its objects. By "Object of a Sign . . . is meant that with which it presupposes an acquaintance in order to convey some further information concerning it" (2.231). Someone must be acquainted with Abraham Lincoln and the present-day sign user who thinks of Abraham Lincoln as a president must be acquainted through other signs and interpretations with the historical person, Abraham Lincoln, and with the idea of presidents. Such acquaintance is "collateral observation" that conditions sign interpretation. It is collateral because it is not internal to the particular series of signs that develop from the initiating object, the proper name referring to an individual. In the case of Abraham Lincoln, collateral observation for us, of course, does not include direct acquaintance with the individual to whom the name applies. Yet our collateral observation does include the constraints of an entire system of historical and political signs and acquaintance with individuals with proper names and presuppositions about acquaintance with the name *Abraham Lincoln* applied to an individual in the nineteenth century. The independent factor that plays a role in sign interpretation will be discussed later in connection with

Peirce's distinction between the dynamical object and the immediate object.

The second point to notice is that, although objects, or something about them, constrain signs, signs themselves not only constrain but create meaning in determining the interpretant. Thus, although there are factors external to the immediate interpretive processes, interpretive processes also include their own developmental conditions that contribute to an evolving system of signs. The developing interpretation of Abraham Lincoln (a president, etc.) illustrates these conditions. As Peirce says in "The Art of Reasoning," a paper of about 1895, "Symbols grow. They come into being by development out of other signs, particularly from icons, or from mixed signs partaking of the nature of icons and symbols" (2.302). Icons, as we shall see, are things that represent objects by virtue of some features intrinsic to the thing that functions as an icon – for example, a photograph. Such iconic conditions, again as we shall see, are presupposed by symbols.

The third point is that the distinction between interpretant and interpretation is implied not only because Peirce uses the word *interpretant* rather than *interpretation* in the first of the two passages quoted, but also because in the second passage he makes a point of capitalizing the word *mind* and qualifying its reference as something potential as well as actual. That there is a distinction between interpretant and interpretation, it may be recalled, was mentioned in the earlier brief account of the triadic nature of signs.

W. B. Gallie nicely shows the breadth of Peirce's conception of interpretants. He points out that for Peirce our determination of whether a thing has been interpreted is found not by inspecting the contents of someone's mind but by seeing what behavior follows from contact with the thing in question.[2] These qualifications are consistent with his aim of avoiding subjectivist consequences for his theory of meaning. At a time late in his career, in a letter to Lady Welby, he expresses regrets that he suggested that interpretation is confined to particular acts of human intelligence, to finite minds, or what he also refers to as "modifications of consciousness." He excuses himself as having assumed that he needed to speak of interpretation as purely mental in the sense of "some mind or other," because he believed that he would not otherwise be understood.[3] He assumed what seems now too to influence our understanding of sign theory, namely, that we are inclined to anthropomorphize and individualize the conditions of sign

---

[2] W. B. Gallie, *Peirce and Pragmatism* (New York: Dover Publications, 1966), pp. 118–20.

[3] See Charles S. Hardwick, ed., *Semiotics and Significs, The Correspondence between Charles S. Peirce and Victoria Lady Welby* (Bloomington: Indiana University Press, 1977), p. 81.

action by regarding interpretative action as purely the function of individual, subjective mental acts.

The move away from the subjectivist version of the conception of meaning is even more strongly affirmed when, following his identification of the three conditions of the semeiotic triad, Peirce makes a distinction between the terms *sign* and *representamen*. The distinction states:

A *Sign* is a Representamen with a mental Interpretant. Possibly there may be Representamens that are not Signs. Thus, if a sunflower, in turning towards the sun, becomes by that very act fully capable, without further condition, of reproducing a sunflower which turns in precisely corresponding ways toward the sun, and of doing so with the same reproductive power, the sunflower would become a Representamen of the sun. (2.274)

In the broadest sense, then, semeiotic may comprise things that are independent of fully functioning signs, but which are capable of being seen as representative. Such things in themselves are not, strictly, genuine signs, because, as we have seen, they are not things that represent something for an interpretant – their status is to be potentially, not actually, interpreted. The sun-directed sunflower, dyadically related to the sun, functioning in just this dyadic way, is not yet a genuine sign. And only if it is also related to an offspring does it function as a representamen of the sun – not as a sign in the mental sense – for the offspring.

To revert to our discussion of the reality of the references of general terms, specifically to the untested diamond, on the broader conception of the way things can be approached through semeiotic, the diamond may be said to function as a sign that represents hardness, among other things, even though it is not seen or touched. This is to say that an untested diamond is a thing that is not subjected to interpretation, but it can nevertheless be regarded as capable of interpretation, in which case, the general disposition to not being scratched by many other substances is something that is potentially a genuine sign – that is, a property or meaning for a possible tester. The relation of nonmental or premental representation to mentally interpreted signs will be considered in a moment.

The fourth point in the passages in which signs are described concerns the fact that in both descriptions, the sequence in which Peirce identifies the three conditions of a semeiotic process places the conditions called a *sign* first, the object second, and the interpretant third. The significance of the ordinal numbers that Peirce uses, however, require that we abstract them from the components that are identified as a first, a second, and a third with respect to describing what a sign is. Thus, what is called a first, a second, or a third will depend on where we are in the semeiotic system. An interpretant, which is a third with respect to mediating between sign and object, becomes a sign standing in "the same triadic relation" to its object as does the initial sign. In the previously cited example, the thought of presidents denoting Abraham Lincoln can be considered a first as a sign. However, it is a second if we attend to the interpretant thought of being human and regard it as a sign. Thus, what was a third is regarded as a first.

With these points in mind, we may move on to identify the conditions of sign processes. Instead of simply identifying the three obvious conditions, sign, object, and interpretant, I shall point out how a fourth condition must be recognized, although this condition functions in the place of one of the other conditions so that recognizing it does not break with Peirce's analysis of semeioses into three working components.

In a fragment of a paper of 1897, and after some introductory remarks in which he identifies logic, "in its general sense," with semeiotic, Peirce offers a description of signs that includes a condition that is generally overlooked in semeiotic studies, which identify only three – sign, object, and interpretant. In this passage, a more complex situation seems necessary for there to be genuine signs that function in genuine semeiotic processes. The description is as follows:

A sign, or *representamen,* is something which stands to somebody for something in some respect or capacity. It addresses somebody, that is, creates in the mind of that person an equivalent sign, or perhaps a more developed sign. That sign which it creates I call the *interpretant* of the first sign. The sign stands for something, its *object.* It stands for that object, not in all respects, but in reference to a sort of idea, which I have sometimes called the *ground* of the representamen. "Idea" is here to be understood in a sort of Platonic sense, very familiar in everyday talk; I mean in that sense in which we say that one man catches another man's idea, in which we say that when a man recalls what he was thinking of at some previous time, he recalls the same idea, and in which when a man continues to think anything, say for a tenth of a second, in so far as the thought continues to agree with itself during that time, that is to have a *like* content, it is the same idea, and is not at each instant of the interval a new idea. (2.228)

This statement is quoted at length because not only does it makes clear once again Peirce's realism, but, and more important for our immediate purposes, it identifies the component of semeiosis that is often overlooked by many who propose sign theories. As Peirce puts it, a sign or representamen is "connected with three things, the ground, the object, and the interpretant" (2.229). As already noted, the conditions of sign situations are usually said to be sign, object, and interpretant. What Peirce here calls the *respect* or *ground* by which the sign stands for its object is thus omitted, even though in the passage just quoted, it is added to these conditions as it is in the better known passage from "Some Consequences of Four Incapacities." Yet this apparently fourth condition is essential in Peirce's analysis. Is a sign situation or semeiotic process, then, essentially tetradic? Is it composed of four terms, rather than three, in spite of Peirce's triadicism affirmed throughout his writing, especially in his discussions of the fundamental categories as well as of semeiotic? The answer, I think, is no.

One way of understanding the place of the ground or respect in triadic semeioses requires seeing signs as the same as semeioses, or units of processes. In the present context, Peirce regards the sign or representamen in its relation to sign situations considered as wholes that are composed of ingredients necessary to the functioning of things as representamens. Thus, a sign is not thought of as one among three components or conditions for semeiotic processes. Rather, a sign is an instance of a semeiotic process. Or, in terms of the identity of such a process, it is the focal factor of a structured whole that is composed of three components that serve as conditions of any semeiotic process.[4] A semeiotic process requires that there be something that has an object for which that thing stands, an interpretant that relates it to its object, and a respect or ground that qualifies the relation between the thing functioning as a sign and its object.

The same kind of analysis also appears in Peirce's early paper, "Some Consequences of Four Incapacities," which we have considered for other purposes. He says there that a sign has three "references; 1st, it is a sign *to* some thought which interprets it; 2d, it is a sign *for* some object to which in that thought it is equivalent; 3d, it is a sign, *in* some respect or quality, which brings it into connection with its object" (5.283). Further, if Peirce's conception of a genuine sign as a triadic relation is taken at face value, a sign must be conceived of as a whole unit that has three tails, or places for subjects that are related. The respect or ground is one of the three subjects related to the two others, object and interpretant. It is the *respect* in which something functioning as a sign can stand in relation to an object by the mediation of the interpretant. Thus, the sign relation may be represented as the sign's being constituted as the whole triad:

A second point concerning this way of understanding the place of grounds or respects in triadic semeioses depends on recognizing that

[4]Max Fisch, I think, suggests this way of understanding a sign situation in "Peirce's General Theory of Signs," in *Semiotics and Significs,* pp. 321–35. See also T. L. Short, "Semeiosis and Intentionality," *Transaction of the Charles S. Peirce Society* 17, no. 3 (Summer 1981).

they qualify the object. Thus, if we relate the triad in which the ground is one of the subjects of the sign in process, we can understand the relation of respects to sign and object as established by virtue of the respects serving as the way the object is represented to the interpretant. This action of an object's being represented in a certain respect, then, constitutes the object as what is immediately given for the sign as it is interpreted. This is what Peirce sometimes calls *the immediate object.* Regarded in this way, the ground merges with the object, but with the object on the interpreted side of the relation between object and sign.[5] Thus, the object on the preinterpreted side is what Peirce sometimes calls the *dynamical object,* which retains independence of the semeiotic process within which the sign arises. The immediate object, then, is a ground or a complex of grounds.

The analysis of a semeiotic process that I have proposed has consequences for the question concerning nonhuman interpretations and the relation of nonhuman to human semeioses. In the first place, as already suggested at the outset, a sign need not be described exclusively in terms of human interpretation. Peirce's use of the term representamen as broader and more fundamental than sign is intended to make this point. Peirce uses representamen in order to show that a thing can represent something without being humanly interpreted. But, in addition, the respect or ground is a condition that functions to qualify the object, and it is identified as having objectivity of the kind that instances of Platonic Ideas or Forms have. We already have seen Peirce's suggestions that his pragmaticist view affirms that the generals that are objects of general terms are objective conditions that function as rules that determine consequences. The respects or grounds that qualify the relation of a sign to its object for the interpretive outcome also function as generals or rules for determining consequences or interpreted meanings. Further, these Forms that qualify the object for the interpretant are what presents the object to the interpretant.

At this point, we should consider further the idea that the complex of Forms that are the respects in which the object determines interpretation may be called the immediate object. This point is important because it is related directly to the issue of determining what objective factors constrain interpretation. Immediate objects are to be distinguished from what Peirce calls dynamical or dynamic objects. Thus, he says that "a sign has two objects, its object as it is represented and its object in itself" (8.333). The object "in itself" is the object of a sign insofar as the object functions as a condition that has some indepen-

---

[5]Peirce's analysis of the formation of propositions in "On a New List of Categories," to be considered later, makes this point in terms of the classical, subject–predicate conception of propositions. The quality abstracted from the substance and expressed by the predicate applied to the subject is said to be the ground of the substance and is "embodied" in the substance.

dence from the interpretive process and that constrains the way objects are represented. The relation of dynamical objects to immediate objects and in turn to semeioses will be pursued further, and the first step in doing this will be to raise the question of when a thing can be said to function semeiotically. Thus, we may ask, How does semeiosis originate? Let me point out, however, that in asking about origins, the idea of originating is to be understood not simply in temporal terms, but also in "logical" terms, or in terms of priority of subjects in their relations considered in abstraction from the times when the subjects enter these relations.

Incipient Signs and Semeiotic Processes

As a first step toward answering the question of origin, we must consider semeiotic processes and things and events that are not interpreted by human intelligence. As an entry into this task, let us return for a moment to the idea of the connection between pragmaticism and semeiotic. We have observed that the connection between semeiotic and pragmaticism is obvious because of Peirce's linking of the theory of meaning with the determination of consequences. In the 1906 paper, Peirce makes this link explicit in saying that the consequences of an idea are found in "the proper significate outcome of a sign," which is the interpretant (5.473). He proposes that the study of interpretants may solve the problem of what the meanings of intellectual concepts are (5.475). The groundwork for this study is an explanation of the nature of triadic action, the test of which lies in the relations between the components or subjects of the relation. If A produces B and, in addition, B produces C, there is no triadic action. But if A produces B in order to bring about C, then the action is triadic. There must be a telos operative within the relation.

An example of dyadic action is a rising pulse rate that is caused by the presence of a fever. The pulse rate is a symptom or *index* of the fever. If the rapid pulse in turn leads to dizziness, we have two dyadic actions, the fever producing a rising pulse rate and the rising pulse rate producing the dizziness. But the conjunction of these dyads is not a triad. The fever did not occur in order to produce, or for the sake of, the dizziness. On the other hand, if a mental representation of the rising pulse rate (that is then regarded as an index of fever) is produced, say in the thought of a physician, a triad is produced, for the physician then interprets this representation of the rapid pulse rate, now understood as an index – an index of fever according to the respects in which the science of medicine discriminates types of symptoms and their causes.

In the 1906 discussion, Peirce introduces a term that complicates his account of the objects that serve as parts of semeiotic triads. The complication is associated with the previously noted distinction between immediate and dynamical objects. In the context of the fever example, this can be seen with respect to the representation that is produced for the thought of the physician. Peirce introduces the idea of the immediate object of the sign (the pulse rate) in identifying the produced representation.

In these cases [cases of dyadic, indexical relations between such things as increases in temperature and their effects], however, a mental representation of the index is produced, which mental representation is called the *immediate object* of the sign; and this object does triadically produce the intended, or proper, effect of the sign strictly by means of another sign. (5.473)

Peirce does not identify the sign of which the mental representation is an immediate object. But we can infer that it could not be the index as symptom, that is, a causal effect, prior to its being interpreted — this is the real or existent object, or what in other contexts would be called the dynamical object. This is what produces the mental representation. The sign, however, does have as its immediate object the mental representation of the index that is a symptom or causal effect. Such a sign, then, must be the indexical sign, or that which is an interpretation of the mental representation of the symptom, the latter being interpreted as the symptom and thus as an immediate object.

Here and elsewhere it is clear that for Peirce immediate objects are the objects of signs as these objects are represented. What determines that a thing enters a semeiotic process, then, is that it either represents or is represented. Let us consider what Peirce means by the term *represent*, or *representation*, and what may be said to *produce* it.

Representation

Often, the term *represent* is used interchangeably with *stand for* or *refer to*. But it should be clear by now that, in Peirce's view of how signs function, this equation is too narrow. Representation has a more complex meaning than is indicated by the definition of it simply as standing for something. As already seen, representamen is more general than sign. In view of the influence of Kant on Peirce, it is reasonable to suppose that Peirce's use of the term *represent* shares common ground with Kant's *Vorstellung*, usually translated as representation. Representation is standing for something representatively, or by means of a presentation, which is present to an interpreter. A representation, then, must be a presentation that refers interpretively. It must stand for its object as representing it, which includes substituting for its object, but not by being simply a duplication of it. It will be seen later that this point needs qualification for certain kinds of (iconic) signs.

What is in question at the moment, however, is the intellectual sign, a sign for an intellectual and general concept.

An intellectual sign depends on an immediate object. The immediate object is a mental representation that is the product of the index: "A mental representation of the index is produced, which mental representation is called the *immediate object* of the sign" (5.473). The mental representation presents an initial, preinterpreted object *as* an object for interpretation. At the risk of introducing a non-Peircean notion of what might appear to be (although it is not intended to be) a cognitive intuition, it might be helpful to refer to this as a presentation of the initial experience of the pulse rate. In the preceding example, the interpretant produced for the physician is an interpretation that is the intellectual sign of the immediate object, mediated by the initial sign produced by the mental representation (presentation). The immediate object is what functions immediately as the representation of the index. In this way a genuine, triadic semeiotic process is initiated.

The initial, pregenuine semeiotic object is part of a dyadic, indexical, causal relation (between the fever and the rising pulse). The rising pulse, which, as will be seen in a moment, is initially a "quasi-sign," becomes genuinely semeiotic by virtue of being interpreted as an index (the rising pulse interpreted as an indexical representation of fever). The interpretation is produced by the mental representation "called the *immediate object* of the sign" (5.473). The fever as a symptom, then, is not an immediate object, and an immediate object is not an object in a causal relation. Nevertheless, the rising pulse as a symptom contributes to determining an interpretation; it produces the mental representation that can become an interpreted object – the immediate object. In turn, the interpretant is itself a sign for further interpretation.

It is significant that Peirce says that the immediate object ("a mental representation of the index") is produced without indicating whether the objects active in the causal relation are responsible for this production. By *responsible for* I mean "serving as the necessary and sufficient condition for." What then is responsible for the representation of the index? Presumably the representation or immediate object is a product of more than one condition. The real object or effect in a causal relation is one condition; but so is the interpreting agent or the interpretant that develops the ensuing triadic action of significate effects or future interpretants. Semeiotic processes are constrained both, on the one hand, from the standpoint of the object that initiates, and relates dyadically to, the immediate, represented object – as Peirce expresses it, "determines" the sign – and, on the other hand, from the standpoint of the agency of interpretation.

The object of thinking, then, is not a directly given existent thing in itself, since our access to things in themselves would be only through concepts or interpretations. In the early paper, "Some Consequences of Four Incapacities," we have seen Peirce taking pains to reject the view that there are things themselves that are inconceivable, or that fully escape cognitive access. As I have been insisting, this does not mean that Peirce rejected the view that there is nothing that is independent of thought. As he says there, although an object is inevitably related to thought, it may be independent of that thought. Merely to be in relation does not require being wholly relative to, much less consumed by, thought. The evolutionary realism (to be discussed later) and the function of the dynamical object indicate the status of this independent condition. In the example at hand, the immediate object is not the fever in itself but the representation of the rising pulse rate that produces another thought or another sign for the physician. This other sign is the proper significate effect or interpretant. The ensuing process of interpretation makes the rising pulse intelligible as an index of fever. The physician first perceives the rise in pulse rate, identifying it as something intelligible – which is to say, as significant, or as a sign. Thus, the rising pulse rate and the physician produce a representation, which, in turn, is an immediate object for a sign to be interpreted by the physician. The physician then interprets the initial experience as a sign, or index, the pulse rate, and in this instance, the interpretation makes the rising pulse intelligible as an index of fever. Interpretation may, and in this case, presumably would, continue the activity of sign interpretation by producing or contributing to other interpretants, which, in this example, may lead to a decision about treatment. The directing factor, or tendency, implied here is the teleological character of semeiosis.

It should be evident from the description of a triadic action – as a relation with a telos connecting two terms through a third – that an instance of semeiosis is "an action, or influence, which is, or involves, a cooperation of *three* subjects, such as a sign, its object, and its interpretant" (5.484). In the example we have been using, the triad, built on the immediate object for the physician's initial interpreting thought, is a genuine triad, for it involves three subjects: (1) the immediate object (the representation in the physician's thought), (2) the interpretation or further sign of the immediate object (the physician's construing of the rising pulse as an index of fever), and (3) the interpretant of this second sign, which ensures that the relation will be teleological, for the interpretant is a construal of this sign as significant, or as a proper significate effect, which, in our example, implies the need of diagnosis. To be sure, the process is more complex than this. If we were to pursue this complexity, one of the issues that would arise concerns Peirce's distinctions among three kinds of interpretants. For our purposes, however, this issue need not be addressed. Suffice it to say that the interpretant identified in the account thus far is what Peirce calls the *logical interpretant*, which is proper to interpretations of intellectual concepts.

Translated into the conception of a sign as a semeiosis unit, the three subjects are (1) the immediate object; (2) the respect in which the immediate object is interpreted – the rising pulse is an index of fever with respect to (or the ground of) the rule or regularity or law of correlated pulse rates and temperature of the body; and (3) the interpretant of (2) as a sign for diagnosis. The importance of recognizing the role of the respect or ground as a component of the sign triad is that it shows one of the ways in which Peirce understood semeioses as inseparable from other processes and regularities in nature. (Thus, I suggest that Peirce's ground here links with his Dynamical Objects.)[6] The constraints on interpretation are from two "sides," the interpreting action and the interpreted compulsion on the course of events. This latter itself is a twofold constraint the sources of which are brute forcefulness of nature and the intelligible lawfulness of nature. These function as the respects in which interpretation contributes to making nature intelligible. And rendering nature intelligible is a semeiotic process, whether some specific human intelligence is or is not an active participant in the process.

It is Peirce's conviction that an instance of semeiosis – an instance in which intelligible meaning occurs – is the supreme example of a genuine triadic relation. A genuine triad is a relation of a sign to an object for an interpreter that cannot be reduced to lower-order relations, that is, dyads or monads. Peirce's insistence on the irreducibility of genuine triads and the "degeneracy" – very briefly, a triad is degenerate if it invites interpretation as being effective at a level, Thirdness or Secondness, although analysis would show that it is reducible to a lower level – of those that are reducible and not genuine will be considered later. At this point, however, it should be noticed that Peirce alludes to the possibility that some signs are not triadic and thus not genuine. He refers to indexes as "quasi-signs":

---

[6]It seems to me that the controversy over whether Peirce did or did not need to include the idea of ground in his later writing – after the appearance of it in the 1868 cognition papers – that engaged T. L. Short and David Savan is not relevant to my point. The idea of respects in which things are related certainly did not drop out of Peirce's system, and his term *ground* is used in the early work as an alternative to *respect*. Savan seems to hold a view that confirms this point. This is not to say, however, that he would agree with my suggestion about linking ground with dynamical objects. T. L. Short, "David Savan's Peirce Studies," and David Savan, "Response to T. L. Short," *Transactions of the Charles S. Peirce Society* 2, no. 2 (Spring 1986), pp. 99–100 and 137–38, respectively.

Whether the interpretant be necessarily a triadic result is a question of words, that is, of how we limit the extension of the term "sign"; but it seems to me convenient to make the triadic production of the interpretant essential to a "sign," calling the wider concept like a Jacquard loom,[7] for example, a "quasi-sign." (5.473)

This terminological proposal reflects the distinction noted previously between the immediate object, or the representation of the index, and the initial object that helps produce the index itself. A non-quasi-sign, a genuine sign, is part of a triadic rather than a dyadic relation with two subjects. An index itself – that is, an index prior to incorporation into an intelligibility-producing process (semeiosis) – is dyadically related to another subject. With respect to Peirce's concerns about how semeiotic issues bear on pragmaticism, the point about indexical reference as dyadic, as prior to entering the triad of semeiosis, shows why Peirce insists that the meaning that is available for human intelligence necessarily includes the function of interpretants. And this is why Peirce initiated his discussion of the linkage of pragmatism with semeiotic by proposing that the problem of the meaning of intellectual concepts would be advanced by the study of interpretants. In order to consider further how interpretants function, once they enter semeioses and thereby make them genuine semeiotic processes, it is necessary to pursue the consideration of Peirce's conception of how semeioses originate in causal action and to focus specifically on his discussion of the relation of interpretants to their objects.

Interpretants and Objects

An interpretant, Peirce says, is "All that is explicit in the sign itself apart from its context and circumstances of utterance" (5.473).[8] The independence of interpretants from variable circumstances entitles them to be called the "proper" significative effects of a sign. Interpretants are repeatable conditions that function as objects regarded in abstraction from the particular circumstances in which they are considered. In this respect, they are generals – dynamic universals or Platonic Forms. This point is reinforced when, in discussing the relation of interpretants to their objects with respect to propositions, Peirce says that "anything belongs to the interpretant that describes the quality or character of the fact, anything to the object that, without doing that, distinguishes this fact from others like it; while a third part of

[7]A Jacquard loom was a machine that used cards that were punched so as to control the loom and it was thus a forerunner of modern computers.
[8]This statement was anticipated by Peirce's early distinction in "How to Make Our Ideas Clear" between belief and the manner of consciousness in which a belief is held.

the proposition, *perhaps*, must be appropriated to information about
the manner in which the assertion is made, what warrant is offered
for its truth, etc." (5.473). Signification, then, is a property of the interpretant, which is a property of qualifying general conditions, which
is found in information about characteristics. This kind of information is independent of the "manner" in which utterances concerning
facts are made and of questions of the truth or falsity of the assertions. Truth and falsity, the applicability of the predicate to its subject,
have to do with the constraints of the subject – which, as will be pointed
out in a moment, is a function of "any individual object the interpreter may select from the universe of ordinary everyday experience"
(5.473).

Because they are effects produced by the sign as it relates to its
object, interpretants have an indirect relation to the real, dynamical
objects of the signs that are interpreted. The direct objects with which
they are related are their immediate objects. Thus, the relation of the
interpretant to what initiated the triadic process, or the semeiosis, is a
mediated relation in which the sign represents the immediate object
in some respect for the interpretant.

In the passages cited, Peirce's exploration of the answer to the question of the relation between interpretants and the objects of signs,
Peirce does not say whether he is referring to the immediate or dynamical object. In this context, it seems appropriate, however, to assume that he has in mind immediate objects, because these are what
he last referred to as the objects of triadic signs. If this is what he
refers to, then his question about the relation of interpretant to object
concerns the relation of the interpretant to the representation that
initiated the triadic process, which is an instance of genuine semeiosis.
This relation is a mediated one in which the sign represents the immediate (represented) object to the interpretant. However, as already
suggested, in his explanation, some of his statements suggest that the
causal or dynamical object also must be acknowledged as having a
function in determining the relation of interpretant to object. Thus,
even though the semeiosis itself necessarily has the immediate object
as the referent of the sign, the application of a sign to what it represents involves the causal or dynamical object that seems to be the remote (preimmediate) initiating condition for the semeiosis.

In order to develop this point, let us return briefly to Peirce's view
that interpretants are predicates and objects the subjects of propositions. We may extrapolate from his discussion of propositions in order to suggest what he would say about the relation of the interpretant to its object in the case of the indexical sign already considered
in the example of the rise in pulse rate. Our purpose is to ascertain
just what Peirce believes to be the relations among the extralinguistic

or extrasemeiotic object in the world (the dynamical object), the initially interpreted object (the immediate object), and the interpretant. Let us first focus on Peirce's own example: the proposition, "Burnt child shuns fire."

Peirce analyzes this sentence in terms of its subject and predicate and also in terms of its object and the information that propositions may communicate. With respect to its subject and predicate, he says:

> The interpretant of a proposition is its predicate; its object is the things denoted by its subject or subjects (including its grammatical objects, direct and indirect, etc.). Take the proposition "Burnt child shuns fire." Its predicate might be regarded as all that is expressed, or as "has either not been burned or shuns fire," or "has not been burned," or "shuns fire," or "shuns," or "is true"; nor is this enumeration exhaustive. (5.473)

In contrast to the predicate, the subject is " 'any individual object the interpreter may select from the universe of ordinary everyday experience" (5.473). We should notice first that although the *objects* in "the universe of ordinary experience" are individuals, the *subject* is the object selected by an interpreter. The subject, then, is not wholly independent of linguistic or semeiotic action. The object in itself, in the sense of a preselected object, is something individual and prelinguistic or presemeiotic. Further, it is noteworthy that the subject applies to any individual object; thus it is general. Intelligible discourse about the objects that interpretation of the proposition selects must employ general terms, or predicates. This implies that the predicate is indeterminate in the sense that it would be true of any or all individuals to whom the proposition is interpreted as applying. What is said is true (fallibilistically) of either this child or that child or any child who has been burned and who shuns fire. The interpretant also, in a way made explicit by the conjunctions into which Peirce suggests the predicate can be translated, implies information expressible in a way different from the specific way it is expressed in the predicate as formulated by Peirce – for he says, "nor is the enumeration exhaustive," which includes the proposition that a child who does not shun fire has not been burned. I take it that Peirce considers the kinds of information provided and implied by the predicate to be relevant to the selection of the subject's object. It seems proper, then, to say that the subject's objects that are selected by the interpreter are immediate objects – representations that initiate semeioses. The constraint of the subject on truth or falsity or applicability of the predicate, referred to earlier (at least insofar as there is something independent of the selectivity of the interpreting sign), must come from the dynamical object, that which is real independently of the particular semeiotic process in which the proposition is formulated. This point deserves elaboration. It is fundamental to Peirce's semeiotic and his evolutionary realism.

With respect to Peirce's analysis of the proposition into information and object, he says, as we observed earlier, that the interpretant is anything "that describes the quality or character of the fact," and anything belongs to the object "that, without doing that [describing the quality or character of the fact], distinguishes this fact from others like it." Is the object here the same as that mentioned in the subject–predicate analysis, that is, the subject's (immediate) object? As pointed out, the subject's object is selected by the interpreter. But in the analysis of information relevant to the predicate and object, Peirce omits reference to the interpreter; thus, the object here seems not to be that which is selected by an interpreter. If so, it must not be identical with the subject's object. If the information said in the analysis to be relevant to the object is not interpreter-dependent or predicate-dependent, then the object in question here must be other than the object as initially represented, or the immediate object. It must be an object dependent upon, or, more strongly, it must be causally productive of an indexical selection, such as an act of pointing or singling out, which is only incipiently semeiotically significant, for it has not yet been made intelligible through interpretation. Consequently, consistent with Peirce's other consideration of objects, we must recognize two objects, or a twofold object: (1) an object for an interpretant, or a subject's object, which is dependent upon a triadic semeiotic act of selection, and (2) an object that has a status that is independent of the semeiotic triadic action: that is, (1) an immediate object and (2) an initiating causal or dynamical object. This interpretation of what Peirce means can be confirmed, I think, by what he says about the way objects distinguish facts without depending on predication.

Peirce says that whatever belongs to the sort of object or objects in question when we consider how a proposition communicates information, distinguishes a fact from others. What is the fact that is so distinguished? Presumably it is the fact stated by the proposition as a whole, which must be expressed by the predicate of an object – here the fact that burned child shuns fire, which is said of an object. And it is the predicate or interpretant that characterizes the object. The fact of the proposition as a whole must be a fact that applies to the subject's object, which we have seen is the object selected by the interpreter. But this is not an object that distinguishes the fact from others like it. Such an object distinguishes the fact from others without the qualification expressed by the predicate or interpretant. How is the distinction between one fact and another made by an object without the function of the interpretant?

The distinction in question is made possible by an object which is independent of the interpretant; consequently, it must be the initiating causal or dynamical object. It is the initiating cause of an instance of semeiosis. Its mode of distinguishing one fact from another must be preinterpretive or presemeiotic. Some child or other, before interpreted as being a child, shuns fire before any intelligent agent recognizes the child who shuns fire as a child shunning fire, much less as a child who has been burned. Once the object, the fire-shunning child, is recognized as a fire-shunning child, the object that functions is immediate, because it is an effect characterizable as a representation – a complex of respects in which the prior object is represented. It is this object that is interpreted, and once it is interpreted, it, as immediate, becomes a sign of a child who has been burned. And this sign in turn is interpreted or gives rise to an interpretant. Consequently, the object of the subject, "any individual object the interpreter may select from the universe of everyday experience," is the immediate object. It is linguistically or conceptually linked, which is to say that it is not presemeiotic, but is caught up in the universe of everyday experience, and it is the initiating condition of an instance of semeiosis. But the object that serves as a condition for distinguishing the fact represented by the proposition is prior to the immediate object. It is a causal object that may function as an incipient object in an instance of semeiosis when it produces an index, which in turn produces a representation.

This way of understanding Peirce can now be turned to the previous example of fever and rising pulse. As a presemeiotic object, fever is an initiating cause or condition that constrains or acts dynamically on intelligent agents or sign-using beings. The presemeiotic object acts dyadically in relation to another object – the rising pulse is in dyadic relation to the fever. The fever is a cause of an incipient sign that may be recognized as an index. Its becoming an index would occur independently of interpretation, though obviously it would not be recognized to have occurred without interpretation. But there is also a presemeiotic, though incipient-semeiotic, relation between the pulse rate and an interpreter on whom the pulse rate acts through a mental representation. As intelligent, the reacting agent (the physician) begins to interpret the rising pulse rate. The agent does so because a representation, an immediate object, has been produced by him or her and the incipient sign. The immediate object, then, produces the fully articulated sign that produces an interpretant so that there is a genuine instance of semeiosis.

The function of the two sorts of objects and sign processes can be seen in light of Peirce's categories, particularly, the relation of what he calls Secondness to Thirdness, the two categories that, as we shall see, cover what is existent, or active and reactive, and what is intelligible in the world. Before turning directly to the Peircean categories, however, it is necessary to consider Peirce's classification of signs. The classes of signs correlate to the classification of things according to the categories; thus, a look at the kinds of signs Peirce identifies will serve as a partial introduction to the categories.

Classes of Signs

One of the key classes of signs – one among the most generally known and influential of the kinds that Peirce distinguishes – has already been taken for granted in our consideration of the semeiotic. This is the indexical sign, the index. Indexical signs probably serve popularly as models for all signs, because indexical signs most explicitly relate to their objects by means of reference or by virtue of standing for some particular thing other than the sign. However, there are other kinds of signs, other ways in which things function meaningfully.

A preliminary point needs to be made about the following discussion of Peirce's classification of signs. It should be helpful if we recognize that the same thing (object or event) can belong to more than one division within the classification that Peirce proposes. Thus, we should think of the classes identified as ways in which the thing classified functions. As will be commented on later, a thing that serves as an index, for instance, as the rising pulse does for fever, may also serve as another kind of sign for the fever – as an icon or as something having a kind of likeness to what it signifies.

In about 1903, Peirce classifies signs with respect to the ways distinct kinds of things function semeiotically. Accordingly, he divides signs into what he calls "three trichotomies," the first consisting of the natures or properties of the things functioning as signs, the second consisting of the way things may function as signs because of their relations to the objects they signify, and the third trichotomy consisting of the ways interpretations of things function as signs that affect future signs.

Signs are divisible by three trichotomies; first according as the sign itself is a mere quality, is an actual existent, or is a general law; secondly, according as the relation of the sign to its object consists in the sign's having some character in itself, or in some existential relation to that object, or in its relation to an interpretant; thirdly, according as its Interpretant represents it as a sign of possibility or as a sign of fact or a sign of reason. (2.243)

Later, and more briefly, in a letter of 1904 to Lady Welby, Peirce describes what he earlier called the trichotomies: "Now signs may be divided as to their own material nature, as to their relations to their objects, and as to their relations to their interpretants" (8.333). We should not be misled into thinking that there is a discrepancy between the two statements of the divisions of classes. It might seem so at first glance, because in the Lady Welby letter the third main division is said to consist of signs insofar as they relate to their interpretants, whereas in the 1903 manuscript, it is the last class within the second main division or trichotomy that consists of signs insofar as they relate to their interpretants. However, in the 1903 account, the third division of the second trichotomy consists of a relation between sign and interpretant that is neither direct nor primary but that obtains between the interpretant and the sign and object together. The sign's relation to its object "consists in its relation to an interpretant." The point is that in this 1903, third division of the second trichotomy, we have a triad in which components, sign, object, and interpretant, are interdependent, the meaning of the sign with respect to its object or reference depending on an interpretant. It is significant, too, that this class of signs is third within the second trichotomy, placed in the ordering of divisions next to the third main division or trichotomy, which consists of three ways in which signs are related *directly* to interpretants.

The first trichotomy, then, is based on what the sign is "in itself" (8.334), what the thing functioning as a sign is apart from its functioning semeiotically. There are three kinds of things classifiable with respect to their constitutions or natures as potentially sign-functioning things. A thing may simply be a quality, or it may be an existent entity – an event or a physical object, for instance – or it may be a general, a repeatable condition functioning as a rule, that is, as a law. More accurately, I think, we can regard any thing with respect to its quality, its being an instance, or its being a kind of instance or object. Thus, a quality such as red or hard (the redness or hardness embodied in a thing); a thing such as a cloud of smoke or a thermometer; an instance, a something, so regarded; and a regularity such as the growth of foliage may each function semeiotically. This trichotomy that includes the kinds of things or aspects of things that can become signs or function semeiotically is important, because the kind of thing a sign is or the aspect of the thing makes a difference to how it can serve as a sign.

The second trichotomy is based on the particular way a thing that is a sign relates, as a sign, to its object. There are three such ways. The kind of thing it is (what it is according to the first trichotomy) affects its way of relating to its object. Thus, a thing may be a sign of its object because of its own intrinsic properties or qualities, for example, as is a portrait; a thing may be a sign because of a causal relation it has to its object, for example, rising pulse and fever; or a thing may be a sign because it is determined by a rule or a law that depends on the interpretant of the sign, for instance, a word established by conventions or usage for which interpretants are responsible, or a regularity such as growth of foliage that is determined by the interpretant laws of biology.

The third trichotomy is based on the way an interpretant represents the thing in relation to making the world intelligible. Again, there are three ways. Thus, a thing may be a sign of possibility for an interpretant without being asserted to be a sign or without connecting itself with other signs or their referents, for example, a term such as a word in isolation. A thing may be a sign of fact; that is, it may be an assertion or something connected with reference to conditions that are not exhausted by interpretation. Thus, a proposition, which affirms something about existence or some part of the world not exhausted or pervaded by signs (here dynamical objects function prominently), is a sign. Finally, a thing may be a sign with respect to its connection with signs of facts and of possibilities; that is, it is a sign with respect to its connection with what are interpreted as propositions composed of terms. Thus, arguments are signs.

The first two trichotomies, especially the second, are more important for our purposes. However, we should recognize the correlations among the hierarchically ordered triads found within and among the trichotomies. The internal relations among the three trichotomies are the basis for Peirce's derivation of ten classes of signs and, finally, for what he claimed could be a system of sixty-six kinds of signs. We shall focus primarily on the hierarchies of triads that are correlated not only among themselves but also with the three categories. The characteristics of the categories underlie the triads that Peirce distinguishes in his classification of signs.

To return to the first trichotomy, we find what will be recognized later as the most direct reflection of the three categories. The first class in the first trichotomy — the division of signs with respect to the sorts of things they are — is "mere quality." A quality, like the preinterpreted rising pulse, is what I suggested earlier is an incipient sign. Peirce calls it a *qualisign.* As a quality taken in itself, it is not (yet) a sign. "It cannot actually act as a sign until it is embodied; but the embodiment has nothing to do with its character as a sign" (2.244). For the quality red to be a sign, to be meaningful, it must have some place in relation to other things. It needs to qualify something. It may do so by embodiment in an instance of the second division of the first trichotomy, which Peirce calls a *sinsign,* and which is an existent thing or event. "It [a sign] can only be so [be a sinsign] through its qualities; so that it involves a qualisign, or rather several qualisigns. But these qualisigns are of a peculiar kind and only form a sign through being actually embodied" (2.245). A red patch, for instance, is a thing that embodies red and which can be interpreted.

The third class of signs in the first trichotomy is the *legisign,* which "is a law that is a Sign" (2.246). As suggested a moment ago, the law may be conventional or natural. Thus, Peirce says, "This law is usually established by men. Every conventional sign is a legisign [but not conversely]. It is not a single object, but a general type which, it has been agreed, shall be significant." But just as sinsigns depend on embodying qualisigns, so legisigns depend on being instanced, just as a law is a rule or condition for ordering consequences that might be actualized. "Every sign signifies through an instance of its application, which may be termed a *Replica* of it. . . . The Replica is a Sinsign. Thus, every Legisign requires Sinsigns" (2.246). Peirce cites as an example, the word *the*, which occurs frequently on this page as a replica, or a sinsign, of the same word, which is a legisign. Elsewhere, in a 1902 manuscript entitled "Syllabus," he makes the same distinction with the word *man* when written or pronounced. As such it "is only a *replica*, or embodiment of the word, that is pronounced or written" (2.292). The distinction here is the same as the more generally known distinction between sign token and sign type. A replica of a word is a token of the sign-type word or the legisign of the word. Consider another example, the word *trichotomy*. Within this paragraph, this same word appears twice, as two inscriptions, once at the beginning of the paragraph where it is used and once, just now, where it is mentioned. It also occurs if it is uttered while reading. These inscriptions (and the sound if it has been uttered) are its examples, its instances, or, in Peirce's words, its replicas, which are sinsigns, because they are actual, existent inscriptions, available to perception. Yet the meaning of the word is not identical with these inscriptions, nor is it identical with any definite set of inscriptions of it. Rather, the word's meaning, what it is as a condition for repeatable inscriptions that are interpretable, is a rule or law – a legisign. Again, the need for Peirce's realism must be invoked. As he says in continuing the passage in which he uses the term *man* as an example, "The word itself has no existence although it has a real being, *consisting in* the fact that existents *will* conform to it" (2.292).

The same sort of hierarchical ordering applies to the second trichotomy, and the second trichotomy as a whole depends on the first, just as the classes within the first trichotomy depend on each other, so that the third (legisign) depends on the sinsign, which in turn depends on the qualisign. In other words, there could be no second trichotomy, according to which things are considered with respect to their semeiotic relations to their objects, unless there were things functioning in accord with the first trichotomy. Thus, for there to be signs with objects, there must be things, qualities, that function as qualisigns that may be embodied as sinsigns that may be instances of legisigns.

What are the kinds of signs within the second trichotomy? In Peirce's words in the 1904 letter to Lady Welby, "In respect to their relation to their dynamic objects, I divide signs into Icons, Indices, and Symbols" (8.335). It is noteworthy that Peirce here uses the idea of the dynamic (which we have encountered earlier as the dynamical) object, instead of the general word *object*, which may include the immediate object, or the object as interpreted. That he does so, of course, shows the importance he places on having an extralinguistic or preinterpreted condition participate in semeiotic processes in which there is reference, that is, a relation of sign to something other than itself, namely, an independently functioning object. But in view of his mentioning the dynamic object, Peirce implies that the object of reference is not fully captured by the interpretive process. It must resist being merely the object as represented, or the interpreted object – which is the immediate object. This point is important for the first two kinds of signs in the second trichotomy, that is, the icon and index, both of which represent something by virtue of factors that are not fully subject to the control of the interpretant. In the context of this letter, Peirce adds comments that highlight further the distinction between dynamical and immediate objects, as we shall see. In any case, as was mentioned earlier, the three classes of signs that are most widely known and discussed belong to this second general trichotomy.

Peirce explains what he means by the terms *icon, index,* and *symbol:* In the letter to Lady Welby, he says of icons, "I define an Icon as a sign which is determined by its dynamic object by virtue of its own internal nature" (8.335). In the 1903 manuscript, he says:

An *Icon* is a sign which refers to the Object that it denotes merely by virtue of characters of its own, which it possesses, just the same, whether any such Object actually exists or not. It is true that unless there really is such an Object, the Icon does not act as a sign; but this has nothing to do with its character as a sign. Anything whatever, be it quality, existent individual, or law, is an Icon of anything, insofar as it is like that thing and used as a sign of it. (2.274)

It should be obvious that a thing functioning iconically, as an iconic sign, must at least be a qualisign; but as already seen, it then must be an embodied qualisign, if it is indeed a sign. A portrait illustrates such an icon. However, it is important that if the portrait does function as a sign, then it must represent something, which means that it does have an object. It is the visual qualities of the portrait that render it representative of the sitter; yet the qualities that enable it to function this way are present in it, even if the sitter did not exist. It is not obvious how a thing may also function iconically when it is a law. I assume that Peirce regarded such things as laws of biological growth in humans as iconic insofar as these laws are like certain laws of biological growth in plants. Or to make use of an example that he mentions to illustrate what he means by the term *index,* a symptom of a disease is a legisign, which is to be a law – that is, a type of occurrence that as a rule signals a certain kind of illness – and such a law may be like the illness of which it is a sign, for example, the key symptom for the illness called mumps, swelling, and the illness it represents.

If laws can be iconic signs, then icons can represent by means of likenesses that are not limited to visual properties, as are likenesses of icons such as portraits. This is another way of saying that such icons are not qualisigns – although this does not mean that they do not depend on qualisigns as conditions for the legisigns that are iconic. The likeness in the case of laws of biological growth must depend on a structure that is common to the sign and what it represents. This point is borne out in Peirce's account of the way the six triads in the three trichotomies can be combined to derive ten classes of signs (2.254–64). It is also borne out by Peirce's brief elaboration of iconic signs. He distinguishes them as follows:

Hypoicons [signs that function iconically] . . . may be roughly divided according to the mode of Firstness of which they partake. Those which partake of simple qualities, or First Firstnesses, are *images;* those which represent the relations, mainly dyadic, or so regarded, of the parts of one thing by analogous relations in their own parts, are *diagrams;* those which represent the representative character of a representamen by representing a parallelism in something else, are *metaphors.* (2.277)

Putting aside for the moment the correlations between iconic signs and the category of Firstness, what can be seen here is that things can be iconic in more ways than simply bearing a perceptual resemblance – an interpretation of icon that often seems to be assumed. In the present context, it is iconicity as consisting of analogous relations that is of importance with respect to the way laws can be iconic. The role of metaphors, the third kind of icon, which is generally overlooked, can be understood in connection with questions of the conditions for evolution in thought and in general in nature, to be considered later.

In defining *index,* Peirce says in the Lady Welby letter, "I define an Index as a sign determined by its dynamic object by virtue of being in a real relation to it. Such is a Proper Name (a legisign [sign type]); such is the occurrence of a symptom of a disease" (8.335). In contrast to the way in which an occurrence such as swelling may be an iconic sign of the inflammation associated with mumps, the same swelling is also an indexical sign of inflammation because the swelling is in a "real relation" with the inflammation. It is caused by the inflammation, as rising pulse is caused by fever, and in that sense the swelling is in a real relation with the inflammation. As iconic, the swelling is qualitatively analogous to the inflammation, according to Peirce's second kind of icon. As indexical, the swelling is an effect of the inflammation. In

the 1903 manuscript, Peirce offers a somewhat more extended definition of index, which bears out this way of illustrating his meaning.
He says:

An *Index* is a sign which refers to the Object that it denotes by virtue of being
really affected by that Object. It cannot, therefore, be a Qualisign, because
qualities are whatever they are independently of anything else. In so far as
the Index is affected by the Object it necessarily has some Quality in common
with the Object [presumably, likeness of structure], and it is in respect to these
that it refers to the Object. It does, therefore, involve a sort of Icon, although
an Icon of a peculiar kind [of the diagrammatic or analogous sort]; and it is
not the mere resemblance of its Object, even in these respects which makes it
a sign, but it is the actual modification of it by the Object [it is the effect of
the object]. (2.248)

Not only do indexes involve icons, but they cannot function fully as
signs without being incipient or potential symbols, the third class of
signs in the second trichotomy. To function fully as a sign, to be a
genuine sign, as we have seen, a thing must represent its object for its
interpretant: "While no Representamen actually functions as such until it actually determines an Interpretant, yet it becomes a Representamen as soon as it is fully capable of doing this" (2.295). A sign "fully
capable of" determining an Interpretant is what I have called an incipient sign.

For a thing to function fully as a sign, as emphasized earlier, it also
must be a component in a process in which the sign mediates for a
purpose. It must function teleologically. The teleological character of
a semeiosis marks the sign in the process as a symbol. This was mentioned when we noticed that the test of triadic action lies in the relation in which one component must produce another in order that a
third be produced. Such an action is a prerequisite for the determination of an interpretant. However, as we already have observed, the
third division of the second trichotomy consists of signs insofar as
their relation to their objects is related to their interpretants, and in
this function, signs are symbols. This is to say that for the more fundamental semeiotic situation – the kind that is not confined to mental
interpretants – a representamen that is a symbol must determine a
mediation between its relation to its object and its relation to its interpretant. This triadic relation depends on a telos, because the representamen functions directionally and with an end that fulfills the process in which it functions. The direction is from the representamen's
relation to its object toward its determined interpretant. The formulation of the interpretant is the end or fulfillment – a provisional fulfillment, to be sure, for the semeiotic process forms an endless series
(e.g., 2.274) – to a complete phase of a semeiotic process.

     This point is put in a way that abstracts from reference to human interpretation in order to emphasize Peirce's intention of constructing a semeiotic for nonhuman as well as human thought, or in the most general terms, for the cosmos as well as for human intelligence. In any case, purposiveness and teleological character is essential to semeiotic processes in general, when the operative representamen is a symbol.

Teleological factors are inseparable from the generality and lawfulness that defines a process as symbolic. The presence of teleological factors is made explicit in Peirce's definition in the 1903 manuscript.

A *Symbol* is a sign which refers to the Object that it denotes by virtue of a law, usually an association of general ideas, which operates to cause the Symbol to be interpreted as referring to that Object. It is thus itself a general type or law, that is, is a Legisign. As such it acts through a Replica. Not only is it general itself, but the Object to which it refers is of a general nature. Now that which is general has its being in instances which it will determine. There must, therefore, be existent instances of what the Symbol denotes, although we must here understand by "existent," existent in the possibly imaginary universe to which the Symbol refers. The Symbol will indirectly, through the association or other law, be affected by those instances; and thus the Symbol will involve a sort of Index, although an Index of a peculiar kind. It will not, however, be by any means true that the slight effect upon the Symbol of those instances accounts for the significant character of the Symbol. (2.249)

It is clear that there is a hierarchical dependency of the sign as symbol on the second class in this trichotomy, indexes – and on the first, iconic, function as well, for indexes in turn depend on icons. Such dependency is to be expected in light of the fundamental role of the dynamical object that constrains a semeiotic system. In this connection, it should be noted that at the end of the passage just quoted, when Peirce says that the "slight effect upon the Symbol of those instances" of the law on the symbol does not account "for the significant character of the Symbol," he does not retract his point that symbols are affected by the instances they denote. Nor does he say that these instances do not contribute to accounting for the significant character of the symbol. What he does is place emphasis on the rule-governing function of the symbol in effecting significate effects (interpretants) in the future.

It should also be clear that symbols are to be contrasted with icons and indexes with respect to the distinction between conditions in contrast to what they condition – between instances and generals and their instances. If indexes are genuine signs, interpreted signs, they must be so through the mediation of the representamen. Thus, to be an index functioning as a sign depends on there being a lawful condition, which is something general, in order to be related beyond itself, to another, *for an interpretant*. Without its being relevant to more than itself and an object, it cannot function semeiotically. However, it is made relevant to more than itself if it not only has some real connection as an effect, but is interpreted as having this connection. And it is by means of a sign that it is so interpreted, that is, by means of its producing a response that yields an interpretation. Such a production must be general, because the products, sign and interpretant, must be capable of being sustained and applicable repeatedly. Thus, symbols are lawful; they are rules, as Peirce says explicitly in an earlier part of the passage quoted previously from the 1902 manuscript, entitled "Syllabus." A *symbol* is a representamen whose representative character consists precisely in its being a rule that will determine its interpretant (2.292). A thing that functions as a rule must have the character of regularity, and it must serve as a condition such that existent instances conform to it. Again, in the same paper, Peirce says:

A Symbol is a law, or regularity of the indefinite future. Its Interpretant must be of the same description; and so must be also the complete immediate Object, or meaning. But law necessarily governs, or "is embodied in" individuals, and prescribes some of their qualities. Consequently, a constituent of a Symbol may be an Index, and a constituent may be an Icon. (2.293)

What Peirce tells us about the way symbols are laws that both govern and are affected by their instances has been set forth in a way that should make clear that, for Peirce, symbols are not only conventions that serve as rules for interpretation but may also and more fundamentally be regarded as rules of habit in nature or in extrahuman processes – processes not confined to particular thoughts. The discussion of symbols as laws also returns us to the question of the relation of signs to their objects. And it is with a reminder of this issue that the present chapter will draw to a close.

We shall not, then, consider the third trichotomy of signs, except to mention its main feature: the inclusion of signs in their relations to interpretants, which is to identify signs that function as symbols in relation to one another. This is not to suggest that the third trichotomy is not important; the function of symbols that articulate meanings that can be brought into relations for purposes of reasoning is, of course, important for Peirce's logic. However, our main concern has been the most fundamental division of signs and their function in relating thought to its object, and, in turn, in relating semeioses to their basis in conditions in reality.

There are other questions that deserve attention, particularly the role of different kinds of interpretants that correlate with the three major divisions of signs. However, this and other issues that are of importance for gaining perspectives on the evolutionary realism at the roots of the architectonic Peirce wished to build can be permitted to arise later in connection with the correlation of the categories with the three kinds of signs and with the metaphysics in which evolutionary realism has its proper setting.

In concluding this chapter, it will be helpful to review quickly the account of the relation of semeiosis to presemeiotic conditions by considering again our accelerating-pulse example. As a presemeiotic object, the fever and the rising pulse rate are initiating causes or conditions that constrain or act dynamically on intelligent agents or sign-using beings. The presemeiotic object acts dyadically in relation to another object – the rising pulse is in dyadic relation to the fever. The fever is a cause of an incipient or "quasi-" sign that may be recognized as an index. Its status as a presemeiotic index would occur independently of interpretation, though obviously it would not be recognized to have occurred without interpretation. But to reiterate, there is also a presemeiotic, though incipient-semeiotic relation, between the pulse rate and an interpreter on whom the pulse rate acts through a mental representation. As a thinking, reacting agent the physician begins to interpret the rising pulse rate. The agent does so because a representation, an immediate object, has been produced by the incipient sign and the interpretant – in this case, the interpretant is in the mind of the physician. The immediate object, then, in turn produces the fully articulated sign that produces an interpretant so that there is a genuine instance of semeiosis.

This way of understanding Peirce is relevant to consideration of his categories, particularly, the relation of what he calls Secondness to Thirdness, the two categories that, as we shall see, cover what is existent, or active and reactive, and what is intelligible in the world. Consideration of the categories is our next task.

3

The Categories and the Phenomenology

The Nature and Function of Philosophical Categories

It should not be necessary to launch a lengthy general discussion of the nature and function of categories in philosophy in order to give an account of what they are and the role they play in Peirce's thought. However, some comments about categories in general are necessary. Briefly, and most generally, categories in philosophy are fundamental conceptions, in the sense that they are conditions of intelligibility. Such conceptions may be regarded as the classes or types of things into which things that are and can be known can be divided. Or they may be considered to be the ways or conditions according to which things can be distinguished and accordingly known. Some things can be made intelligible because they can be located in space and time – as substances that serve as referents for subjects in sentences or propositions. These belong to the category of substance. Some things can be made intelligible because they can be determined to be contingent (Abraham Lincoln's beard, which may or may not be shaved off), whereas others are regarded as necessary ($2 + 2 = 4$ in a number system based on 10). These belong to the category of modality, which includes contingency, possibility, and necessity. Fundamental classes or conditions of intelligibility are not unlimited in number. They are necessary for identifying, classifying, and relating what may be an unlimited number of things in the universe (or universes of discourse) encountered in any and all domains of experience, including the domain proper to science and that which is available to common sense. However, one may distinguish what Peirce called a "long list" and a "short list" of categories. Aristotle's categories belong to the long list. They result from his analysis of the way things can be said. Kant's categories owe their identification to his analysis of how we form judgments. In general, if a philosopher constructs a long list, we would expect to find categories, as types or classes of things, that are not found in all things at all times and all places. We find, for example, that not all things are necessary, or that all things are substances in the sense of being in space and time. Peirce's concerns throughout most of his career were with formulating a short list to be identified much in the way Kant sought to explain them, except that, for Peirce, as will be pointed out in a moment, (1) the conditions of forming conceptions expressed in propositions took the place of forms of judgment, and (2) he wanted his categories to apply to everything at all times and all places, that is, to be universal and necessary in scope.

In a long list, not all things fall under any one of the categories. For instance, subjects and their references, or substances, belong to a class of things that is different from the class of predicates or properties that are attributable to the subjects or substances. Although all things do not fall under any one of the categories in the long list, all things do fall under all the categories when the list is considered as a totality – if we assume the philosopher has found an exhaustive list. In contrast, the short list is composed of categories that are without limit general; each and all of them apply to all things. Not only does the whole set apply to all experiences and things that are and can be experienced or conceived but so does each one of the categories in the list. Each of them is universal and necessary both to all experience (for the experiencer) and to what is experienced (that to which the experiencer attends).

As universal and necessary, the short list of categories cannot be determined by means of actual observation alone, that is, they cannot be derived only inductively, for they are conditions under which inductive inference, among other kinds of inference, is intelligible. Hypothetical inference (Peirce's "abduction") is necessary. Peirce formed his list on the basis of two approaches. One approach can be called, broadly, *logical*. The other is called by Peirce *phenomenological*, which is in a special way observational. Our attention will be directed primarily toward the categories as phenomenologically derived. Peirce's phenomenology not only consists of a systematic study of the categories but it is also characterized by Peirce as the foundational science or division of philosophical studies, which, of course, includes logic. Thus, it seems to take a more fundamental place than logic and must be established independently of an a priori method. Additional consideration of the priority of phenomenology and some observations about its relation to Husserl's phenomenology and Hegel's conception of the categories will be addressed later.

As a way of seeing what the categories are for Peirce, there are advantages in beginning with one of his earliest statements of the concepts that in his more mature thought are identified as the categories of the short list. This statement is his article, "On a New List of Categories," published in 1867 in the *Proceedings of the American Academy of Arts and Sciences*.[1] One advantage in starting here can be seen if we ask

[1] Vol. 7 (May 1867), pp. 287–98.

about the implications of the fact that this relatively early statement refers to five rather than three categories. The five categories are being, quality, relation, representation, and substance. What happens to two of these, being and substance, in his later theory of categories has implications for his metaphysics. A second advantage is that his formulation of the categories in the "New List" is accomplished through setting them forth in terms of semeiotic concepts. What become the categories are at the same time what become the conditions of sign processes and classes of signs. But perhaps most important is that his analysis in this article fits the framework of both logic and, loosely, a phenomenological method.

I shall offer an account only of certain points in Peirce's discussion.[2] The focus will be on some of Peirce's key assumptions that inform his thought in general and the highlights of the main conception that become the categories in his later discussions.

The Origin of the Categories in "On a New List of Categories"

The purpose of Peirce's "New List" is to specify the general conditions necessary to the formation of conceptions, which he states occur when impressions are unified in propositions. These are conditions of intelligibility, because propositions are the basic products of the articulation of knowledge. They are expressions, or the meanings and utterances, that can be applied truly or falsely to what we experience. Thus, as Peirce indicates in later commentary on the "New List," he is concerned with fundamental categories of thought (1.561).

At the outset, working within the Kantian framework for understanding what theoretical judgments do, Peirce says that "the function of conceptions is to reduce the manifold of sensuous impressions to unity" (1.545). The major problem addressed in the article, then, concerns the identification of the conceptions required to articulate experience by unifying its components, which is to form a proposition: "The unity to which the understanding reduces impressions is the unity of a proposition" (1.548). Three crucial features of Peirce's attack on the problem should be noticed, however, before the outcome of Peirce's analysis is sketched. First, the conceptions with which Peirce is concerned are universal – "This theory [about the function of con-

---

[2]See Murray Murphey, *The Development of Peirce's Philosophy* (Cambridge, Mass.: Harvard University Press, 1961), chap. 3, esp. pp. 65–89, which contains probably the most extended discussion of this article that has been published thus far. Christopher Hookway's examination of this essay also provides a straightforward and insightful explanation of Peirce's argument; see his *Peirce* (London: Routledge & Kegan Paul, 1985), argument; pp. 90–7.

ceptions] gives rise to a conception of gradation among those conceptions which are universal" (1.546). Thus, they must be necessary to the intelligibility of all propositions, that is, to the determination of impressions that otherwise would be chaotic. And, as universal, the conceptions are categories – what I have suggested are conditions of intelligibility.

Second, the conceptions that are required cannot function independently of one another. They are ordered, giving "rise to a conception of gradation" (1.546). This gradation is hierarchical, just as we have seen in the ordering of the classes of signs. "For one such conception may unite the manifold of sense and yet another may be required to unite the conception and the manifold to which it is applied; and so on" (1.546). The hierarchy, then, is delineated by a structure in which conceptions serve their function through the mediating of other conceptions that serve their own functions.

The importance of the order into which the categories fall is illustrated in part by a suggestion already mentioned. There are two universal categories of the "New List" that are later excluded from the short list. These are *being* and *substance*. The order in which they appear is as the first and the last, respectively. This suggests that Peirce may have later viewed them not as dispensable but as superfluous when listed separately. In any case, their positions as beginning and ending, or framing, the intermediate categories are an indication that they have a special relation to the other three categories and perhaps especially the second and fourth.

The order of the categories and their relations can, I think, best be understood if we note that Peirce disclaims giving a psychological, introspective description of the order in which what the categories apply to are discriminated. His perspective is intended to be that of description combined with logic. It is directed toward stating a structure of presuppositions and their order of dependency. As Murphey puts it, "so far as they [the categories] constitute simply the concepts of connection among signs and their objects necessary to that unity [of propositions, they] may be discovered by the analysis of the structure of that proposition which brings the manifold to unity."[3] Within this order can be understood cognitive processes by which experience is made intelligible – processes that are themselves psychological. This point will be expanded in a moment.

Finally, because of the location of each category within the order in which they relate to one another, the identification of each depends on a special process of abstraction called *prescinding*. Prescinding is a process required to distinguish the categories insofar as they are dis-

[3]Ibid., p. 65.

covered phenomenologically as well as logically and, as in the article now being considered, quasi-logically. Thus, his method in this early work not only anticipates his later logical but also his phenomenological approach to the categories. Prescinding is also a process for distinguishing the components of triads – of signs, for example – that are threaded throughout all Peirce's thought; consequently, it plays a role in the explanation of his evolutionary realism, and an account of it must be given in a moment. At present, however, we must complete and expand our observations of the three crucial features of Peirce's account of the necessary conceptions for the formation of propositions.

The third crucial feature of Peirce's discussion is linked to the point about hierarchical dependence. What Peirce analyzes is what can be distinguished among a multiple of conditions for the formation of a proposition *once it has been completed.* We begin in the midst of things, with ready-made experiences and completed propositions. And we focus on such experiences and propositions in order to consider what makes a proposition possible as the completed expression of a cognitive experience. This point is a way of reinforcing Peirce's purpose of drawing out the logical structure underlying cognition. Let us next turn to the highlights of his analysis.

It will be helpful in anticipation to adopt an overview and summarize the results of the analysis. There are three intermediate universal conceptions between substance and being. As the first intermediate category, Peirce identifies what he calls *quality,* which functions as "reference to a ground." The relation of quality to reference to a ground will be considered later. Suffice it to say here that, as we have seen in connection with semeioses, qualities may be respects by which an object is interpreted; thus, they may serve as grounds of what we come to know about objects. At the moment, however, what is important is to observe that Peirce begins with the most general and most abstract intermediate conception, with the category that is closest to the final unifying conception needed for the complete proposition. This does not mean that Peirce regards the first conception he mentions as first in a temporal sequence. It is logically first, because it is the most fundamental and general concept to be abstracted from the complex of constituents of the proposition.

The second category is *relation,* which Peirce defines as "reference to a correlate." This category depends on the first, because there could be no relating of one thing to another without there being a first thing, which is what Peirce refers to as a quality, and which requires reference to a ground in order that it can stand, as ground, in relating one thing to another. The third universal conception is *representation,* or "reference to an interpretant." This category depends on the second in that it presupposes that there are things to be interpreted. The quality or ground is then related to impressions, by being interpreted as determining them so that they function as the substance – that which is to be indicated by the subject of the completed proposition. The third conception is the interpretation of the two things in relation, the quality and the substance that it is interpreted as qualifying. This summary now must be expanded by a closer look at Peirce's analysis.

Peirce opens his analysis by saying that what is nearest to sense (the manifold of sensuous impressions) is the universal conception of *"the present in general"* (1.547). Although referring to what pertains to sense may seem to introduce a psychological observation, as already said, it is not Peirce's intention to engage in psychological description. Rather, he wants to call to our attention one of the conditions (this one is a framing condition) that is a universal conception or category, that is presupposed by the assertion of a proposition. A proposition must have something or other to "work on," to be denoted and interpreted. The present in general, which he says is also called in philosophy the *It,* or *substance,* is the purely denotative condition of a proposition. It is what makes possible the presence of something to be determined as intelligible by the interpreting function of the subject and predicate. There must be something interpreted, and the present in general provides that condition.

At the same time, there is something asserted of the subject, or of that which is denoted, and what is asserted is the predicate that is brought into unity with the subject. What is predicated is a quality. But there are intervening conceptions that must be presupposed in order to account for the unifying function of the predication of a quality to a subject.

In order to elicit these conceptions, Peirce focuses closely on subject and predicate. Thus, after referring to the sensuous manifold that is nearest to sense, he continues by describing constituents that must be distinguished in order to account for predication. The first distinction leads him to the quality that can be abstracted from its embodiment in the substance that is to be denoted by the subject. "Quality, therefore, in its very widest sense, is the first conception in order in passing from being to substance" (5.551). That is, quality is the first conception – it is closest to the final, framing category, being – in the order of bringing unity to the manifold by means of the copula that unites subject and predicate.

At this point, it is important to emphasize what has been said about the fact that the conceptions fall into a certain order. Thus, when Peirce says that quality is the first conception, he does not mean that it is an observed datum that appears to perception. "Quality seems at first sight to be given in the impression. Such results are untrustworthy" (1.551). Quality is not an immediate datum; the present in general is, but it is not yet brought into focus so that it is determinate enough to justify the predication of a quality. Quality is a "mediate conception," that is, it has a function in establishing an assertion and relates conditions of the assertion – components to be brought into a unity. It mediates the mass of unrelated impressions that comprise the present in general.

It is essential to keep in mind also that the impressions of which Peirce writes are not intuitions, or the referents of intuitions, which are first, or immediate, cognitions – that is, cognitions that, for Peirce, are not determined by previous cognitions. The impressions that provide the concept of the present in general are not yet cognitions; so they could not be intuitions in the sense of first cognitions – cognitions not determined by any previous cognition. But neither is quality something cognitively intuited; it is the first mediating conception that makes possible the unifying of substance. In its capacity of mediating, it relates and is related by determining and being determined by other conceptions. Further, quality is derived by abstraction from considerations concerning the structure of propositions, and, as such, it cannot be a first cognition.[4]

The conception of being for Peirce in the "New List" is the basis of the connecting link expressed by the copula *is* of the proposition. "The unity to which the understanding reduces impressions is the unity of a proposition. This unity consists in the connection of the predicate with the subject; and, therefore, that which is implied in the copula, or the conception of *being*, is that which completes the work of conceptions of reducing the manifold to unity" (1.548). In this connection, we have already noted that Peirce refers to "passing from being to substance" because being is presupposed by the unifying function of the term *is*, a function performed when a proposition asserts a predicate of a subject. And the completed predication requires the function of the universal conceptions, presupposing, finally, the unifying function of the copula, *is*. The analysis follows the order of conditions that follow from the most fully abstracted – abstracted from the completed proposition that is given for analysis – to those that are least abstract or general in relation to the completed proposition. Quality, then, is the first conception in the order of the most fundamental, abstract presuppositions between substance and being. It is

---

[4]It is significant that Peirce does not deny that there are intuitions in the sense of immediate experiences or unmediated mental acts. What he denies is that such experiences or acts are cognitive. This point has been made in the explicit, although brief, account of the way Peirce uses the term *intuition*, in the later article, "Questions Concerning Certain Faculties of Man."

the most general category required so that the *is*, or the conception of being that is presupposed by the thinking or saying that something is something else, can unify the manifold. This point should be clearer once we have considered the kind of abstraction Peirce thinks is necessary in order to make such distinctions. This kind of abstraction, prescinding, is what has been mentioned and remains to be considered as the kind of abstraction Peirce thinks necessary in order to make the distinctions that compose his analysis.

Precision, is one of three kinds of abstractions, the other two being discrimination and dissociation. Peirce characterizes prescision by comparing its way of abstracting from the other ways. In his early thought, Peirce conceived of abstraction in general as attending to one element or aspect of something while neglecting the others. Peirce characterizes the three kinds of abstraction as kinds of separation of elements. Each involves attending to something distinguished within experience. Abstraction, then, operates on a whole, or on something that is general and not simple, something that has more than one element or aspect, within which analysis can mark distinctions or differences. The procedure of sorting out elements or aspects is abstraction because it requires focusing attention on something while not focusing attention on other aspects.

Abstraction by discriminating is the weakest kind of abstraction in the sense that, of the three ways of abstracting, it covers the most cases. It presupposes a distinction only between the senses, the meanings, of the things abstracted. "I can discriminate red from blue, space from color, and color from space" (1.549). The meaning of each item is distinguishable from the others, even though those meanings may be interdependent. Abstraction by dissociation concerns the associations of images that can be separated and involves psychological considerations of what consciousness can be about. It is the strongest kind of abstraction in that it concerns the fewest things that can be abstracted. "I can dissociate red from blue, but not space from color, color from space, nor red from color."

Precision is not as broadly applicable as discrimination or as restricted as dissociation. "Pre[s]cision . . . supposes a greater separation than discrimination, but a less separation than dissociation." "I can prescind red from blue, and space from color (as is manifest from the fact that I actually believe there is an uncolored space between my face and the wall); but I cannot prescind color from space nor red from color" (1.549).

It is probably evident by now that Peirce's use of prescision in the "New List" and, as will be seen, in his later account of the categories is important because of the order of the terms, specifically, the universal conceptions, that can be prescinded from one another. Prescision is integral to his later analysis in which he inquires about the categories phenomenologically. It should be emphasized that in prescinding, the kinds of components prescinded cannot be abstracted reciprocally. "Precision is not a reciprocal process. It is frequently the case, that, while A cannot be prescinded from B, B can be prescinded from A" (1.549). Color cannot be prescinded from space, but space can be prescinded from color, because color is an impression that "occasions" (1.549) the necessary conception of space. Color must be extended, spread out, and so it occasions in the sense that it presupposes space. But space does not occasion or presuppose color; it is possible to suppose that there is uncolored space. Peirce's point in characterizing prescision near the beginning of the "New List," then, is that he needs to explain the procedure by which he identifies the universal conceptions or categories. By prescinding, he can specify those conceptions that must be presupposed by the graded constituents or conditions of propositions and by the propositions composed by these constituents.

Now if a conception does not reduce the impressions upon which it follows to unity [does not succeed in completing or contributing to the completion of a proposition], it is a mere arbitrary addition to these latter; and elementary conceptions do not arise thus arbitrarily. But if the impressions could be definitely comprehended without the conception, this latter would not reduce them to unity. Hence the impressions (or more immediate conceptions) cannot be definitely conceived or attended to, to the neglect of an elementary conception which reduces them to unity. . . . The explaining conception may frequently be prescinded from the more immediate ones and from the impressions. (1.549)

Each category, then, is a necessary condition or presupposition for a richer or more complex conception or category. And each category must be prescinded from the more complex and immediate conception. But the process cannot be reversed. By analogy, color is more complex than space in the sense that color requires space, while space does not require color. Space can be attended to, to the neglect of color, but not vice versa. The same order and relationship holds for the data and conditions into which Peirce analyzes propositions.

Let us now return to the first conception, quality. We must examine the sense in which a predicate asserts a quality of the unified substance or subject. Peirce says, "Since this [the applicability of the mediate conception, quality, to the more immediate one, the substance] is *asserted,* the more mediate conception is clearly regarded independently of this circumstance" (1.551). To predicate a quality of a subject is the first occasion of the first conception, quality, because asserting the predicate presupposes something distinct to be predicated, the quality; and this is to presuppose an abstraction of the quality from its presence or embodiment in the subject. As abstracted, the quality is attributed to, and in the future would be attributable to, other substances. However, insofar as any given quality is considered in its own right, it is taken immediately, and as such, it is distinguished and prescinded from what is given, that is, from the present manifold of impressions that are to be made intelligible. Thus, of quality, Peirce says, "But, taken immediately [by which I interpret him to mean, "considered in itself as prescinded"], it transcends what is given (the more immediate conception [the present in general, substance]), and its applicability to the latter is hypothetical" (1.551).

Predication, then, is a form of hypothesizing, for the predicate is applied to the subject by virtue of being considered an interpretation of a part of the manifold of impressions that are being brought to unity. The predicate is a sign of these impressions in the sense that it interprets the subject as denoting them insofar as they are of the sort to which the predicate applies.

The abstraction of a quality, however, is more complicated than is suggested by what we have observed thus far. The complications can be seen if we consider the example Peirce cites to clarify his analysis. The example is, "This stove is black." He points out that "black" indicates that there is something that is black (and is a stove) and that this is discernible by virtue of a recognition of a quality, blackness, abstractable from the manifold of impressions and then made applicable to those impressions insofar as they function as the present in general and, in turn, as a substance.

Take, for example, the proposition, "This stove is black." Here the conception of *this stove* is the more immediate, that of *black* the more mediate, which latter, to be predicated of the former, must be discriminated from it and considered *in itself*, not as applied to an object, but simply as embodying a quality, *blackness*. . . . The same thing is meant by "the stove is black," as by "there is blackness in the stove." . . . Moreover, the conception of a pure abstraction is indispensable, because we cannot comprehend an agreement of two things, except as an agreement in some *respect*, and this respect is such a pure abstraction as blackness. Such a pure abstraction, reference to which constitutes a *quality* or general attribute, may be termed a *ground*. (1.551)

There are, then, two occasions for the need to refer to the first conception, quality. As noted earlier, before we turned to a closer examination of the analysis, the first occasion is that the predicate is *asserted*, so that what is asserted must be regarded as abstractable. The second occasion is that for there to be an assertion and thus an abstraction, there must be an agreement between what is predicated and the subject of predication. Notice that Peirce refers to the agreement not in a vague, general way, or in some indefinite way, but as an agreement in some *respect*. The respect in the example of the stove is *blackness*.

However, it is significant that, at this point, what is referred to as the quality is not the abstraction itself. He points to "a pure abstraction, reference to which constitutes a quality." Thus, the quality is the "reference to" the abstraction. If this shift in identifying the quality is compared with Peirce's remarks about the equivalence of embodying the abstraction, blackness, and the predicate, black, which is the abstraction insofar as it is applied to the subject, we can discriminate three constituents that serve as occasions of quality. First, there is the subject, or linguistic sign that refers us to a substance – which results from asserting the hypothetical or the interpretive condition, the quality, of some of the impressions confronted in the present in general. Second, there is the abstraction that is required to be acknowledged in order that asserting can take place. Finally, there is the third, embodied abstraction, which mediates between the pure abstraction and the substance.

Insofar as it is attended to within the initial sense-manifold, a quality, then, is relational, in the sense of reference to an abstraction (the ground), and insofar as it is an interpretive conception that brings the substance under a condition of intelligibility, or a unification. Thus, it must be emphasized, at least at this stage of his thought, that for Peirce quality attached to a substance is not itself an abstraction, although it depends on the pure abstraction (blackness) and as such, the pure abstraction is the ground of the embodied quality. This third function of quality is its serving as the respect or ground of the interpreted impressions – the respect of the agreement, that is, between what is predicated and what the predicate is applied to, is the ground of the applicability of that which is predicated. Thus, there is the perceived stove. There is presupposed blackness. And there is perceived black. Perceived black is the embodied blackness; black mediates the abstraction and the substantial thing – the thing that is recognized *as* manifesting a certain quality. Black, or embodied blackness, can serve this function in its capacity as the *respect* in which some of the impressions resemble and differ from other impressions in the present in general. Some of these impressions are in agreement (and thus deserve to be the subject of predication) with other components of the experience, that is, with those indicated by the abstraction, blackness. In short, being black requires being relational in two ways, being blackness embodied in the referent of the subject, the stove, and being different and like other impressions of what is not black and what is like the impression, black. Blackness, the abstraction, however, is itself just what it is apart from a relation.

This part of the analysis suggests a clear anticipation of at least part of Peirce's later account of semeioses when he says that a sign refers to its object in some respect, which is a ground. It may also be suggested that what Peirce refers to here through the example is an immediate object, namely, the object of the proposition with respect to its being a stove that embodies blackness – that is, a complex of characters that serve to make impressions intelligible. These suggestions, and Peirce's identification of the occasions of the first category, lead directly to the second intermediate, universal conception, which Peirce calls *reference to a correlate*. And it will also be seen that the third conception must consequently be identified – that is, the conception of representation or reference to an interpretant, which already has been seen to emerge because of the need to hypothesize with respect to the applicability of the predicate. Such hypothesizing depends on a comparison and determination of some way that there is agreement between the things compared.

Let us focus briefly on the second intermediate category. Peirce says, "The occasion of reference to a correlate is obviously by comparison" (1.553). What exactly is compared? Presumably, and as already suggested, some or all of the impressions given in the present in general are compared with either other given impressions or with remembered or inferred impressions or conditions. Peirce suggests both alternatives. And I think he means to say that both given and mediate or inferred constituents are the sources of the relate and correlate that are compared.[5] His examples suggest this. For instance, in one example, he explains how *b* and *p* can be compared by means of superimposing one, turned on its axis, on the other. The result, he says, is "a new image which mediates between the images of the two letters, inasmuch as it represents one of them to be (when turned over) the likeness of the other" (1.553). Presumably, *b* and *p* represent immediate images in the sense that they are simultaneously present to perception. In his second example, one of the correlates is not given immediately as an actual impression that is compared with another actual impression. The example is "a murderer as being in relation to a murdered person; in this case we conceive the act of the murder, and in this conception it is represented that corresponding to every murderer (as well as to every murder) there is a murdered person; and thus we resort again to a mediating representation [the act of murder] which represents the relate [murder] as standing for a correlate [murdered person] with which the mediating representation is itself in relation" (1.553). Here the need to abstract from a more immediate conception to a second, correlated conception is explicit. But the need for abstraction, or prescision, is also present in the first example, because the new image of the superimposed *b* and *p* must be something

[5]Murray Murphey presents a detailed discussion of the problem of determining what Peirce considers to be the things compared in Peirce's analysis; see *The Development of Peirce's Philosophy*, pp. 76–87.

thought about from which b and p are prescinded in order that the image represents one to be "in the likeness of the other." Further, if we consider what is involved in the example, "This stove is black," we can see that the abstraction, blackness, requires the role of memory from the standpoint of psychology and inference from the standpoint of logic. Not only is its application to *this stove* hypothetical but blackness must be discriminated from any number of other instances to which it is applicable. The multiple instances together form the basis for the distinctions among qualities referred to their abstractions. And the instances are also required so that a repeatable image can be derived.

Once we see the conceptions that are prescinded from a more immediate conception – from the $b–p$ image in the first example and the conception of the act of murder in the second – we see that they are occasioned by the more immediate conception and we recognize the function of the more immediate conception. And once this function is recognized, we can see that there is a representative role, an interpretant, that must be acting so that the prescinded conceptions or images both can be prescinded and be intelligible by virtue of the way they are represented by the occasioning, more immediate conception. "Every reference to a correlate, then, conjoins to the substance the conception of a reference to an interpretant; and this is, therefore, the next conception in order in passing from being to substance" (1.553).

To the answer to the question of what is compared with what, that is, what is the source of the correlate that is compared with the relate, Peirce adds several more suggestions. These indicate that Peirce thinks there are two parts of the impressions that are given in the present in general.

Reference to an interpretant is rendered possible and justified by that which renders possible and justifies comparison. But that is clearly the diversity of impressions. If we had but one impression, it would not require to be reduced to unity, and would therefore not need to be thought of as referred to an interpretant, and the conception of reference to an interpretant would not arise. But since there is a manifold of impressions, we have a feeling of complication or confusion, which leads us to differentiate this impression from that, and then, having been differentiated, they require to be brought to unity. (1.554)

From this statement, Peirce concludes that there is a need for the interpreting function that we, who are driven to form the proposition, provide by "the holding together of diverse impressions" and uniting "directly the manifold of the substance itself" (1.554). Relate and correlate seem to have their sources in the given impressions, but the determination of them taken as relate and as correlate, that is, as two impressions or groups of impressions, ready to be compared, takes us beyond their immediate presence. Intelligibility requires our prescinding away from where we are when we begin to try to understand how we render experience intelligible.

It is necessary next to consider how the three intermediate categories Peirce has identified serve as the basis of his phenomenologically and logically derived categories in his later thought.

From the Categories of the "New List" to the Phenomenology

The transition from the categories of the "New List" to Peirce's phenomenological derivation of them is in part conditioned by the connection between the "New List" intermediate categories and the components of semeioses. Peirce himself offers some of these connections, and some of them have already been mentioned. First, it is clear that the third intermediate category is a representation, which constitutes a semeiotic function, which is to say that it is a sign. Further, the representation or sign, requires an interpretant, and if there is an interpreted sign, there must be an object to which the sign refers for the interpretant according to the interpretation. Third, the second intermediate category constitutes the referential relation between object and sign, which the interpretant brings together. The relate is an object for the correlate, or vice versa, by virtue of the function of the interpretant that gives rise to inferential comparison of the relate and correlate. Thus, the thought of a murderer is a sign of a murdered person by virtue of the conception of the act of murder in which "it is represented that corresponding to every murderer (as well as to every murder) there is a murdered person" (1.553). Finally, the abstraction that constitutes the first category is the ground or – as is referred to a few years later in Peirce's definition of a sign – the respect. The respect or ground, it will be recalled, is one of the three conditions of an instance of semeiosis, one of the three components that make up a sign as it functions for an interpreter and its object. And, as was noted earlier, the grounds or respects in which the sign is interpreted as qualifying the ways the sign refers to its object constitute the immediate object.

In addition to the explicit connections between semeiotic conditions and the categories that already have been seen as integral to Peirce's analysis, there are correlations that become crucial to his later categoriology. After his account of the intermediate categories, he says:

The five conceptions thus obtained, for reasons which will be sufficiently obvious, may be termed *categories*. That is,

> *Being*
> Quality (reference to a ground)
> Relation (reference to a correlate)
> Representation (reference to an interpretant)
>   *Substance*
> The three intermediate conceptions may be termed accidents.
> (1.555)

Let it be noted that to refer to the intermediate conceptions as accidents is obviously not intended as a retraction of the point that they are categories and thus universal and necessary. It is rather a way of indicating their status in relation to the framing foundations of categories, that is, to their serving as a means to the end of making intelligible what otherwise would be chaos, which is to serve the purpose of unifying the diversity of what is encountered in experience.

Peirce continues his explanation of what he has identified by first introducing explicitly the idea of assigning numerical terms to the categories. Thus, he says:

> This passage from the many to the one is numerical. The conception of a *third* is that of an object which is so related to two others, that one of these must be related to the other in the same way in which the third is related to that other. Now this coincides with the conception of an interpretant. (1.556)

This description of the third intermediate conception anticipates Peirce's later phenomenological identification of the semeiotic condition by which phenomena are interpreted and thus rendered intelligible. This category is called Thirdness.

Peirce adds further remarks that anticipate the numerical naming of the phenomenological categories. He continues the passage just quoted, pointing out that "an *other* is plainly equivalent to a correlate. The conception of second differs from that of other, implying the possibility of a third" (1.556). Although he does not refer to quality as the category of the first, or as Firstness, which later is part of his phenomenologically categoriological terminology, the terms are implicit, given the characterizing of the conception of a third and of a second and given the numerical ordering itself. The remainder of the "New List" is devoted to an explanation of how the categories are fundamental in logic. Here he anticipates his division of logic as a complex of the branches of semeiotic. The discussion does not bear directly on his theory of the categories in their mature form. And it is to this theory that we must now turn.

The Origin and Scope of Peirce's Phenomenology

It was suggested that the categories of the "New List" resulted from both formally logical and observational considerations. That Peirce persisted in thinking that the derivation of the categories requires both approaches seems obvious in his statement in 1894 that "The *list of categories* . . . is a table of conceptions drawn from the logical analysis of thought and regarded as applicable to being" (1.300), to which he adds, "each category has to justify itself by an inductive examination which will result in assigning to it only a limited or approximate validity" (1.301).

We should expect that Peirce sees the need to look beyond the analysis in the "New List," because its scope is confined to the conditions of the proposition. Thus, the list is not obviously extended to all experience, or to all aspects of what makes experience in all its dimensions intelligible. Peirce's broadened scope within which he discusses the categories is the main topic of this section and the remainder of this chapter. The extended context in which the categories are exposed is made finally by moving from the conditions of propositions to the phenomenology. However, Peirce's first step in moving toward his developed phenomenological theory of the categories is made through a broadening of his conception of logic. And this broadened conception is accompanied by developing and adopting a logic of relations or of relatives.[6] It is this logic that served the moves made after the "New List" with respect to his formal approach to the categories.

In some later remarks (c. 1905) concerning the "New List," Peirce says that about the time he wrote this article he had been introduced to De Morgan's logic of relations.[7] Although, as he said a bit earlier, in 1894, "Thorough study of the logic of relations confirms the conclusions which I reached before going far in the study [of the logic of relatives]" (1.293), his acquaintance with the logic of relations at the time of the "New List" did not contribute to the analysis of propositions that he offered there. It was twenty-five years before his study of the logic of relations approached a "provisionally final result." During that study, he modified his understanding of the predicates of propositions: "Indecomposable predicates are of three classes: first, those which, like neuter verbs, apply to a single subject; secondly, those which like simple transitive verbs have two subjects each . . . and thirdly, those predicates which have three such subjects, or correlates" (1.562).

The central idea in this classification of indecomposable predicates – predicates that are irreducible, each serving distinct, necessary, and unifying functions in making objects intelligible – is a classification of three fundamental kinds of relations. These relations represent the three intermediate categories that Peirce proposed in the "New List." They exhaust all possible kinds of relations among things and so ex-

---

[6]Peirce sometimes uses the expression *logic of relatives* in place of *logic of relations*. He distinguishes between these by indicating only that the expression *logic of relatives* is more accurate because it refers to the terms or subjects as distinct from the relations in which the terms occur.

[7]This reference is found in the *Collected Papers* (1.562).

haust all possible categories of the short list. Being and substance no longer stand as separate categories. They are not distinct relations. Instead, they are, or seem to be, integral to the other three kinds of irreducible relations. However, this evolution of thought about how categories are identifiable in terms of propositions that express monadic, dyadic, or triadic relations is not itself an enrichment of the observational approach. Thus, we need to see the way in which Peirce added his phenomenological basis for identifying the categories.

It should be noted that there is no evidence that Peirce introduces the terminology of the later, phenomenological categoriology until, apparently, no earlier than 1894 (see, e.g., 1.302). Herbert Spiegelberg says that the term *phenomenology* itself was not introduced until 1902.[8] At this time, presumably, he begins to make explicit use of his study of the logic of relations as a way of understanding the fundamental conceptions that make things intelligible. But in doing so, he anticipates the variations on terminology that reflect his phenomenological approach. The categories now are explicitly identified by ordinal as well as cardinal numbers made into hypothesized substantives as well as adjectives. But more important is that we can see a transition from his earlier "New List" when he makes some explicit remarks about the changes he introduces. Because his work on the logic of relations seems to be at least partially responsible for these changes, we should observe further the main features of this logic that suggest them.

Peirce's modification of his understanding of predicates is related to a recognition that predicates may be understood as including the copula *is* and, as we have seen, may apply to multiple as well as single subjects. Thus, a proposition is regarded no longer in terms of the classical subject and predicate united by a copula but rather as a relation in which the predicate is a relation that applies to one or more subjects.

To say that the relation functions as the predicate means that the relation is what is said of the subjects; it is what connects them so that they are made intelligible. In order to do this, they include a copula or some active conception that brings a subject or subjects together under some respect or ground in which the subject is qualified or the subjects are related. Accordingly, the proposition "This stove is black" is a monadic relation, for it has only one subject. "Is black" is the monadic predicate that applies to the subject. Thus, the copula "is" is internalized. But the expression "A is the father of B" is a proposition that is dyadic, because it has two subjects, "A" and "B." And, using

---

[8]Herbert Spiegelberg, *The Phenomenological Movement: A Historical Introduction* (The Hague: Martinus Nijhoff, 1960), p. 18.

one of Peirce's favorite examples, "A gives B to C," we have an example of a triadic relation, because it has three subjects. The three kinds of relations, then, may be named "monad," "dyad," and "triad."

In later remarks on what he developed in his logic of relations, Peirce also says:

> I have, since 1870, written much about the logic of relations. In those writings, I have *usually* restricted the terms "relation" and "relationship" to *existential* relations and relationships. By a relationship I understand the conception of a fact about a set of things abstracted from the representation of the things themselves, or, in other words, a predicate which requires more than one subject to complete a proposition, or conception of a fact. A relation only differs from a "relationship" in that one of the two subjects is regarded as being taken account of first, and is usually called the *subject nominative,* while the others are called the *direct* and *indirect objects.* (MS 200, 2–3; K. 5–6)

The consequences of this application of the predicate for identifying the categories are that the universal conceptions or categories are to be found in kinds of relations. Of course, the categories of the "New List" are also characterized with reference to relations. The second, obviously, is itself called relation, and it is applicable to two terms, one being the relate or thing that is compared with another thing, the correlate. The first intermediate category that is identified by the expression, "reference to a ground," is a monadic relation, having one subject that is qualified by the ground. And the third intermediate conception is described as reference to an interpretant, or representation, which is a triadic relation that brings together the things compared with a third thing, an interpretant. Peirce's characterization of the intermediate categories with reference to the way predicates imply relations is not, however, the same as treating the predicate as itself a relation. And it is the latter treatment that marks the later categoriology.

In the later framework, the copula, *is,* is externalized. However, Peirce also moves toward a less formal terminology for describing the categories. In the mid-1880s,[9] Peirce suggests ways in which he begins to bridge the earlier and later ways of referring to the categories. He says:

> By the third, I mean the medium or connecting bond between the absolute first and last. The beginning is first, the end second, the middle third. The end is second, the means third. The thread of life is a third; the fate that snips it, its second. . . . Continuity represents Thirdness almost to perfection. (1.337)

[9]In the *Collected Papers,* this manuscript is dated c. 1875. However, a more recent dating made at the Peirce Edition Project dates it as c. 1885. This later dating is more consistent with the way Peirce explains the categories in all his other discussions. Indeed, even 1885 seems a few years early with respect to the expressions Peirce uses, especially, in view of his use of the word *Thirdness* and his reference to it as continuity.

A bit later, in 1890, he formulates his conception of the categories in a way that also suggests a transition from the categories in the logic of relations to the application of the logic of relations to the phenomenological approach. In a draft of a work entitled, "Notes for a Book, to be entitled 'A Guess at the Riddle,' with a Vignette of the Sphynx below the Title," he begins with a discussion of the role of the triad in reasoning (1.354). Specifically mentioning the triad in physics, he uses the term *Thirdness* to indicate a conception that is necessary to the purposes of a kind of explanation that does not presuppose any form of absolute (1.354). Moreover, he confesses to his own leaning toward the use of threefold divisions in all his reasoning. Thus, he says of his inclination to think in triads, "I mean no more than the ideas of first, second, third – ideas so broad that they may be looked upon rather as moods or tones of thought, than as definite notions, but which have great significance for all that. Viewed as numerals, to be applied to what objects we like, they are indeed thin skeletons of thought, if not words" (1.355). If the numerical identification of categories provides no more than a skeleton of thought, then we need additional considerations to complete the search. Further, because philosophy aims at distinctions that "go down to the very essence of things," Peirce insists that "it behooves us to ask beforehand what are the kinds of objects that are first, second, and third . . . in their own true characters" (1.355). Peirce then initiates one of his earliest phenomenological approaches to describing what he takes to be the three categories of the now-revised short list. This description begins as follows: "The first is that whose being is simply in itself, not referring to anything nor lying behind anything. The second is that which is what it is by force of something to which it is second. The third is that which is what it is owing to things between which it mediates and which it brings into relation to each other" (1.356).

The development of Peirce's ordinal and cardinal terminology used to identify and describe his categories, however, seems fairly well entrenched a bit earlier, specifically, by 1894. In that year, in his essay "The List of Categories: A Second Essay, X" he refers to the ideas of both first and Firstness (1.302). And, in 1898, Peirce refers to the result of his earlier search for universal conceptions as "what I call my categories." He mentions "Quality, Relation, and Representation," omitting any reference to substance and being (4.3). In explaining how he arrived at the three that he does mention, he states explicitly his preference for a new way of identifying the categories. He says, "But I was not then aware that undecomposable [*sic*] relations may necessarily require more subjects than two" (4.3). He then adds that

for this reason *Reaction* is a better term. Moreover, I did not then know enough about language to see that to attempt to make the word *representation* serve for an idea so much more general than any it habitually carried, was injudicious. The word *mediation* would be better. Quality, reaction, and mediation will do. But for scientific terms, Firstness, Secondness, and Thirdness, are to be preferred as being entirely new words without any false associations whatever. How the conceptions are *named* makes, however, little difference. (4.3)

Why is *reaction* a better term? Because it indicates the brute, dyadic character of the second category. And *mediation* is more direct than *representation* in directing attention to the essential structure of representation. This direct reference to structure is important because of the generality of the idea Peirce has in mind for his third category. In any case, if, as Peirce says at the end of the quoted passage, the names of the categories make little difference, they nevertheless are suggestive of Peirce's ways of regarding the categories. In fact, some of the terminology and explanations of his terms that he is now using belong to the language that most pervades his phenomenological descriptions of the categories. Reaction, for instance, is critical in his account of the second category; the term *mediation* bridges logical and phenomenological descriptions of the third category; and *Firstness, Secondness,* and *Thirdness* are preferred terms that he constructs by means of the substantives he makes of the ordinal terms when he adopts his phenomenological approach. Let us turn to this way of describing the categories.

In a 1905 letter to Lady Welby (Draft), July 1905, he says, "I have been overhauling my classification of signs with the result of throwing the matter into a state of confusion which I hope with time will heal up into some connective tissue."[10] He then refers to his categories in their most recent form as having resulted from two years of incessant study in the direction of "trying to do what Hegel tried to do. It became apparent that there were such categories as his." Further, he says:

Alongside of these, however, which may be called material categories, there are formal categories, corresponding to his [Hegel's] three grades of thought. These are much more important as all classifications according to structure are than classifications according to material. [By *phaneron*] I mean whatever is before the mind in any way whatever & regardless of whether it is possible that there are indecomposable elements of the elements of the *phaneron* which have different grades of structure. (Ibid.)

We are, then, ready to consider the phenomenological categories in somewhat more detail.

The Phenomenological Description

The Foundational Role of Phenomenology

As preparation for further discussion of Peirce's phenomenological description of the categories, it is necessary to consider his view of the

[10]The most recently published appearance of the letter is in *Semiotic and Significs: The Correspondence between Charles S. Peirce and Victoria Lady Welby*, ed. Charles S. Hardwick, assisted by James Cook (Bloomington: Indiana University Press, 1977), p. 189.

purpose and method appropriate to phenomenology as a science. My comments in the present context will omit a comparison of the scope and method of Peirce's phenomenology with that of Edmund Husserl. A brief comparison of these will be made a bit later after some initial explanation of Peirce's purposes. Not only does phenomenology constitute a systematic way to develop Peirce's categories empirically but it is characterized by Peirce rather late in his career as a foundational branch of philosophy that, with mathematics, serves as the foundation of the other two branches, which are what he calls the "normative sciences" of aesthetics, ethics, and logic, and the third branch that depends on these, metaphysics.

As has just been suggested, the point that phenomenology is foundational depends on Peirce's later classification of the sciences. This outline should be described briefly. Peirce classifies philosophy as one of the sciences of discovery, a kind of science that uses inquiry for advancing knowledge rather than simply classifying or reasoning with what is already known. The other branch of the science of discovery, referred to as *idioscopy*, consists of the special sciences, those that depend on specific assumptions and principles and methods of observation appropriate to the aims and subject matter of the science – for example, what we now refer to as physics, chemistry, or biology.

Idioscopy depends on philosophy. Further, within philosophy, the branches are ordered hierarchically, as we have seen, so that the most fundamental is phenomenology on which rests the normative sciences – ethics being dependent on aesthetics and logic on ethics – and finally, metaphysics, which rests on all other branches of philosophy. Of particular interest to us is whether all the branches of philosophy depend exclusively on phenomenology.

It is important to take into account that Peirce not only places phenomenology as foundational within his outline of his classification of the philosophical sciences, but he also says that mathematics, which is not identified as a philosophical science, serves directly as a basis for the normative branch, and for phenomenology itself. We should also note that if the branches of philosophy were to stand only on phenomenology, then the categories as phenomenologically derived would seem to be more fundamental than the categories as logically derived, because logic is a normative science that rests on phenomenology. However, Peirce did not sharply separate logic, or at least the formal part of it, from mathematics. I suggest that the categories derived logically are not separable from one of the jobs of mathematics. Hence, the categories logically and mathematically derived in the logic of relations share a foundational role with the categories phenomenologically derived. What more can be said about this relationship of serving as a shared foundation, and what can be said about the possibility that the logically formed categories are, as is mathematics, somehow more basic than phenomenology?

In standing as a foundation for philosophy, phenomenology also stands as a foundation for the special sciences. However, mathematics, or at least mathematics as it overlaps formal logic, also is said by Peirce to serve as a foundation for all the sciences. In 1903, Peirce says that normative science rests on both mathematics and phenomenology (1.186). Yet Peirce has said in 1902 that all the sciences of discovery, among which he includes mathematics, rest on observation 1.239–40). Presumably, however fundamental mathematics may be, it is insufficient to support all the sciences, for these include sciences that are observational and dependent on observation. This is consistent with Peirce's statement in about 1896 that mathematics is "only busied about *purely hypothetical questions.* As for what the truth of existence may be the mathematician does not (*qua* mathematician) care a straw" (1.53). Mathematics is "cut off from all inquiry into existential truth" (1.53). That mathematics is not more fundamental than phenomenology is also borne out by the statement that "The business of collections enter into mathematics. It is represented in the theory of substantive possibility, and this flows from Categories. Therefore the doctrine of the categories must precede mathematics" (MS 339c Kentner page number 458, ms. p. 222r).[11]

Let me suggest here that as a way of sorting out the relation between the foundational roles of mathematics and phenomenology with respect to deriving the categories, we may exploit Peirce's method of prescinding, which, as seen in the "New List," showed the relative interdependencies of the categories. If mathematics is the most abstract of the sciences in being the most hypothetical and removed from existential considerations, then it is reasonable to suppose that mathematics can be prescinded from phenomenology, which itself is prescindable from the normative sciences. This, of course, is consistent both with Peirce's insistence that phenomenology is dependent on the "conditional or hypothetical science of *Pure Mathematics* (5.40) and with Peirce's idea that normative sciences are dependent on phenomenology. The suggestion of prescinding mathematics from phenomenology should be expected to the very extent that Peirce thought out his categories in terms of the abstract relations appropriate to the logic of relatives. Furthermore, phenomenology can be supposed without normative considerations. But then mathematics presumably can be supposed without recourse to actual observations (although not necessarily without *possible* observations of actualities). If this is correct, then mathematics is fundamental as the most abstract or hypothetical

[11]I am indebted to André Etienne for calling this passage to my attention.

foundation; phenomenology is fundamental as the most purely observational foundation.[12] Moreover, it should be added that mathematics as it overlaps aspects of logic is fundamental in providing techniques and procedures for the thought appropriate to phenomenology and in turn all the sciences.[13]

If we assume that phenomenology is the primary general (coenoscopic) empirical observational science, then, it must share with mathematics the foundational function for philosophy and, in turn, the other sciences. The foundational function of phenomenology or phaneroscopy is evident in Peirce's description of its method and scope. A brief consideration of Peirce's description of phenomenology will confirm the pervasiveness and fundamental role it plays.

The Aim, Method, and Scope of Phenomenology

The term *phenomenology* or *phaneroscopy*, which Peirce sometimes uses alternatively for the same science, is not introduced until 1902. However, the terminology of what Peirce does designate as phenomenology is present as early as 1894, as has been suggested already. However, I believe that the aim of phenomenology was anticipated as early as his "New List" of 1867, in which he uses the procedure of prescinding. Thus, it will be recalled, he attends to conditions of the intelligibility of phenomena, and these conditions are regarded as universal conceptions, or categories, that we find in his phenomenologically described categories beginning in 1894. It may be noted, too, that in 1902, just prior to his systematic description of phenomenology, he may have anticipated this description. He explains that philosophy "contents itself with observations such as come within the range of every man's normal experience, and for the most part in every waking hour of his life." In this context, Peirce calls philosophy *coenoscopic*. In a footnote, he quotes Bentham as saying, "*Coenoscopic ontology*, then, is designated that part of science which takes for its subject those properties which are considered as possessed in common by all the individuals belonging to the class which the name *ontology* is employed to designate, i.e., by *all individuals*" (1.241). In the same work, Peirce points out that philosophy is not like idioscopy in being "split from

[12]The idea of prescinding mathematics from phenomenology as a way of deciding on which of the two sciences is foundational occurred to me in conversation with Nathan Houser and André Etienne at the Peirce Edition Project in September 1988.

Let me add that it may also be suggested that if phenomenology is open descriptively to every appearance, then it must also be descriptive of even the most abstract considerations or aspects of phenomena, such as those proper to the abstractions of mathematicians. It may be regarded also as continuous with descriptive mathematics.

[13]The function of mathematics in providing techniques and procedures was emphasized by Christopher Hookway in conversation about the issue of how mathematics and phenomenology are related in Peirce's thought.

top to bottom into an efficient and a final wing," because philosophy has the task of "comparing the two stems of causation and of exhuming their common root"⁺ (1.273). Nevertheless, philosophy is distinguishable into two groups of studies. He says that "besides what constitutes . . . the main body of philosophy, resting exclusively upon universal experience, and imparting to it a tinge of necessity, there is a department of science which, while it rests, and can only rest, as to the bulk of it, upon universal experience, yet for certain special yet obtrusive points is obliged to appeal to the most specialized observations, in order to ascertain what minute modifications of everyday experience they may introduce" (1.273). The first of these groups, presumably, is either phenomenology itself or at least what is concerned with experience in its universality. I believe that Peirce is here thinking of the branches of philosophy, normative sciences and metaphysics, insofar as they require the kind of generalized attention to experience such as comes into "the range of everyman's normal experience." And this is to think of the branches of philosophy as they rely on phenomenological considerations.

In 1903, in his lectures on pragmatism and pragmaticism, the idea of a science that concentrates on the general task of philosophy seems to be clearly confirmed. In explaining pragmaticism, he resorts to an explanation of phenomenology.

Be it understood, then, that what we have to do, as students of phenomenology, is simply to open our mental eyes and look well at the phenomenon and say what are the characteristics that are never wanting in it, whether that phenomenon be something that outward experience forces upon our attention, or whether it be the wildest of dreams, or whether it be the most abstract and general of the conclusion of science. (5.41)

This requirement of phenomenology that it concerns characteristics recognized independently of the source or force of the phenomena that they qualify is consistent with the idea that phenomenology must be neutral with respect to the ontological and epistemological status of phenomena. Thus, in 1905, he says:

Phaneroscopy is the description of the *phaneron;* and by the *phaneron* I mean the collective total of all that is in any way or in any sense present to the mind, quite regardless of whether it corresponds to any real thing or not. If you ask present *when,* and to *whose* mind, I reply that I leave these questions unanswered, never having entertained a doubt that those features of the phaneron that I have found in my mind are present at all times and to all minds. (1.284)

A few paragraphs later, Peirce adds that

phaneroscopy has nothing at all to do with the question of how far the phanerons it studies correspond to any realities. It religiously abstains from all speculation as to any relations between its categories and physiological facts, cerebral or other. It does not undertake, but sedulously avoids, hypothetical explanations of any sort. (1.287)

At this point, we should note that the epistemological and meta-physical neutrality of Peirce's phenomenology bears common ground with the program of phenomenology initiated and developed by Edmund Husserl. There is little evidence about the extent to which the two men knew about each others' work. In a passing reference, Peirce acknowledges an admiration for Husserl, referring to him as "distinguished" (4.7), while at the same time saying that Husserl was not faithful to his own antipsychologism.[14] In an article comparing Peirce's and Husserl's phenomenologies, Spiegelberg observes that the term phenomenology was used by both in print for the first time just one year apart – Husserl's use in 1901 and Peirce's in 1902. Spiegelberg, however, recognizes that the conception of a "science" or form of systematic study later called phenomenology certainly appeared in Peirce's writings long before 1902 – a point to be discussed later. Moreover, at the time both men proposed phenomenological programs, the term *phenomenology* was being used in various circles ranging from the Hegelians to positivists like Ernst Mach. In general, Peirce's use of the term shares with Husserl's the requirement that the investigator refrain from introducing any assumption about the existence or inexistence, reality or unreality, or truth or falsity of the phenomena studied. Thus, Peirce as well as Husserl conceived phenomenology as a science in which questions of the basis or explanatory conditions for its phenomena must be bracketed – at least in the initial stages of investigation. Phenomenology for both concerns what appears before consciousness just as it appears. Its aim is to find the structures common to phenomena. Moreover, in its approach – and this seems to be the only point of agreement that Peirce recognized sharing with Husserl – phenomenology is not a form of psychology, for it excludes the use of the methods of psychology and instead relies on a logical method, which, for Peirce depends on prescinding. Finally, Peirce and Husserl agree that phenomenology is the foundational science, except that for Peirce certain aspects of mathematics are even more fundamental.

The differences between Peirce and Husserl are at least as significant as their agreement. Most basic are Peirce's aim to use phenomenology to describe his categories – categories that, as we have seen, were already evident to him and, further, which were indicated by his own logic of relations, which, as he pointed out long after he wrote the "New List," might have helped him when he wrote that paper. In addition, his aim was to understand them as ontological conditions. Thus, his aim was not to provide a pure phenomenology for its own sake and as an independent foundation for the other sciences, but

---

[14]Spiegelberg, *The Phenomenological Movement*, in which references to Peirce are made throughout both of two volumes, and in "Husserl's and Peirce's Phenomenologies: Coincidence or Interaction," *Philosophy and Phenomenological Research* 17 (1957).

rather to use phenomenological procedures to determine the most fundamental and universal modes of being. Furthermore, he did not, like Husserl, turn his sights on the way phenomena are intended by consciousness. Peirce confined his attention to the universal aspects of the phenomena as they are given, in themselves, not to the act of attention that is directed toward the phenomena, an interest that motivated Husserl.

The other conception of phenomenology that was alive and noticed by Peirce is Hegel's. Unlike his tenuous conscious relation to Husserl, his attention to Hegel is explicit. He admits a similarity as well as a difference from Hegel, whom he considers weak on the side of the logical structure of the description of the stages of thought. "[Hegel] was . . . right in holding that these *Categories* are of two kinds; the Universal Categories all of which apply to everything, and the series of categories consisting of phases of evolution." Peirce says that Hegel had not "catalogued" the latter adequately (5.38). He also suggests a difference over the structure of the science in question. In fact, Peirce claims that he uses the term *phaneroscopy* in place of *phenomenology* in order to mark a difference between himself and Hegel. But he does admit that Hegel "is so nearly right" about the universal categories that his own "doctrine might very well be taken for a variety of Hegelianism," although, he adds, his view was determined by considerations "entirely foreign to Hegel," for whom at that time he had contempt (5.38).

Let us return to Peirce's conception of the nature of phenomenology. As we have seen, in insisting on the neutrality of his own observations of phenomena while he is engaged in phenomenological description, Peirce refers to those phenomena that "are perfectly familiar to everybody." Thus, what he describes phenomenologically is open to everyone, and Peirce invites the reader to "actually repeat my observations and experiments for himself" (1.286). Phenomenology or phaneroscopy is "that study which, supported by the direct observation of phanerons and generalizing its observations, signalizes several very broad classes of phanerons; describes the features of each; shows that although they are so inextricably mixed together that no one can be isolated, yet it is manifest that their characters are quite disparate; then proves, beyond question, that a certain very short list comprises all of these broadest categories of phanerons there are; and finally proceeds to the laborious and difficult task of enumerating the principal subdivisions of those categories" (1.286). Let us, then, survey Peirce's descriptions of the categories that he discovers phenomenologically. In doing this, it will be helpful to bring together from a variety of places the key components of Peirce's different descriptions. For the most part, we shall be less concerned than before with placing Peirce's accounts in chronological order.

The Categories Phenomenologically Described

Terminology The various phenomenological descriptions of the categories may be grouped into those that relate the categories primarily to words appropriate to logic, psychology and descriptive ontology, and speculative metaphysics. These groupings overlap, and they also suggest that the neutrality with which phenomenology begins cannot be sustained. Thus, the categories arrived at phenomenologically are integrated with Peirce's entire philosophy, especially his speculative metaphysics. His overall conception of evolution, in fact, is given a framework in terms of the phenomenologically formed categories.

Before reviewing the descriptions themselves, it should be noted that an implicit reason that the neutrality of phenomenology is provisional for Peirce is that the neutrality of the terminology one must employ in descriptions intended cannot itself be sustained. Particular descriptive words are proper to particular domains of what we experience; yet each category is claimed to be present in all domains of what we experience. This point is especially relevant to the attempt to describe the first category and is especially problematic because it should, at first, presuppose nothing; it should be primary and not dependent on relations beyond whatever it makes intelligible. Thus, the descriptions of the first category face an inherent limitation. This problem will be obvious in the summary that follows.

Firstness The first category, we have seen, is referred to as Firstness. Although the term originated as a way to call attention to a logically derived first category, as it did in 1894, it became increasingly used with reference to the first category phenomenologically derived. A bridge from logical to phenomenological derivation is, I think, suggested by some of Peirce's discussions of the categories in terms of monads, dyads, and triads, where these are not understood simply as names for kinds of relations. Thus, he proposes that, as monadic, the first category is that element of any phenomenon that gives it its character independently of anything else – that is, independently of any other phenomenon and any other character. Later, in 1908, the idea of the monadic aspect of phenomena is related to another approach to the categories. They are explained not strictly in terms of the logic of relations but here in terms of indecomposable elements classified either according to "the form or structure of the elements," or according to "their matter."

It is important to notice that the structure that Peirce refers to is what he calls *external*, that is, the structure of the phenomenon's "possible compounds" (1.288–9). Thus, making use of an idea essential to chemistry, he treats the categories as valencies. "If, then, there be any formal division of elements of the phaneron, there must be a division according to valency; and we may expect medads, monads, dyads, triads, tetrads, etc." (1.291). It is interesting that Peirce includes the term *medad* as one kind of valency.[15] That tetrads are mentioned fits Peirce's view that there are relations that are more complex than triads, although they are analyzable into triads. However, in contrast to tetrads and higher-order relations, the medad is a valency of zero and thus seems to be prior and somehow simpler than the simplest relation, which has a valency of one: the monad. I should like to concentrate for a moment on this possibility.

Although Peirce says relatively little about medads, the fact that in the context of discussing the categories he does cite them in addition to monads may have implications for his phenomenological descriptions. What, then, is a medad? It should be pointed out first that there is another place where, in 1897, the medad is discussed in connection with reading propositions in terms of the logic of relations. In that context, Peirce refers to the medad as a kind of closed relation, or, more precisely, as a completed proposition (3.470–87). However, although using the term *medad* in this sense must have some bearing on Peirce's purpose in the context of explaining his categories, the connection between the use of the term in both contexts is not clear. I shall only briefly speculate about this connection in a moment. My main focus at present will be on the context in which the idea of the medad is drawn from chemistry insofar as he uses the idea to help explain his categories. This latter context, it may be noted, is some ten years later than the context in which medads are cited in connection with the logic of relations; so it may be reasonable to suppose that Peirce viewed the relevance of the idea of the medad from a different perspective at this later time.

If a medad exemplifies one (or more?) of the categories, then it is an aspect of phenomena that must be understood without respect to the application of a predicate to a definite subject. It must be a condition of a phenomenon such that the phenomenon in no way appears as related and in no way appears as having a structure or distinguished, definite parts or aspects internal to it. Thus, the medad is not related to any other aspect of another phenomenon, or even of itself. It is independent of anything to which the phenomenon for which it is a condition might be attributed or in which it might be embodied. As Peirce points out in another place, a medad is a *rheme*,

---

[15]It is my understanding that the term *medad*, referring to elements with no bonding properties, that is, with zero valency, is no longer used in chemistry. In Peirce's day, however, it appeared in chemistry dictionaries and, because Peirce himself had worked in chemistry, we may suppose that he found the idea of medads to be useful along with other ideas of valencies.

that is, a character or term that might function as a relation applicable to referents or subjects, but which in fact has no referent or subject (e.g., 2.272). Thus, a medad is a rheme that has no blank to be filled in, in order to complete a proposition. Medads, then, are distinct from monads. Let us examine this distinction a bit more closely.

Although a monad is a character or relation without reference to any other character, it is nevertheless a relation in which a character is relevant and applicable to a subject. Moreover, the thought of it is expressible in the logical form of a relation appropriate to a single-subject proposition. Consequently, if medads are unlike monads because they do not apply to subjects, then they are something other than characters that are attributed to something. The way they are thus different is illustrated by Peirce. He refers to medads as events: "A medad would be a flash of mental 'heat-lightning' absolutely instantaneous, thunderless, unremembered, and altogether without effect" (1.292). It seems, then, that if attention is given to a medad, then there is necessarily a recognition that nothing is said of anything. We simply have some wholly unrelated character. Such a character cannot be an abstraction or a general, that is, something recurrent or repeatable, because it is exemplified as an event, as something momentary and unattached. Thus, we should not suppose that blackness, for example, would be a medad simply because, as an abstraction, it is unattached and unembodied. Presumably, an individual medad cannot be a phenomenon appearing as a quality describable in abstraction from something it qualifies, for any particular medad is "unremembered." The abstraction *blackness,* then, does not illustrate a pure medad, not because, as an abstraction, it has no subject, but because it is something that is distinguishable as referring to a color that belongs to a place in relation to a color chart or to some characterizable set of relations among other colors. As instantaneous, a medad must be indescribable. As I shall suggest later, I believe that an abstraction of this sort should be understood in the light of the third category, having the status of what Peirce calls *degeneracy,* as well as in light of the aspect of phenomena that Peirce describes as Firstness. It belongs to the third category in a peculiar way insofar as a third manifests an element of pure possibility that can become a potentiality or tendency. And this is what an abstraction manifests.

What, then, is the relevance of the idea of the medad for the categories? Specifically, what is its relevance for explaining Firstness? This point depends on the idea that a medad may be thought of as a charge that is unattachable to any atom or any particle. Such a charge, as Peirce suggests in his figurative description, would be like "heat-lightning" that has no effect. Heat-lightning strikes nothing, is not a bolt moving from cloud to ground, joining oppositely charged poles. It is therefore significant that Peirce describes the medad as heat-lightning rather than a bolt of lightning, which would, after all, be or at least involve a case of Secondness, because there are two relata in the case of a lightning bolt. In contrast, heat-lightning and thus the medad have an autonomy requiring no other in order to be what it is as a medad or as lightning.

Firstness thought of in terms of medads, then, is a momentary charge that has no content or subject that is charged. To be effective as a charge, a second is required. So medads suggest Firstness in its purest, prescinded form. Firstness is the momentary, wholly unrelated aura or tone that gives presence to any phenomenon. The suggestion that Firstness is a tone or presence may be relevant to a possible connection between the context in which the medad is discussed here and Peirce's earlier discussion of it as a completed proposition. A completed proposition does not have dangling tails. All its tails have become bonded in connections within the proposition. Thus, we might regard the whole proposition as the wholeness of an integration of components, subjects, and predicates. Such a whole might then be viewed as the presence or overall condition for intelligibility that is found within the proposition and must be articulated by a reading that sorts out and mentions components in various orders as they relate to one another. The proposition thought of this way, then, may also be viewed as a gestaltlike holistic condition that itself cannot be pinned down or articulated except through its contributing parts, which are first monads. The medad then may function as a monad, a completed proposition related to its subject, which is related as one condition in a dyad and which through the whole proposition is in turn related to other propositions in a triad. Transferred from functioning like heat-lightning to functioning with respect to completed propositions suggests that medads are less like initiating sparks and more like general ("enveloping") conditions of the presence of intelligibility. However, it may be that Peirce saw his first category as functioning in both ways. Whether this suggested connection is consistent with Peirce's two perspectives on the medad is an issue that I shall not try to carry further here.

This description of Firstness has consequences for another issue raised when Peirce cites as examples of Firstness particular qualities, such as redness, or tones. These are abstractions and, as identifiable and thus classified, they must be impure as examples. They are what they are as other than something else – some other color or tone – in order to be classified as this or that color or tone. Thus, they are ready to be embodied, that is, they are what they are with respect to monadic predication. Medads must be prior to monads, functioning as the sheer momentary presence that is the possibility of a quality that can enter a monadic relation.

In any case, whatever Peirce has in mind in identifying medads when he explains categories in terms of valencies, we can perhaps see more sharply the way in which he thinks of instances of Firstness in terms of monadic predication. They have single subjects but do not depend on these or some other subject to give them their character. They are whatever they are apart from whatever other things are. Any relation they may have, temporal, spatial, or classificatory, is not relevant insofar as we attend to a phenomenon in its Firstness. Firsts are presences of some sort not yet determined with respect to other categories.

In addition to his logical and chemical entry to describing the categories, Peirce uses the terminology of psychological and ontological description. Accordingly, he identifies elements of the first category as qualities and feelings (5.44). And it is with respect to this way of identifying Firstness that special problems of description arise.

Contemplate anything by itself. . . . Attend to the whole and drop the parts out of attention altogether. One can approximate nearly enough to the accomplishment of that to see that the result of its perfect accomplishment would be that one would have in his consciousness at the moment nothing but a quality of feeling. . . . It would be unlike any other such quality of feeling. In itself, it would not even resemble any other; for resemblance has its being only in comparison. (1.318)

This quotation exemplifies the paradoxical character of trying to describe Firstness. We should notice, initially, that Peirce says that we can *approximate* the accomplishment of attending to the phenomenon in its Firstness, as singular and without parts. And the result is something that *would* be in one's consciousness. Further, as already indicated in the overlapping logical description, Peirce uses as illustrations qualities such as red, bitter, tedious, hard, heartrending, noble. These examples, as suggested earlier and now in the passage just quoted, are necessarily misleading insofar as each implies other examples and other kinds of things in order that the example referred to be identifiable. Peirce is conscious of this problem, as already indicated, and that is why he cautions the reader that attempts to describe Firstness involve the paradox that once an example of it is discriminated, named, and described, it is "gone," no longer a first. In discussing feeling as something that illustrates Firstness, and after remarking that "of whatever is in the mind in any mode of consciousness there is necessarily an immediate consciousness and consequently a feeling," he adds that "all that is immediately present to a man is what is in his mind in the present instant. . . . But when he asks what is the content of the present instant, his question always comes too late. The present has gone by, and what remains of it is greatly metamorphosed" (1.310).

What is referred to as red or tedious, and so on, then, is what has been related – for example, to other red or tedious instances and other instances that are nonred or nontedious that provide occasions for the classification being employed. Thus, we miss the mark when we try to identify something that is genuinely first – as if we were to try to characterize a medad further than the suggestive remarks Peirce uses. What is it, then, that is accomplished in the descriptions of what belongs to the first category? It seems to me helpful to regard instances of the category of Firstness as conditions of properties or qualities. As conditions of qualities, they are indeterminate waiting to be determinate. This suggestion is supported, I think, by Peirce's statement that "A quality is a mere abstract potentiality" (1.422). And in another manuscript, he says that "Firstness is the mode of being which consists in its subject's being positively such as it is regardless of aught else. That can only be a possibility" (1.25).[16] Further, with respect to Firstness, as long as things do not interact, Peirce insists that it is meaningless to say that "they have any being, unless it be that they are such in themselves that they may perhaps come into relation with others" (1.25). This independence from attachment to something else, including a subject, is reinforced when Peirce compares qualities with examples of the category of Thirdness. Pointing out that there is a difference between instances of Firstness and Thirdness, he says that "a quality is eternal, independent of time and of any realization" (1.420).

The abstractive process of prescinding is essential to Peirce's description. Because Firstnesses are what they are prior to relation, and we cannot articulate their intelligibilities without treating them as in relation, we must attend to them by prescinding. This is to attend to the condition of quality to the neglect of the other aspects of the phenomenon. It is to attend to the potential determinate qualification that becomes a particular quality while not attending to the quality itself. Thus, pure Firstness is the condition of qualitative determination. It is what is presupposed by prescinding away from the occasions of abstractions that are particular properties, that is, are embodied abstractions.

It is important to emphasize that a first is a condition of quality rather than a quality itself. And the point that prescinding is the appropriate procedure for identifying Firstness suggests why it can be said that Peirce treats it as a condition of qualitativeness, which, in

---

[16]It should be remarked in passing that Peirce's conception of abstract potentiality is used as an alternative to the conception of possibility. In turn, real possibility is potentiality not thought of merely as abstract, but as having a tendency to embodiment.

turn is instanced by conditions for particular qualities. Further, the idea of a first as a condition of quality is consistent with the analysis in the "New List" in which the first intermediate category is found in reference to a ground. A ground, it will be recalled, is an abstraction that is presupposed by the relation in which an abstract quality is embodied and thereby concrete or functioning as a qualification helping to unify a substance. As a condition of differentiated firsts, then, Firstness may be said to function in what may be called a "logical way." At the same time, however, Firstness is experienced. It is the tone of phenomena – their suchness or way of being present.

For Peirce, then, Firstness is an abstraction that is concrete; that is, it is something that is experienced. First of all, Firstness must at least be something conceived. But it is more. Firstness can be felt. It can be felt, as indicated earlier, as a presence, though not one that has sufficient determination to be classified. The experiencing of the first category is necessarily integral to the enterprise of phenomenology. In introducing a discussion of the application of phenomenology, Peirce says:

> Be it understood, then, that what we have to do, as students of phenomenology, is simply to open our mental eyes and look well at the phenomenon and say what are the characteristics that are never wanting in it, whether that phenomenon be something that outward experience forces upon our attention, or whether it be the wildest of dreams, or whether it be the most abstract and general of the conclusions of science. (5.41)

Clearly, Peirce assumes that what is identified as a universal characteristic is something discerned, something that has an impact on consciousness. Indeed, the categories, and it is Firstness that is of concern at the moment, must be manifest, even if we cannot identify the specific character of what is manifest. Thus, a bit later in the same discussion, Peirce asks, "When anything is present to the mind, what is the very first and simplest character to be noted in it, in every case, no matter how little elevated the object may be?" And he answers, "Certainly, it is its *presentness*" (5.44). With Hegel, he agrees that this first and simplest character is immediacy. But he adds that, contrary to Hegel, as he sees it, he is not asking us to view Firstness as an abstraction identifiable as "Pure Being."

> Go out under the blue dome of heaven and look at what is present as it appears to the artist's eye. The poetic mood approaches the state in which the present appears as it is present. . . . Imagine, if you please, a consciousness in which there is no comparison, no relation, no recognized multiplicity (since parts would be other than the whole), no change, no imagination of any modification of what is positively there, no reflexion – nothing but a simple positive character. . . . In short, any simple and positive quality of feeling would be something which our description fits that it is such as it is quite regardless

of anything else. . . . But as they are in their presentness, each is sole and unique; and all the others are absolute nothingness to it. (5.44)

An instance of Firstness, and Firstness itself, then, no matter how remote in abstraction from definite predication, is unique and concrete in being felt.

It should not be surprising that if Firstness is felt, it functions in continuity with the complexities of all experience. What we feel occurs in a context in which we react and, in turn, may engage in thought. Peirce's point that we react leads at once to the second category, called Secondness, which is the element of all phenomena by virtue of which they act in relations to other phenomena. Before turning to this category, however, we should notice that Firstness can be described in terms that not only reflect the psychological-ontological and logical approaches but also fit the metaphysical implications of Firstness. The metaphysical dimension of Firstness follows inevitably from Peirce's insistence that firsts have an impact on us. Thus, he says that "the idea of First is predominant in the ideas of freshness, life, freedom" (1.302). "Freedom can only manifest itself in unlimited and uncontrolled variety and multiplicity; and thus the first becomes predominant in the ideas of measureless variety and multiplicity" (1.302). The metaphysical character of this description is not evident in the reference to variety and multiplicity, which is appropriate to ontological description for which no immediate explanatory considerations are required. Rather, the metaphysical issue arises in connection with the reference to freedom and the qualification that variety and multiplicity are uncontrolled. Freedom and being uncontrolled have to do with conditions or with causal considerations. To say that a universal aspect or category of all phenomena is found in the respect in which it manifests freedom is to call attention to its autonomy in relation to other phenomena and to other aspects of the phenomenon in which freedom is manifest.

That Peirce conceived of his categories in terms of metaphysics, even though his descriptions that have metaphysical implications are offered in the context of a phenomenological approach, is evident in a manuscript in which he characterizes them as modes of being. "My view is that there are three modes of being. . . . They are the being of positive qualitative possibility, the being of actual fact, and the being of law that will govern facts in the future" (1.23). With respect to the first category, the addition of "positive" to "qualitative possibility" directs us toward the role of Firstness in the world, that is, its function in the context of facts. It is to this context that we must now turn in order to see how Peirce describes Secondness.

Secondness From the logical perspective of phenomenological description, Secondness is that indecomposable element of a phenomenon that relates it to something else by virtue of its dependency on the other thing. Thus, Secondness is regarded as the category of aspects or phenomena that make them manifest the dependency of all things on one another. But the dependency is dyadic. That is, the relation that all phenomena manifest with respect to Secondness is a relation in which one thing is connected with another independently of any other, any third, thing. Pure instances of this aspect of phenomena are found in causal relations. "The idea of second is predominant in the ideas of causation and statical force. For cause and effect are two; and statical forces always occur between pairs" (1.325). For example, a bullet hole is related to a second, a bullet – although the characterization of the things causally related, it must be remembered, is, with respect to the relation, neglected.

The characterization of Secondness in terms of causality, of course, overlaps the metaphysical terminology that Peirce sometimes uses to describe Secondness. With respect to the logical perspective, however, it is the dyadic nature of the relation that is at issue. The dyadic relation that exemplifies Secondness is prescinded from a description in which we can say what kind of things are related, a description that initiates and presupposes a system of cognized properties and relations such as firearms, gunpowder, agents capable of operating firearms, and so on.

It should be obvious that such a relation already has been encountered in Peirce's semeiotic in the form of the indexical sign, which, regarded as prescinded from a fully functioning sign activity, involves no interpretation. Thus, because it is supposed insofar as it is prior to interpretation, Secondness is that aspect of phenomena that is encountered as brute resistance, the obdurate force of presence. It is as yet uninterpreted and thus is as yet not relevant to that aspect of phenomena by virtue of which they are intelligible.

Just as Firstness is describable as a logical relation that is also felt, so Secondness is described as a relation that is felt. Indeed, it is a mode of phenomena by which Firstness itself has a link with the world, a link that takes it from its prescinded status as autonomous to its connection to something other than itself, so that we can react to it and then prescind it from what we experience. Secondness is indispensable to the presence of phenomena. It is indispensable to Firstness insofar as phenomena must have some impact as the occasion for prescinding sheer, autonomous presence. (It will be recalled that in the "New List" Peirce regards the conceptions from which precision starts as occasions for what is prescinded.)

The point that Secondness is felt suggests a twofold way in which Peirce illustrates the category. The first moves us to the perspective of metaphysics, the second to psychological considerations. There are two domains of the world in which Secondness is manifest. The first has just been mentioned. It is the domain of causality – or, more broadly, we may add, the domain of dynamic, active relation of one thing to another. The dynamic relation is manifest as the aspect of phenomena that we notice when attending to them in relation to one another and as having parts that react to one another. But there is another domain in which seconds are experienced. It is that aspect of phenomena insofar as they stand over against us as experiencing or conscious, attending agents. Thus, in the same place where Peirce says that idea of second is predominant in the ideas of causation, he says, "In sense and will, there are reactions of Secondness between the *ego* and the *non-ego* (which non-ego may be an object of direct consciousness)" (1.325). The point that there is this second domain in which Secondness is experienced is reinforced by Peirce's statement in another manuscript that "We live in two worlds, a world of fact and a world of fancy. . . .[W]e call the world of fancy the internal world, the world of fact the external world." We control the second only by "voluntary muscles" so that we can develop habits of reacting to the external world – a point that, as we shall see, is essential to the third category. But the point is that there is an aspect of experience that forces itself on us, an aspect that, if we could not control our habits, would "every now and then" disturb our internal world by "brutal inroads of ideas from without" (1.321).

If Secondness is experienced as resistance and constraint, as we have already noted in connection with Secondness as causation, it is also experienced in struggle. "The second category that I find . . . is the element of struggle" (1.322). We encounter it in "effort opposing change," and perhaps in its most extreme form, in shock (1.336). In characterizing the duality of pure instances of Secondness as struggle, it is implied that there are two things that are interdependent. One thing is what it is because of its linkage to the other. This is essential in the idea of causation; an effect depends on its cause in order to be what it is as an effect, and a cause depends on its effect in order to be what it is as a cause. The importance of this point will be seen later when Peirce's ideas about genuine and degenerate cases of the categories are considered.

Peirce's reference to struggle and externality and brute intrusions within our experiences points to other ways of describing Secondness. For Peirce, the experience of something that forces itself on us and produces reaction is the way facts are encountered. Secondness, then, may be regarded as the category of facticity. We have seen this in his description of the categories as modes of being. The second element is said to belong to the mode of being "of actual fact" (1.23). In this respect, Secondness is the category of fact as "actuality" (1.24). It appears in happenings *then* and *there*. Seconds, then, can be found in instances of experience that are put into spatial and temporal schemes – a result that, as we shall see, depends on the third category for which interpretation is integral to it. Such instances also are referred to sometimes as the appearance of existents – the aspect of phenomena by which resistance and insistence on taking a place in experience are revealed.

The metaphysical framework in which Secondness is described is implicit in the idea of constraint, resistance, compulsiveness encountered as over against our wills. Such encounters are sometimes described by Peirce as manifestations of matter, as the matter of any phenomenon in contrast to its form. The matter of a phenomenon is its resistance, its intractability in relation to our wills (1.419). This conception of matter should be kept in mind when those who conclude that Peirce was an idealist because he said that matter is effete mind. Matter is the resistance to what is active and changing in phenomena. However, as the resistant element that is characterized as one of the ways Secondness is encountered, it is inseparable from the resistance that for Peirce would be inevitably encountered if inquiry were to continue into the infinite future. Further, it should be noted that Secondness is the category of intrusion within experience. Thus, if it is effete as mind, it is not effete in playing the role of brute impact on mind that is active.

I have made much of the point that Firstness and Secondness are not categories in which interpretation and thus intelligibility participate directly, insofar as the category is considered in itself. Both Secondness and Firstness must be attended to by means of prescinding. They are prescinded from interpreted phenomena. Interpreted phenomena belong to the category of Thirdness. But what interpretation requires that is universal in all phenomena remains to be set forth. The results consist of Peirce's description of Thirdness.

Thirdness As for Firstness and Secondness, one range of descriptive terms for Thirdness is an appropriate ingredient of logic as semeiotic. Thirdness is the category of triads. This can be seen in light of our previous considerations of the conditions of sign situations. A genuine sign process includes an interpretant that is a third relative to an object and the sign or representamen. An instance of semeioses is, for Peirce, paradigmatic as an illustration of Thirdness. Thus, he says in sketching a proof of the irreducibility of the third category that "every genuine triadic relation involves meaning, as meaning is obviously a triadic relation" (1.345). A means B is necessarily dependent on a third thing, C, because A can mean B only if it does so for an interpretant, C.

Triadic relations, or instances of Thirdness, are found in any domain that is meaningful or intelligible. One such domain consists of certain facts in physics. "Take any fact in physics of the triadic kind, by which I mean a fact which can only be defined by simultaneous reference to three things, and you will find there is ample evidence that it never was produced by the action of forces on mere dyadic conditions" (1.345).

The necessity of presupposing triads is also evident in common-sense situations in which we make experience intelligible. Ideas of direction presuppose three conditions, or triadic relations. Thus, "your right hand is that hand which is toward the *east*, when you face the *north* with your head toward the *zenith*. Three things, east, west, and up, are required to define the difference between right and left" (ibid.).

Generally, as we have seen, every triad involves meaning, which may be illustrated not only by the triad of semeiosis itself but by meaningful actions. Thus, Peirce explains that "every genuine triadic relation involves thought or *meaning*. Take for example, the relation of *giving*. A *gives* B to C. This does not consist in A's throwing B away and its accidentally hitting C. . . . If that were all, it would not be a genuine triadic relation, but merely one dyadic relation followed by another" (1.345). There need be no notion of the thing given. Giving is an action that relates three things or subjects. Each of these requires both of the others by virtue of the act that relates them. And the action that relates the three things requires all of them in order to be what it is, in this example, an agent that gives something to a receiver. Peirce makes the point that the relation of giving would lose its essential character of giving unless there were three subjects. He insists on this as one of his reasons why genuine triads cannot be broken into and reduced to two dyads and monads. We have seen both that symbols presuppose indexes and icons and, with respect to categories, that Secondness, simple two-term relation and reaction, presupposes Firstness, something to be related and to be present, ready to act and react. Accordingly, Thirdness presupposes Secondness and Firstness. Thus, triads presuppose dyads and monads. Nevertheless, neither dyads nor monads are sufficient to perform the function of triads. As Peirce puts it in the passage from which the quotations we have just noted appear, "A triadic relation is inexpressible by means of dyadic relations alone."

It should also be observed that Peirce not only wants to show the irreducibility of the three relations, and especially of Thirdness, but he also insists that all higher-order relations can be reduced to triads.

This point is essential to Peirce's commitment to the principle that intelligibility is achieved through triadic thought. Thought itself can occur only where there is meaning or mediation in which a third connects a first and a second. Whether intelligibility does or does not require a fourthness of some sort is an issue that we cannot settle here, if, indeed, it could ever be settled with finality. Peirce, I think, does sustain a kind of fallibilism with respect to the issue, because his argument for the reducibility of higher-order relations consists on the one hand in showing that in the logic of relations, relations more complex than triads can be analyzed into triads and on the other hand of challenging the reader to identify more complex and irreducible relations or categories.[17]

The interdependence of the three subjects of genuine triadic relations shows us that for Peirce relations that are triadic are continua. That is, they are indivisible with respect to their parts. In this way, they exemplify what we have encountered before in the form of generals, or rulelike conditions. Thus, Peirce characterizes Thirdness as that aspect of phenomena that is both thought and law. "The third category of elements of phenomena consists of what we call laws when we contemplate them from the outside only, but which when we see both sides of the shield we call thoughts" (1.420). To refer to instances of Thirdness or thirds as laws is, of course, to introduce the metaphysical framework for discussing the categories. In fact, it may be recalled, in one of his references to categories, he equates the third category with law by calling it a mode of being (1.23). But at the same time, the framework of descriptive psychology seems to emerge when he suggests that thirds are thoughts.

We must keep in mind that for Peirce thoughts are not confined to subjective states or actions. If this is not already clear from what has been said about his realism, it should be unquestionably clear when we later review his conception of mental activity, which is constituted in continuity with the world. At the moment, however, it is Peirce's conception of the generality and consequent continuity found in instances of Thirdness that is at stake. And what is important for his purposes is not whether thirds are exemplified in consciousness or objects in the world. As instances of a category, they must, of course, be found in both. It is important in understanding Peirce's conception of Thirdness, however, to notice what is distinctive about the kinds of things that exemplify it. And the distinctive feature to be noted in

---

[17]I have addressed the issue in a response to Carl Vaught, who argues that Peirce should have recognized the need for fourthness. "Fourthness: Carl Vaught on Peirce's Categories," *Transactions of the Charles S. Peirce Society* 24, no. 2 (Spring 1988), pp. 265–78.

what has been said about the irreducibility of triadic relations is that they are generals and thus they instance continuity. Things are not seen to be meaningful or intelligible by being simply associated with one another. They must also be components in a system. Thus, they are what they are by virtue of that to which they are connected through some third component, and this kind of interdependence requires more than discrete items in relation. Further, intelligibility requires conditions in the form of the relations that do the relating – conditions that are more than the things related. Thus, giving is a relation that can be considered by prescinding it from the things related in an act of giving. These relations that are not reducible to their relata are generals, the continuities that function as laws that govern what they relate.

Generality has been seen to be essential to Peirce's pragmaticism and his semeiotic. Meanings are determined by consequences that follow rulelike or general patterns. These rulelike patterns, or generals, it will be remembered, are the constituents of Peirce's realism. Accordingly, Thirdness is a foundational category because it is the category that consists of the essential constituents of his realism.

We have also encountered generals or rulelike conditions in semeioses. The need for the presence of generals in semeioses is obvious because meanings depend on triads and intelligible meanings require irreducible triads, a requirement that relations not be broken or be capable of division into their relata without remainder. These irreducible relations are generals. With respect to the function of signs, meanings are determined by interpretants that are themselves functions of generals in the form of respects or grounds. Thus, when Peirce says that all genuine triadic relations involve meaning, he implies the architectonic that is founded in part on pragmaticism and semeiotic. The third category provides the intelligible thread that shows how the distinct components of his philosophy are linked.

There are other characterizations of Thirdness that must be mentioned before we move on to further discussion of the architectonic in the next chapter. One description points us in the direction of the evolutionary dimension of Peirce's realism. In a passage that calls on psychological and ontological considerations, he says:

Five minutes of our waking life will hardly pass without our making some kind of prediction. . . . Yet a prediction is essentially of a general nature, and cannot even be completely fulfilled. To say that a prediction has a decided tendency to be fulfilled, is to say that future events are in a measure really governed by law. . . . If the prediction has a tendency to be fulfilled, it must be that future events have a tendency to conform to a general rule. . . . This mode of being which . . . *consists* in the fact that future facts of Secondness will take on a determinate general character, I call a Thirdness. (1.26)

Thirdness, then, is the category that accounts not only for mediation and thus meaning, or, generally, intelligibility, but also that reveals continuity and thus futurity. In another place, Peirce reinforces the point about Thirdness as a condition of our recognition of futurity:

...But we constantly predict what is to be. Now what is to be, according to our conception of it, can never become wholly past. In general, we may say that *meanings* are inexhaustible. . . . For this reason I call this element of the phenomenon or object of thought [meaning] the element of Thirdness. It is that which is what it is by virtue of imparting a quality to reactions in the future. (1.343)

It seems clear that Peirce views Thirdness as a key to understanding evolution. The extent to which there is spontaneity, or some form of deviation or departure from regular conformity to law, in the "imparting of a quality to reactions in the future," remains to be determined in the next chapter. Before moving to this chapter, two final points about the interrelations must be introduced.

We have already seen that the categories are related in a hierarchy structured by the procedure of prescinding from a phenomenological attitude in which phenomena are considered with respect to the way they appear before we analyze them. Once we begin to regard them with respect to the ways they appear, we abstract from what I think Peirce believes is the richest object of attention, the phenomenon viewed as a whole, in all its aspects, whatever they may be. The proper way of abstracting is by prescinding. Thus, as we have noticed, Secondness can be prescinded from Thirdness – the latter being the "richest" aspect of the phenomenon, because as triadic it requires there to be dual relations and reactions to which Thirdness gives character and, in turn, because it requires quality as that which is present to be involved in dyadic reaction. The kind of hierarchy functioning here has been seen in sign action and in the categories delineated in the "New List."

The point that the hierarchy is at work in the "New List" suggests two issues, one addressed by Peirce and the other left for the student of Peirce to address by inferring an answer. The first issue concerns what Peirce calls *degenerate cases* of the categories. The second concerns questions raised earlier about the absence of the two limiting categories, being and substance of the "New List," in Peirce's mature categoriology.

I shall treat the first issue briefly, only sketching the basic idea underlying Peirce's attributions of degeneracy to certain ways in which the categories are manifest. The main reason for noting that categories may be degenerate is to throw additional light on their irreducibility and to prepare for some of the suggestions to be made in the next chapter about the intelligibility of the growth of laws where there is spontaneity.

A relation or category that is genuine is one that cannot be reduced to a lower-order category. Another way in which Peirce explains genuineness is to say that the things that make up a genuine category must be characterized by that category. Thus, in genuine Thirdness,

the first, the second, and the third are all three of the nature of thirds, or thought, while in respect to one another they are first, second, and third. The first is thought in its capacity as mere possibility; that is, mere *mind* capable of thinking, or a mere vague idea. The *second* is thought playing the role of Secondness, or event. That is, it is of the general nature of *experience* or *information*. The third is thought in its role as governing Secondness. (1.537)

A sign situation illustrates this. Each component is itself a third because of the role of interpretation. Thus, it may be recalled, in sign action, the series of signs is endless, object and interpretant being signs of further signs and objects. At the same time, we can pause and single out each, treating it as first or second or third to the other in relation to the other. "Every sign stands for an object independent of itself; but it can only be a sign of that object in so far as that object is itself of the nature of a sign or thought" (1.538). In genuine Thirdness, its first must be a law or thought, its second a law or thought determined by the first, and its third the law that mediates the first and second. Thus, in the case of giving, the thing given is a law in the sense of playing the role of the possibility of being imparted; the receiver is a law through playing the role of reacting; and the giver is a law through the act or relation of giving that governs the Secondness of the thing that becomes a gift, thereby bringing about the reaction of the receiver.

In the case of genuine Secondness, both the first and second in the relation must be of the nature of seconds themselves. "That is, being a second involves Secondness. The reaction still more manifestly involves the being what another makes the subject to be" (1.525). We have noted this point earlier in seeing that in Secondness, the two subjects in relation depend on one another to be what they are as second to the other. A bullet and a bullet hole depend on each other, having a real connection that makes each function according to Secondness to the other, although the Secondness of the one is different from the Secondness of the other. To use Peirce's example in the passages where he discusses genuine and degenerate cases, "To kill and to be killed are different" (1.527). The Secondness is more accidental to the former than to the latter, Peirce adds, presumably because the former initiates the action and the second is the reactor.

A degenerate case of a relation or category is one that appears to be of a higher order than one in terms of which it can be understood. Accordingly, as Peirce says, there can be no degenerate case of First-ness. But there can be degenerate seconds and degenerate thirds. A degenerate case of Secondness is exemplified when two things are related so that both are not seconds in relation to one another. A thing, or some matter in which a quality inheres, is something that is second to the quality and the quality is second to the matter, because there are two distinguishable relata. But both do not involve Second-ness, because the quality is, as quality, a first. "The mode of being of the quality is that of Firstness. That is to say, it is a possibility. It is related to the matter accidentally; and this relation does not change the quality at all, except that it imparts . . . this very relation of inher-ence . . to it" (1.527). The quality does not require the matter in order to be a first that is brought into relation with the matter, although the matter attains its very existence – its embodying function because of the quality. Without the quality embodied in it, it would be nothing, whereas the quality would be what it is as possibility without the mat-ter.

Thirdness is degenerate when a sheer quality, or an image, is con-strued as something directly experienced as a predicate attributed to some object. The experience is itself of the quality as a first. The con-struing of this as an attributed or predicated quality is an interpreta-tion and includes more than what is claimed to be seen.

In the last degree of degeneracy of Thirdness, there is thought, but no con-veyance or embodiment of thought at all. It is merely that a fact of which there must be, I suppose, something like knowledge is *apprehended* according to a possible idea. . . . For example, you look at something and say, "It is red." Well, I ask you what justification you have for such a judgment. You reply, "I *saw* it was red." Not at all. You saw nothing in the least like that. You saw an image. There was no subject or predicate in it. (1.538)

Thus, we can regard every instance of Firstness as more than it is, as including interpretation and thus knowledge. Analysis shows that what is directly experienced can be reduced to a first. Alternatively, the first can be construed as a third if Thirdness is added to it, that is, if thought or interpretation is added and yields, for example, the cognitive expression, "It is red."

Peirce offers another illustration of the degeneracy of Thirdness. Here it appears in the attempt to treat a triad as explainable by two dyads. We have noted the example earlier. If giving is analyzed into two acts, A's laying down B, which C subsequently picks up, we would have a "degenerate form of Thirdness in which Thirdness is exter-nally appended" (8.331). There is no Thirdness in each pair taken alone. There is no law bringing together the two actions, unless this is added on the ground that there is one thing that is the same in both pairs, namely, the thing that passes from one to the other, from A to B. However, such a thing is not a gift unless it passes from A to B because of the law of giving that characterizes the act as giving and that constitutes the thing that passes from A to B as a new relative, namely the thing that has become a gift. The importance of Thirdness as a way of accounting for the introduction of newness by incorporating lower-order relations that are transformed into instances of it is, I think, suggested by Peirce's brief discussions of degenerate cases.

An answer to the second question about the conceptions of being and substance can be most adequately addressed in the context of the discussion of Peirce's metaphysics, which is to follow. It is appropriate, however, to indicate what I believe accounts for Peirce's dropping reference to being and substance in his phenomenology. It is clear that he has not abandoned these conceptions completely, because he does refer to them in other contexts. Why, then, are they not distinct categories as they were in the "New List"?

There are two considerations that suggest an answer. First, once Peirce treats the categories from the vantage point of the logic of relatives, the supposition of a proposition that brings unity to a manifold by uniting subject and predicate is not needed in order to determine what conceptions are universal in phenomena. Recall too that the copula expresses the category of being in the "New List." But in the mature treatment, the copula is the larger relation that is applicable to the subjects. Thus, on the basis of the introduction of the logic of relations, Peirce could include the expression of being, or the unifying condition of experience within the expanded copula. Substance is also included within the relational treatment in the sense that it is present as the diversity of the subject or subjects that is given approximated determinateness by the character of the relation that applies to it or them. But it still may be asked whether both substance and being are not implicitly functioning in ways that are distinguishable so that they might be said to be additional categories, as they are in the "New List."

One way to answer this question is to note Peirce's commitment to the principle that triadic experience is fundamental to intelligibility. This means for Peirce that intelligible experience is both irreducible to lower-order relations and is exhausted by triadic relations in the sense that higher-order relations are reducible to triads. Thus, if being and substance are distinguishable conceptions, they nevertheless should be reducible to, or understandable without recourse to, the triadic account of the categories. This point seems to me to be consistent with Peirce's aims and discoveries in approaching the categories through phenomenology.

Phenomenology claims to be framed by brackets that exclude metaphysical considerations. Thus, being and substance, which have their homes in metaphysics, should enter the results of phenomenological analysis only insofar as universal aspects of phenomena manifest them. And a case can be made for the suggestion that being is internal to Peirce's description of all the categories and that substance is internal to Firstness and Secondness together. In his metaphysical framework for describing the categories, not only does Peirce refer to them as modes of being, but he also describes Firstness as manifesting the sheer possibility of being, that is, as the possibility of any and all determinate manifestations of being in seconds and thirds. Further, Thirdness is the category of unification by means of giving character to things and accordingly bringing things into the accord of continuity. Being, then, is understood with respect to its modes. What other conception of being would then be necessary for analysis to distinguish? In turn, substance is that which is to be made intelligible. It is represented if the subject terms referring to substances are determined by means of expressions found in monadic, dyadic, or triadic relation. When these are applied to their subjects, which is to have their subject places filled in, then substances are determined and to that extent made intelligible. Predication mediates them. Being unifies the manifold and articulates the subjects to which it applies.

Phenomenologically, this same point is made in terms of the mass of qualitative presences, the counterpart to a manifold of diversity, that acts and reacts, the counterpart of particular instances of the manifold that are discriminated and demanding to be made intelligible through the unifying function of generals or character that Thirdness furnishes in its mediating capacity. This attempt to account for being and substance in the mature list of categories may be developed in part by the discussion of Peirce's evolutionary realism. The extent to which Peirce's three categories provide a structure is such that a more fundamental conception that might ground the categories is not needed. I shall maintain that any independent, foundational condition would undermine the evolutionary thrust of Peirce's realism. The very nature of the categories must contain within them the intelligibility of an evolving universe.

In summary, then, we may highlight the main features of the phenomenologically derived categories. Firstness is the category of me-dads, and of monadic relations. It is thus the category of qualitative, autonomous presence, of qualitative possibility, or the condition of specific qualities. By virtue of its functioning as a condition of what may be, it is the category of freedom and spontaneity.

Secondness is the category of dyadic relations that are dynamic, causal connections between two terms. The two terms may refer to objects in the world that contrast with, and thus manifest some resistance to, one another, or the two terms may be ego and nonego. Thus, Secondness is a category of otherness and, to some degree, of struggle. In manifesting otherness, it manifests matter. Secondness is present where there is facticity and existence, where there is brute action within the world or on consciousness. Thus, seconds are also instances of actuality.

Thirdness is the category of intelligible meaning. It is present in all phenomena because all phenomena insofar as they are intelligible involve mediation. Mediation is irreducible with respect to the significance of the phenomenon; consequently, Thirdness is the disclosure of continuity and our sense of anticipation of future consequences, our sense of prediction. Thirdness, then, is the category of law, and the law is not constituted by a finite collection of facts, but rather law constitutes the potentiality, the tendency for there to be future facts that follow a pattern given by the law and thus take on a determinate character. However, this is to say that Thirdness is the category that directly presents us with continuity, which is the condition at the basis of synechism. Let us then turn to this topic.

4

Synechism and
Peirce's Evolutionary Realism

Introduction

A theme central to the discussion in this book has been the expression
of the belief that Peirce's philosophy presupposes an architectonic
founded primarily on a form of realism. There are reasons for resisting this interpretation, however, as I have already suggested. It has
been claimed that Peirce was fundamentally an idealist.[1] This difference is understandable, for there is a sense in which he was an idealist
and a sense in which he was a realist. Hence it may be claimed that he
was a kind of metaphysical idealist and, at the same time, an epistemological realist. On this view, he was an idealist metaphysically in the
sense that the final object of thought in general, the final aim of investigation, is regarded as not only completely thought-dependent but
also mental in nature. He was a realist epistemologically, then, in the
sense that in the context of any theoretical investigation, what investigation is about is independent of that investigation, but what is independent is thought or theory that is not exhausted by the particular
theoretical framework at the time. I think this is a misleading suggestion. My purpose in the first section, then, will be to show why it is
misleading and to propose that Peirce's conception of the constraints
of an extrasemeiotic or extraepistemic condition has a fundamental
function that aligns him with a special form of metaphysical realism
– what I have called evolutionary realism.[2]

---

[1] I have in mind especially comments of Joseph L. Esposito in *Evolutionary Metaphysics:
The Development of Peirce's Theory of Categories* (Athens: Ohio University Press, 1980).
For instance, he says that "it would be with Hegel that he would ultimately reconcile
himself in later life" (p. 3). This in itself need not be understood to mean that Peirce
fully agreed with Hegel. However, it does suggest that their views were not opposed
to one another – yet Peirce takes pains to dissociated himself from Hegel, as will be
emphasized in what follows. In any case, evidence that Esposito opts for the idealist
interpretation is found in other parts of his book. For instance, he says, "And it may
be safe to say that by 1863 Peirce already had settled on the rudiments of his lifelong
philosophic perspective – objective idealism" (p. 82).

[2] My approach intentionally disregards a suggestion made by both Max Fisch and Christopher Hookway that Peirce changed his view from idealism to realism after 1890,
because of the influence of Francis Abbot. I do so first because my primary concern is
to lead to the issue as it is focused on the status of the object of the final opinion or

The proposal that his is an evolutionary realism will, I hope, make clear that I believe Peirce wanted and managed to push beyond the traditional labels *idealism* and *realism*. Thus, he should be identified with neither the idealisms nor the realisms that he took seriously in his own philosophy. Before proceeding, however, at the beginning of the first section, some consideration will be given to what I mean by the terms *idealism* and *realism* as they are relevant to Peirce. What I shall say about them is intended to get at the most general and basic assumptions underlying various traditional forms of both views. With respect to our initial question, these underlying conceptions are directly connected with the evolutionary realism that I shall attribute to Peirce's thought.[3]

In any case, consideration of Peirce's special kind of realism brings us to the conception of continuity and Peirce's metaphysical underpinning for pragmaticism, that is, his synechism. In other words, what I shall treat as evolutionary realism flows out of synechism, which is grounded in a conception of continuity. Thus, the argument for the realist interpretation of Peirce is an introduction to the second section and culminating topic of this book: Peirce's synechism, which is the core of his architectonic.

I shall address this topic in three stages. First, I shall offer a more extended account of what I mean by *realism* and *idealism* and try to show how these terms relate to Peirce's view. Second, I shall turn to the conception of evolution that undergirds his unique realism. I shall begin by considering Peirce's attack on necessitarianism, or metaphys-

---

convergent conclusions of inquiry. And I do not think that either Fisch or Hookway concentrates on this issue in their considerations of the way Abbot influenced Peirce. In addition, it seems to me that although Peirce suggests that he adopted a realism after 1890, there are passages that suggest that he leaned not only toward realism before 1890, but also toward idealism after 1890 – indeed, well into the 1900s, as I shall point out in a moment. Max H. Fisch, "Peirce's Progress from Nominalism toward Realism," *Monist* 51 (1967), p. 169. The passage from Fisch is in part the basis for the discussion of changes in Peirce's thought concerning his realism and idealism in Christopher Hookway's *Peirce* (London: Routledge & Kegan Paul, 1985), p. 113.

[3]It is appropriate to repeat here a comment made in the Preface about Peter Skagestad's *The Road of Inquiry: Charles Peirce's Pragmatic Realism* (New York: Columbia University Press, 1981). I said that Skagestad supports a kind of realism in Peirce that recognizes its openness to indefinitely continued departures from law and convergences of opinion. This is a kind of fallibilistic realism, for which there may not be a final realization of completed convergence and thus there may not be truth in the sense of final truth. There are only local truths that are provisional and dependent on local convergences. What I shall say about evolutionary realism is in large part consistent with Skagestad's view. However, my account is different in tying the conception of departures to cosmological speculation about the evolutionary changes that flow from such departures, and my account of the final opinion as an ideal limit of convergence is not quite, so it seems to me, what Skagestad sees as indefinitely pursued end. This point should be clearer in the next chapter where the notion of the ideal limit is discussed in connection with what I say about some of Peirce's sympathetic critics who are currently affirming antimetaphysical realism.

ical determinism, and his discussions in his 1890s *Monist* series of evolution and the law of mind. There is, I think, a strategic advantage in moving immediately from Peirce's argument against necessitarianism and its consequent defense of the hypothesis that chance and spontaneity are real ingredients in the universe to his account of his theory of evolution. The argument against necessitarianism and for spontaneity lays the basis for his theory of evolution. Thus, I shall treat the *Monist* articles of the 1890s by taking up the third and then the last, which is devoted wholly to his conception of evolution. I shall then turn back to the penultimate article, "The Law of Mind," the topic of which presupposes and elaborates Peirce's idea of continuity.

At least one advantage in proceeding in this way is that it shows rather dramatically what I believe is the most fundamental tension in Peirce's philosophy. We see that the conception of spontaneity is central to Peirce's thinking from the 1890s on (if not earlier). As we shall see, even though Peirce defends the hypothesis that there is spontaneity, he does not claim that spontaneity itself makes any specific event or particular law intelligible. Regularities, or generals, are what render phenomena intelligible. And the continuous flow of experience is what characterizes the connections among ideas so that experience is intelligible. This point is articulated forcefully in "The Law of Mind," which is to be treated after we have considered the hypothesis of spontaneity and the theory of evolution. Thus, we shall see that the insistence on the reality of spontaneity, or what Peirce means by *chance*, of unpredictable origins in the course of evolution, is held in the face of Peirce's persistent commitment to the necessity for continuity as an underlying condition of generality and thus of intelligibility.

The final discussion, then, will launch us into speculations about Peirce's synechism, which I believe is the lifeblood of his architectonic. This architectonic is constituted by the evolutionary realism that transcends the views known to him that were assigned the labels *idealism* and *realism*.

Before turning to the main task, a remark is in order concerning one way of viewing his metaphysical speculations in general. Interpreters frequently are and have been intent on suggesting that Peirce may have been inconsistent, on the one hand, in developing his logic and epistemology and the pragmatic maxim intended to purify philosophy by excluding metaphysical speculation, and, on the other hand, in speculating rather freely about metaphysical issues. The notion that there are two Peirces has been alluded to in the Preface. Occasionally, recent discussion echoes this possibility. Hookway, for example, surveys various views about this possible inconsistency and says: "It is easy to conclude that Peirce's interests drew him in two conflicting directions. He was blinded to the incompatibility of these metaphysical excesses with his work in logic."[4] Hookway's comment should not be interpreted as a sign that he did not take Peirce's views about metaphysical issues seriously. His point is that there is, at least ostensibly, some degree of discrepancy between these two dimensions of Peirce's thought as a whole.

To take this discrepancy as fundamental, as has been done by those who interpret Peirce as divided between two philosophical orientations, is, however, curious. First, if Peirce was a logician, he hardly could have been at such odds with himself that he would not have recognized what is a very obvious alleged inconsistency. Second, Peirce may have seen beyond what has been the rather narrow scope of what inheritors of early analytic philosophy admitted as intelligible philosophical utterances. With respect to this latter point, it is obvious that Peirce recognized the significance of issues that cannot be adequately dealt with in terms of the maxims that early in his career seemed to be what guided his conception of meaningful philosophy. And if he was a logician, surely he would not have been blind to the tension within his thought. Awareness of this tension is evident in his attempts to combat his nominalism in commenting on his early interpretation of general terms subjected to the pragmatic maxim. His insistence on the reality of generals (which is integral to his metaphysical speculations) was viewed as essential to his conception of meaning. Once this much is given over to metaphysics, the possibility of pursuing metaphysical issues is not closed. Thus, it seems to me that the explicit antagonism to metaphysics sometimes found in Peirce's writing must be placed in context and seen in light of his larger vision. His opposition is to uncritical theological speculation and to metaphysical systems, such as the Cartesian and, with qualification, the Hegelian. These, for him, were unfounded with respect to intuitive origins and to an abstract, "wooden" logic that seems to take unrelenting flight from ordinary, (critical) commonsense experience. Observation, then, does play a crucial role in what Peirce proposes as hypotheses that have metaphysical rather than idioscopic, that is, special, scientific application. And at least to that extent, Peirce remains true to his maxim.

Epistemological Realist and Metaphysical Idealist or Epistemological Idealist and Metaphysical Realist?

The Terms Idealism and Realism

I shall assume, as already suggested at the beginning of this chapter, that the minimal expectation of anyone who affirms idealism is the

---

[4]Hookway, *Peirce*, p. 263.

conviction that the source or foundation of knowledge is thought itself, or is mental in character. To be somewhat more cautious, for the idealist, the condition of knowledge is in itself at least mindlike and not like anything nonmental. In order to refine this characterization, it will be helpful to make use of Hookway's assumption about the claims of idealism. He says:

Idealism has, I shall assume, two components:
   1. The claim, in some area of discourse, that the range of the real does not exceed the range of the knowable;
   2. Claim (1) is to be explained in some constructivist fashion: realities other than thoughts or experiences are understood as supervenient upon, or arising out of, or constituted by, mental or intentional facts.[5]

The crucial point is that whatever form idealism takes, it requires that what is thought of as real be constructed by mental conditions, whether those conditions be limited to human agents or a transhuman agency, understood as divine or as the Absolute. Realism, on the other hand, in the minimal sense requires that what is real be to some extent or in some way independent of mental construction – indeed, what is real determines, contributes to, or at least resists the activity of mental activity, human or transhuman.

Realism has taken many forms. A straightforward realist claim is that there are external things or at least something external to mental activity and conceptualization. What is left undetermined in this formulation is the nature or status of what is external. We are concerned, of course, with the answers Peirce gave or implied, and this has been suggested in part in the earlier chapters. From the beginning of this book, I have insisted that Peirce leaves open the possibility that he is a realist in two senses: (1) scholastic realism for which generals, which can be understood as repeatable conditions, have an ontological status in the world, independent of particular thoughts or language and (2) realism as a view that insists there is a condition independent of thought in general or of all systems, taken singly or as a whole, for which thought and language are internal to those systems. The first sense is the realism of dynamic universals, and this kind of realism is consistent with objective idealism. The second sense of realism affirms an extramental condition, and it is what I consider anti-idealist.

This anti-idealism takes two directions. Both concern "where" one locates the source or condition for constraints encountered in interpretation. The first has been mentioned and reiterated; it is the extramental condition implied by the notion of convergence that is nonac-

---

[5]Christopher Hookway, "Pragmatism and 'Kantian Realism,' " *Peirceanna, Versus Quaderne di studi semiotici* 49 (January–April 1988), ed. M. A. Bonfantini and C. J. W. Kloesel, p. 105.

tual or ideal and that is, if it were actual, a goal that recedes into the infinite future. The condition of constraint that recedes in this way is a function of the dynamical object as a teleological condition. It must be emphasized, however, that this teleological condition functions in a developmental teleology and is itself not a fixed End. Rather, it is open-ended. The idea of developmental teleology will be introduced and, at least to some extent, made clearer later in this chapter.

The second form of anti-idealism already has been suggested, but it has not been sufficiently emphasized. It is present in Peirce's second category, the category of resistance and constraint that forces itself on conceptual frameworks at certain moments in history and that constrains the way frameworks shift and are modified in fitting (or sometimes unfitting) rather than arbitrary ways. This function of instances of Secondness is, I think, a manifestation of dynamical objects or of *the* dynamical object functioning in local contexts.

There are other senses in which Peirce might be thought of as a realist. One of these was mentioned in the Introduction: epistemological realism, which applies to the view that there is something independent of the concepts and language that constitute theory at definite times and definite contexts in the history of science and of societies. With respect to science, this view is a form of scientific, or more generally, empirical realism. It may or may not accept the reality of generals in the sense in which Peirce did in the name of scholastic realism. The reality of generals could be restricted to concepts and regarded as having mental status. What is crucial for this kind of scientific realism is that theory is grounded in something independent of any given theory, and this something is a condition of the convergence of other theories with it. The convergence that is independent of the results of definite investigation at a definite time may itself be limited to a definite later time. On the interpretation of Peirce as a scientific realist, however, convergences eventually would reach an ultimate convergence, or culmination in the final opinion, which, for the scientific realism referred to here is after all mental insofar as it is understood as a system of concepts that are not independent of thought in general. This view, it seems to me, is an idealism rather than a realism – it turns out to converge with idealism as defined by Hookway's two "components."

A metaphysical realist in the sense I am suggesting for Peirce, then, in contrast to idealism, is one who insists that the condition for constraints lies in something to be reckoned with that is not exhausted by what is mindlike or by a fundamental source or condition that is constituted exclusively as thought. This residue is not in itself mental in nature.

This characterization of idealism and realism avoids considerations of whether there are material things that resist understanding in terms of thought. The concept of matter is itself at issue, as I think it was for Peirce. If matter is simply whatever is mind-independent, then my formulation of the difference could be stated in terms of whether one is committed to the view that there are irreducible material resistances to thought activity. However, I then see no reason for using the term *material*. In any case, the key term here is *mind* or *thought* and the issues turn on whether there is something that is not exhausted by them.

It is necessary to consider what may be meant by the term *thought*. The term, I believe, is derived at least in part from the questioner's own self-awareness of what goes on when one is conscious of anything. Thus, if one is an idealist, then one understands this self-reflective model as primary in serving as the proper way to account for what exhausts what is known and knowable. The alternative is to understand this model as restricted, and thus as not serving exhaustively for determining the conditions of knowing. The realist, then, affirms the irreducible function of a mind-independent residue of compulsion or resistance that constrains thought.

It may be helpful to expand my characterization of realism with reference to Hookway's discussion of the issue concerning whether Peirce's view may be described as a Kantian realism. Hookway points out that in his late writing, Peirce denied "that reality was 'relative to thought in general,'" although he adds that he believes Peirce "did retain its 'anthropocentric' character during the last two decades of his life."[6] His reason for this qualification is based on the point that Peirce's categories by which he gives a general description of reality have an *a priority* "in spite of being developed through an observational inquiry."[7] My concern here, however, is not to consider the force of Hookway's argument, but to draw briefly on his characterization of the realisms that are at issue. Suffice it to say that Hookway's suggestion that Peirce remained Kantian is based on a conception of realism that is tied to the role of the categories in understanding what reality is, could be, or may be. The point I am making is that the realism to which Peirce is committed is unique and is not simply a function of what any categories could tell us about its structure, if indeed it had a structure.

Another way to put this is to say that at least some if not most conceptions of realistic foundations that have led recent writers to affirm the inevitability of cultural and linguistic contingencies have been based on what I call an *overdetermined* reality. The reality that is thought to

[6]Ibid., p. 105.
[7]Ibid., p. 111.

be standing over against thought has been viewed as determined in specific structured ways, with external objects existing quite independently of thought, and this structure is supposed to be waiting for thought to be adequate to it, or until thought is perfected, partially inadequate to it. Thus, the view rejected by recent linguistic and cultural contingency theorists, is that there is a real, actual, shaped world that ideally corresponds to thought. I shall develop this point in the final chapter. What I shall argue for is not this rejected metaphysical realism, but rather what may seem to be a weaker kind of realism, although one that is unique to Peirce. Thus, I agree with Hookway that Peirce never abandoned the view that reality is relative to thought in general and that "the concerns and practices of inquirers shape their conception of reality."[8] I do not think it follows, however, that being relative in this way makes reality dependent on thought in general or that reality is exhausted by the intelligibility standards brought to bear on it by inquirers. There will be occasion later to refer once more to Hookway's insights into this issue.

With this comment on my understanding of realism and idealism in mind, I shall begin with a brief examination of one passage that provides probably the most obvious support for the view that Peirce was committed to metaphysical idealism. After showing that this passage deserves a subtler interpretation than it is normally given and that it, and several others, should be qualified when understood in context, I shall discuss some of the passages that most clearly support a realist interpretation. I shall then explain how Peirce's conception of cosmic evolution indicates that he leaned toward a metaphysical, evolutionary realism.

Peirce as Idealist

A passage in Peirce's writings that provides obvious evidence for classifying him as an idealist appears in a discussion in 1891 of the answers that have been given to the question, What is the nature of the universe? He identifies three types of answers – dualism, materialism, and objective idealism – and he indicates a preference for the third. The basis for this preference centers on his rejection of materialism. He insists that materialism construes feeling as "a kind of mechanism," which he thinks is unreasonable.[9] Thus, he says, "The one in-

---

[8]Ibid.

[9]In this connection, later in the *Monist* 1890s series (6.35–65), he offers other arguments, the major thrust of which is the rejection of a view that reduces growth to mechanistic, reversible, and immutable law. Such a law itself needs to be accounted for; thus, the view that reduces all phenomena to it does not serve as an adequate answer to the question of the nature of the universe.

telligible theory of the universe is that of objective idealism, that matter is effete mind, inveterate habits becoming physical laws" (6.24).

An illustration of the influence and authority of this passage can be seen in Sandra Rosenthal's thoughtful account of Peirce's treatment of the three metaphysical commitments. She interprets Peirce's remarks about his preference as a "self-proclaimed idealism."[10] Reinforcing the conclusion that Peirce is a self-proclaimed idealist are other, even more explicit assertions. For instance, in an 1886 letter to Francis E. Abbot, referred to by Max Fisch, Peirce claims himself "not only phenomenalist, but also idealist."[11] He says (probably in 1892) that "everything is of the nature of mind" (MS 954.00012–13). And in 1903 he indicates that his doctrine "might very well be taken for a variety of Hegelianism (because Hegel is so nearly right)" (5.38).

In the first quoted passage, Peirce's statements that the one intelligible theory of the universe is objective idealism and that matter is effete mind are probably generally considered conclusive support for classifying Peirce as a metaphysical idealist. There are, however, three reasons to withhold this conclusion. In the first place, it may be based in part on overlooking what Peirce understood in referring to matter. Matter is what is fixed as inveterate habit. It is immutable law, law no longer subject to any spontaneity whatsoever. Given this conception, one could rewrite Peirce's characterization of the relation of mind to matter to read, "Mind is lively matter." Would this make him a materialist? I think not.

The possible interchange of mind and matter is in fact discussed by Peirce in an essay on the connection between the two (6.272–86). He proposes that in view of the continuity between the characters of mind and matter, one could hold the "mechanistic hypothesis" insofar as it "attributes to mind the properties of extension" and attributes to matter a low grade of feeling (6.277). It should be acknowledged that he adds to this remark the idea that the law of mind is more basic, mechanical laws being only special results of it. However, with respect to all the quotations mentioned here, my point is that the concepts of mind and matter for Peirce belong to a continuum and should be understood in the context of the architectonic at which Peirce aimed. Thus, when they enter Peirce's discussions, they do not have quite the meanings they had in the traditional discussions of realism, material-

[10]Sandra B. Rosenthal, *Speculative Pragmatism* (Amherst: University of Massachusetts Press, 1986), pp. 114–16.

[11]Max H. Fisch, "Peirce's Progress from Nominalism toward Realism," *Monist* 51, p. 169. The letter to Abbot is included in the chronological edition of Peirce's works: *The Writings of Charles S. Peirce*, vol. V, (Bloomington: Indiana University Press, forthcoming). This passage from Fisch is mentioned in a discussion of changes in Peirce's thought concerning his realism and idealism by Hookway, *Peirce*, p. 113.

ism, and idealism. Matter is not some mind-independent collection or congregation of substantial entities. Nor is effete mind equivalent to effete mental experiences, the model for which lies in personal consciousness. Effete mind is rigid regularity of events – process without spontaneity.

The second reason for not concluding that Peirce adopted metaphysical idealism is that saying that objective idealism is the one *"intelligible* theory of the universe" does not preclude the possibility that this one intelligible theory will not exhaust all that is intelligible. Other theories, because fallible – like all theories (presumably including objective idealism) – may offer the promise of less intelligibility, although nevertheless contributory to understanding the whole of experience. Moreover, other theories might contribute to accounting for the successes and failures of inquiry. Indeed, I shall later mention a passage in which Peirce makes this point explicitly. I should emphasize that I do not intend to claim that Peirce deliberately implied this possibility. I mean only to claim that he did not necessarily claim that his own view is identical with objective idealism. And it seems to me that his preference leaves open the possibility of hypotheses that concern the universe insofar as it includes but is not exhausted by regularities or laws that constitute the necessities of an objective idealist's universe. Peirce's own view, as will be emphasized later, affirms an inescapable resistance to intelligibility.

In the third place, even if Peirce did mean to affirm the truth of objective idealism to the exclusion of all other views – an option for him that is not demonstrated – we are still faced with the possibility that Peirce's own view would be a very peculiar version of objective idealism, one so peculiar that it perhaps had better not be called by the traditional label that was applied to views that were, in Peirce's time, popular – for instance, those of Royce, W. T. Harris, and the St. Louis Hegelians.

The idea that, insofar as Peirce leaned toward objective idealism, his was of a peculiar brand, is explicitly suggested in 1906 in Peirce's identification of his pragmatism as *conditional idealism*. In saying this, he adds a comment about this condition, "That is to say, I hold that truth's independence of individual opinions is due (so far as there is any 'truth') to its being the predestined result to which sufficient inquiry *would* ultimately lead" (5.494). In the present context, the relevance of *would* is its exclusion of the conception of an actual predestined result, or an actual final opinion. The word "would," emphasized by Peirce, is particularly important for understanding the conditionality of Peirce's idealism, for, as I have noted earlier, Peirce's conception of would-be's also supports what he calls his realism. But let us next move beyond qualifying the quotations that are supposed to support Peirce's adoption of idealism and recognize his equally strong, if not stronger, self-proclamations that he was a realist.

Passages Supportive of Peirce's Realism

There are at least two kinds of passages in which Peirce proclaims realism. Before considering these, however, two preliminary points should be made. It should first be noted that both Sandra Rosenthal and Christopher Hookway, who, as already observed in the case of Rosenthal, point to the idealistic side of Peirce, also include in their discussions consideration of his realist leanings. I am not sure that either of them wants to assert decisively that the realist side is more fundamental or to be given more weight. Rosenthal in fact says that Peirce's realism is not opposed to idealism.[12] I should point out, however, Rosenthal, in conversations, has said that she leans more in the direction of realism of the kind I want to propose. In any case, without actually counting passages, it seems to me that there are at least as many that align him with realism. Thus, as will be argued later, considerations that reach beyond his self-proclamations must be brought to bear on the issue.

The second point has to do with what Peirce means by the terms *real* and *realism*. As early as his 1878 papers on belief and the maxim of meaning, he uses what he says is the commonly adopted meaning, namely, that the real is what has characters that are independent of how you or I think (5.405). And as late as 1906, Peirce says, "Whether the object immediately before the mind is the Real object or not seems to be a question from which it is difficult to extract any clear meaning; but it [is] quite certain that no thinking *about it* will at all modify the Real object, since this is precisely what is meant by calling it Real," although, he continues, it is "sometimes an object shaped by thinking" (MS 634.00010). Part of this quotation, then, explicitly suggests that thinking may occasionally function by giving character to what it is about. However, thought also is restricted insofar as the real object is not identical with the characters attributed to it. This, I think, reflects what in his semeiotic is the distinction between the immediate and dynamical objects. It will be recalled that the first is the object as represented by a sign and the second is the object insofar as it is indepen-

---

[12]*Speculative Pragmatism*, p. 120, n. 34.

Robert Jacques has written a paper in which he collects typical examples of Peirce's references to realism, forthcoming in the *Transactions of the Charles S. Peirce Society*. He concludes that an emphasis on Secondness serves as a key feature of a kind of realism that tends to be overlooked by many interpreters of Peirce.

dent of the representation and is thereby resistant, serving as a condition that restrains the determinations coming from the side of the interpreter. This distinction is important for our topic and will play an important role later.

In 1910, Peirce says, something is what "I call 'real,' be it anything asserted or imagined, or conceived, or any element of such assertions, image, or concept, or of whatever other sort it may be, if, and only if, it possesses characters which it would possess, just the same whether or not, you or I, or anybody else, or everybody living during any limits of time, opines, fancies, or otherwise thinks it possesses *some* characters that are *not* of this description" (MS 663.00006). We have, then, two ways of understanding reality. The first concerns a condition of resistance to whatever "shape" or interpretation a thinker considers appropriate to the object. The second is the condition of the possibility of a final or invariant shape, in the form of the characters of the object that are independent of any particular interpretation at any actual time. Such characters would then be accessible only at the terminus or limit of inquiry.

A Distinction Between Two Kinds of Supporting Passages Passages in which Peirce declares his allegiance to realism may be sorted into two overlapping kinds. The first consists of those in which he explicitly refers to himself as a realist, including the self-proclamation that his view is a scholastic realism and that it includes the insistence that generals, which he sometimes suggests are like Platonic Ideas, are real. The second kind of supporting passages includes those that implicitly suggest realism – at least insofar as some form of realism follows from anti-idealism. These may be distinguished into three species. First, there are those that include his insistence that his view is to be distanced from Hegel's. This insistence, of course, does not necessarily imply realism. It does show, however, that Peirce did not regard himself as an objective idealist of the kind best known in his philosophical community. The second species relates to the first way of understanding the term reality, namely, as what resists mind-dependent conditions of interpretation. It consists of some of his affirmations of critical commonsensism, some of his accounts of perceptual judgment, and those passages that introduce Peirce's insistence on Secondness and the dynamical object. The third species relates to the second way of understanding the term *reality*. It includes his accounts of the final opinion and, again, the dynamical object. The third species, it may be observed, must be considered in light of the envisaged overall architectonic.

Self-Proclamations I shall cite only a few examples of the two kinds of passages and devote only a moment to those passages in which he refers to himself as a realist. The most obvious example of this first kind of passage occurs in the context of Peirce's attempts to show how pragmaticism is opposed to nominalism. He says, for instance, "I am myself a scholastic realist of a somewhat extreme stripe" (5.470). And in another place, he says:

> Another doctrine which is involved in Pragmaticism as an essential consequence of it, but which the writer defended . . . before he had formulated, even in his own mind, the principle of pragmaticism, is the scholastic doctrine of realism. This is usually defined as the opinion that there are real objects that are general, among the number being the modes of determination of existent singulars. (5.453)

The second sentence in this passage indicates why Peirce's declaration that he is a scholastic realist is supported by his repeated insistence on the reality of generals. As observed earlier, he occasionally suggests that generals have a kinship with Platonic Ideas rather than Aristotelian universals. I do not mean to claim that Peirce's conception of generals is anti-Aristotelian, as his avowed scholastic realism indicates. However, the extent to which Peirce suggests that he has Platonic leanings – at least regarding the status of respects or grounds (in which signs refer to objects), which are generals, by which phenomena are interpreted – is, I think, based on, first, his insistence that no general is exhausted by actual instances and that its possible instances are infinite and, second, the dynamic character of generals. The idea, to be discussed in a moment, that this dynamism is evolutionary departs from the traditional understanding of a Platonic Idea or Form. In any case, Peirce says when lecturing on his category of Thirdness, "In short, the idea of a general involves the idea of possible variations which no multitude of existent things could exhaust but would leave between any two not merely *many* possibilities, but possibilities absolutely beyond all multitude" (5.104). Further, a general is dynamic, subject to growth and teleological effectiveness: "The evolutionary process is . . . a process by which the very Platonic forms themselves have become or are becoming developed" (6.194). The tychistic assumption behind this passage will be considered later; it provides perhaps the most significant clue to Peirce's special realism.[13] The impor-

---

[13]The relevance of Platonic Ideas for Peirce is found not only in late developments of his thinking when he was concerned with cosmology, but it can be seen also in one of what I think is its most significant manifestations, (as observed in the second chapter) his semeiotic. In the context of his early thinking about how signs function in cognition, there is reference to the function of Platonic Ideas in the second cognition paper of 1868. There he defines a sign as follows: "Now a sign has . . . three references: first, it is a sign *to* some thought which interprets it; second, it is a sign *for* some object to which in that thought it is equivalent; third, it is a sign, *in* some respect or quality, which brings it into connection with its object." Later (c. 1897), he associates the re-

tance of the references to Platonic Ideas and generals is evident in Peirce's insistence that his pragmaticism and philosophy in general gave a crucial place to the function of would-be's or conditionals that function in the processes that constitute nature. In short, the reality of Platonic Ideas or the reality of generals is the reality of would-be's. And this is to insist on the reality of Thirdness, because Thirdness is a category applying to generality and is found wherever there are would-be's, or real possibilities (5.453). In the lecture on Thirdness mentioned earlier, Peirce says that *"Thirdness is operative in Nature,"* and in order to convince his audience, he asks how we can know, that is, predict with assurance, that an unsupported stone will fall if released. The answer, he says, is that there must be something real in the course of events that functions as the object of our thoughts (5.93–6).

As pointed out earlier, being a scholastic realist may be understood to be consistent with objective idealism. Thus, the evidence of scholastic realism is not sufficient to establish his position as a realist in the sense drawn at the beginning of this chapter. Let us, then, turn next to the second kind of supporting passages for realism, those in which Peirce's commitment is implicit.

Anti-idealism

Peirce's Distance from Hegel In insisting on the crucial role of Thirdness in his conception of pragmatism, Peirce does not want to commit himself to Hegelianism. He says, "The truth is that pragmaticism is closely allied to the Hegelian absolute idealism, from which, however, it is sundered by its vigorous denial that the third category (which Hegel degrades to a mere stage of thinking) suffices to make the world, or is even so much as self-sufficient" (5.436). Unlike Hegel, Peirce holds all three categories to be "independent or distinct elements of the triune Reality" (ibid.).

Closely related to this way of distinguishing himself from Hegel, Peirce points out in another passage how his conception of the reality of Thirdness distinguishes his own view from Hegelian idealism along with six other metaphysical systems, which he seems to think exhaust all possible types. His purpose here is to show the conceptual value of his three categories. He uses these to classify metaphysical systems according to their acceptance or rejection, or ignoring, of one or two of the categories, and he concludes that his includes all three. I shall

spects or qualities that connect sign and object with Platonic Ideas. He says that the sign stands for its object, "not in all respects, but in reference to a sort of idea, which I have sometimes called the *ground* of the representamen. 'Idea' is here to be understood in a sort of Platonic sense" (2.228).

not consider all the types he identifies. What is important, however, is what he says about Hegelianism and those views that come closest to his own. He says that Hegelianism "of all shades" is to be commended because it opposes the reduction of everything to mechanical force and in this opposition, "regards Category the Third as the only true one." But he adds that in the Hegelian system the other two are only introduced in order to be *aufgehoben*" (5.77–9). Further, in a note to paragraph 77, he explains that, in addition to his own system, the "metaphysics that recognizes all the categories . . . embraces Kantism, Reid's Philosophy, and the Platonic philosophy of which Aristoteli-anism is a special development." And he adds the interesting obser-vation, "I should call myself an Aristotelian of the scholastic wing, approaching Scotism, but going much further in the direction of scholastic realism." What more explicit evidence is needed to show that Peirce did not mean to equate his view with objective idealism – unless somehow the interpreter finds a way to construe Scotism or scholastic realism (perhaps in terms of affirming the intelligibility of individuals with reference to complexes of universals) as a species of objective idealism. Yet given his denial of Hegelianism and his avowed scholastic realism, such an interpretation surely would affirm a very peculiar form of objective idealism.

Finally, Peirce's distance from Hegelianism and his resistance to being identified with idealism in general are found in his statement that he includes idealism as only part of his overall view. Thus, although he does affirm objective idealism as at least relevant to his own philoso-phy, he says also at the end of one of the 1890s papers, "The Law of Mind," that synechism, which he elsewhere referred to as the basis of pragmaticism, "carries along with it . . . first a logical realism of the most pronounced type; second, objective idealism; third, tychism, with its consequent thoroughgoing evolutionism" (6.163). The idea that synechism, or his conception of the foundation of pragmaticism, is formed of increments that include some of the traditional philosoph-ical positions suggests again that Peirce wanted to move beyond the options, including idealism and realism, as they were available at the time.[14] In any case, the passage just quoted makes clear that Peirce's idealistic tendencies constitute only a component of his architectonic rather than its final commitment.

Critical Commonsensism, Percepts, and the Dynamical Object The second species of implicit realism is suggested in some of Peirce's discussions of critical commonsensism and perceptual judgment. Peirce identifies

[14]Hookway and Rosenthal suggest that Peirce was headed toward a view that could not be reduced to one or the other, even though, as Rosenthal says, he did not make this clear.

six characteristics of critical Commonsenism, which he calls a consequence of pragmaticism. The sixth characteristic is suggestive for our
purposes. This characteristic calls for a modification of Kantianism.
The modification concerns the need for the "Kantist . . . to abjure
from the bottom of his heart the proposition that a thing-in-itself can,
however indirectly, be conceived." With the correction of the "details
of Kant's doctrine," one "will find himself to have become a Critical
Common-sensist" (5.452). Immediately following this statement, Peirce
launches into an account and defense of scholastic realism. This defense, however, is not an elaboration of the correction of details of
Kant's doctrine. It is the introduction of another consequence of
pragmaticism. What, then, are the details of the Kantian view that are
to be corrected? Presumably, they concern at least the points at which
a substitute for the abjured notion of a thing-in-itself plays a role in
the critique of understanding. I suggest that there are at least two
ways in which Peirce might thus modify Kant.[15] These follow from
his suggestions about how interpretations of experience are subject to
constraints, the source of which is not in the inquirer. The condition
of these constraints may be understood as taking the place of things-
in-themselves that must be rejected insofar as they are somehow related to phenomena without being cognizable. I would like to suggest,
specifically, that the modifications to which Peirce refers are correlated with Peirce's conception of the function of percepts in relation
to perceptual judgment and the function of the dynamical object for
percepts and, more generally, in the growth of knowledge.

Peirce writes about percepts in two ways.[16] In the first way, they are
the uncontrolled, compulsive moments when something in experience is forced on attention so that conscious interpretation initiates
the formation of a perceptual judgment. In these moments, the percept is not intelligible, for it is as yet not subject to the mediating
process of interpretation. Thus, in a manuscript of 1903, he says that
percepts are "absolutely dumb" (7.622). As precognitive, they are
preintelligible and contain only Firstness and Secondness (7.630). Yet
the percept compels a reaction that is subjected to critical control and
that becomes integrated into interpretation. Thus, although the percept is not itself intelligible, its *effect* is not arbitrary. The responsibility
of interpretation is to be adequate to it.

In the second way in which Peirce writes about percepts, he treats

---

[15]Vincent Colapietro proposed to me the likelihood that Peirce also had in mind modifications of Kant's view of the self or deliberative agent. This proposal seems reasonable, but it is not one that bears directly on the concerns crucial in the present discussion.
[16]Elaboration of this point is offered in my "In and Out of Peirce's Percepts," *Transactions of the Charles S. Peirce Society* 26, no. 3 (Summer 1990), pp. 271–308.

them as the results of interpretation and therefore as the objects of perceptual judgments. Thus, he sometimes illustrates percepts with reference to external, perceptual objects. For instance, he says, "I see an inkstand on the table; that is a percept. . . . What I call the inkstand is a generalized percept, a quasi-inference from percepts. . . . Subsequently, when I accept the hypothesis of an inward subject for my thoughts, I yield to that consciousness of resistance and admit the inkstand to the standing of an external object" (8.144). As the objects of completed perceptual judgments, percepts have an autonomy with respect to the judgment that functions as a sign of them. Like percepts that *precede* judgment, those that are *subsequent* to judgment have an obdurate presence, and they cannot be changed at will. The inkstand cannot be willed away; it insists on being there in front of the interpreter who has judged it to be an inkstand. Thus, there are constraints here, too, but they are postjudgmental constraints that appear as the respects in which the object perceived is an inkstand rather than a chair or cup. It seems to me that it is in his conception of percepts and perceptual judgments that Peirce reveals one side of his scientific realism and what perhaps is the basis for the idea that he was an epistemological realist. However, the conception of percepts in relation to perceptual judgments is also suggestive of a metaphysical realism. This, I think, is indicated by what he says about the dynamical object and the way this can be brought to bear on the function of percepts.

The dynamical object, it will be recalled, is the object of a sign insofar as the object is the condition for constraints on interpretation. It is that which is or remains to be interpreted and is present as Secondness in a phenomenon and as the residue of what is never exhausted by interpretation in any finite time. "We must distinguish between the Immediate Object, – i.e., the Object as represented in the sign, – and the Real . . . say rather the Dynamical Object, which, from the nature of things, the Sign *cannot* express, which it can only *indicate* and leave the interpreter to find out by *collateral experience*" (8.314). The point should be emphasized that the role of the dynamical object as a semeiotic-independent condition is for Peirce the role of a thought or mind-independent condition. A relatively long quotation may serve as evidence of this point:

I have already noted that a Sign has an Object and an Interpretant, the latter being that which the Sign produces in the Quasi-mind that is the Interpreter. . . . But it remains to point out that there are usually two Objects. . . . Namely, we have to distinguish the Immediate Object, which is the Object as the Sign as the Sign itself represents it, and whose Being is thus dependent upon the Representation of it in the Sign, from the Dynamical Object, which is the Reality which by some means contrives to determine the Sign to its Representation. (4.536)

In this connection, we may return briefly to Hookway's treatment of the issue. In an article in which he discusses Peirce's rejection of nominalism, he hits the nerve of the issue when he asks, "What basis has Peirce for preferring the hypothesis that realities exist prior to their discovery to the alternative that they spring into existence as investigators come to acknowledge them?"[17] My answer is that on Peirce's view, the alternatives are not so sharply drawn. Indeed, Peirce does not prefer one to the exclusion of the other. He prefers both. Paradoxical as this might appear, it can be understood through Peirce's idea of the distinction between the dynamical and immediate objects. Thus, the experience of instances of Secondness provides evidence of constraint and by a kind of transcendental deduction – showing what is required hypothetically in order to justify what appears to function in a certain way in experience – Peirce is led to suppose a dynamical object that *"must"* be a condition functioning so that constraints lead and sometimes compel investigators to acknowledge and adopt certain interpretations in preference to others. This does not commit him to a view of preexistent real objects *in themselves*. However, it does resist the idea that dynamic, existential (conditions of instances of Secondness) realities spring into existence when they are acknowledged. What does spring into existence is the immediate object. What functions independently of this is the dynamical object, the compulsive force of which is manifest in instances of Secondness.

In addition to functioning as a constraining condition in particular cognitive situations, Peirce suggests that the dynamical object may serve teleologically in the final aim of investigation. He says that an object of a sign "may be the Object in such relations as unlimited and final study would show it to be," which is the dynamical object (8.183). The relation of this condition to the question of the independence of the object of the final opinion from thought in general must now be considered. And this moves us to the third kind of statements that suggest Peirce's realism.

Before considering these, however, it is proper to acknowledge a possible objection to what I have just cited as evidence of realism. My comments about the object of the final opinion suggest that just as the quotations cited in support of the idea that Peirce was an idealist were qualified, so should the statements supporting his self-proclaimed realism. In the first place, it might be said that asserting the reality of generals is not incompatible with objective idealism. As pointed out, objective idealism might recognize generals as realities that are independent of the thought of any individual or group of individuals,

[17]Christopher Hookway, "Reference, Causation, and Reality," *Semiotica* 69 (1988), pp. 331–48. The quotation is from p. 337.

although not of thought in general. Further, Peirce's self-declared realism was sometimes proposed in opposition to nominalism, and idealism is also opposed to nominalism, in particular, in its affirmation of the independence of repeatable experiences and the necessity of uniformities or laws that transcend particular mental processes. Thus, his rejection of nominalism may have been made from the perspective of an idealism. He occasionally suggested as much, especially in the 1868 articles on cognition published in the *Journal of Speculative Philosophy*. Let us, then, briefly explore this opposition to nominalism. If Peirce's opposition was not exclusively an expression of an idealist's orientation, then his insistence on the independent ontological status of would-be's or generals may be linked to an overarching realism that undergirds his envisaged architectonic.

In the cognition papers, Peirce proposes what might be taken as an idealist principle that rejects the conception of an incognizable thing-in-itself. This leaning toward what might seem to be an idealism, however, seems to me to be restricted. Peirce reaffirms his characterization of the conception of the thing-in-itself as absurd in the much later discussion of commonsensism, quoted earlier, which was written after he had begun to make repeated references to the realism to which he was committed. Moreover, within approximately two years of the cognition papers, he affirmed an alignment with realism. This is evident in his review of the works of Berkeley in 1870, where he concentrated on the difference between realism and nominalism. And this distinction seems to have played a crucial role in the way he conceived of realism throughout his career. He regarded as nominalistic any view that supposed that the only realities are individual things and that these are unrelated to thought. He opposed the idea that such realities could serve as things-in-themselves severed from lawful, recurrent realities or real generals, and which are real only as confined to mental acts. And, as already suggested, we may suppose that Peirce was driven to his self-identification as a realist in large measure because of his anathema to nominalism. This anathema was tied to his conviction, presumably based on his acquaintance with science, that there are real generals, regularities in nature that are effective in relation to thought and to other generals. In any event, it is with antinominalism in mind that he sometimes called himself a scholastic realist even of an extreme kind. Whether his scholastic realism is subsumed under some form of objective idealism or is integral to an architectonic realism needs to be considered in the context of the third species of passages that support realism.

The Final Opinion and the Dynamical Object The third group of implicit affirmations of realism concerns the final opinion and the dynamical object. One of the earliest examples, referred to in the first chapter of this book, is found in the relatively early article, "The Fixation of Belief," where he discusses the presuppositions of the scientific method. As we saw, science presupposes what he calls the *realistic hypothesis*, that there is an external permanence, "something upon which our thinking has no effect"; to quote at length:

There are Real things, whose characters are entirely independent of our opinions about them; those Reals affect our senses according to regular laws, and, though our sensations are as different as are our relations to the objects, yet, by taking advantage of the laws of perception, we can ascertain by reasoning how things really and truly are; and any man, if he have sufficient experience and he reason enough about it, will be led to the one True conclusion. The new conception here involved is that of Reality. (5.384)

This statement should be joined with what Peirce says about the aim of inquiry in the next article in the series, "How to Make Our Ideas Clear." Again, let me rely primarily on Peirce's own words. He says that "the progress of investigation carries [the minds of scientific researchers] by force outside of themselves to one and the same conclusion" – to a foreordained goal; thus, "the opinion which is fated to be ultimately agreed to by all who investigate, is what we mean by the truth, and the object represented in this opinion is the real" (5.407). If the object of the final opinion is the real, then we seem to have a clear acceptance of a realism for which there is something that is independent of mind – that is, what has mental ontological status. In explaining further what he means, however, Peirce raises the question whether his definition of reality "makes the characters of the real depend on what is ultimately thought about them," and, as pointed out earlier, his answer reveals that he had not decided conclusively one way or the other, for he says:

But the answer to this is that, on the one hand, reality is independent, not necessarily of thought in general, but only of what you or I or any finite number of men may think about it; and that, on the other hand, though the object of the final opinion depends on what that opinion is, yet what that opinion is does not depend on what you or I or any man thinks. (5.408)

This statement has led some to suppose that Peirce is here affirming an idealism in the sense that the object of the final opinion collapses into or is identical with thought in general. The one little expression *not necessarily*, however, indicates that this may not be so – even at this early stage of his thought when he was struggling against nominalism. Peirce simply leaves open the possibility of the identity of the object with thought in general.[18] This is not to propose that Peirce did not

[18]That the "not necessarily" is generally ignored is exemplified by the fact that it is not mentioned by Hookway when he discusses the passage in question as part of his considerations of the ways in which Peirce avoided a commitment to realism in his early 1877–8 papers.

lean toward an idealistic principle in this relatively early essay. Rather, it is to suggest that he was uncertain, or perhaps unconcerned, at that moment about accommodating realism to his repudiation of nominalism. In order to push this point further, we must consider what Peirce says later about the terminus of inquiry in the infinite future; and it is here that the idea of evolutionary realism emerges as what I believe is Peirce's special brand of realism.

The question that faces us, specifically, is, What sort of thing is the object of the final opinion? What is its status? There are two directions from which to pursue this question. First, we may ask what the dynamical object is insofar as it functions as the condition that will be or *would* be encountered in the future, at the end of inquiry. Second, we may ask, What sort of referent of thought could terminate inquiry? The first question is suggested when Peirce says that an object of a sign "may be the Object in such relations as unlimited and final study would show it to be," which is the dynamical object (8.183). The second question is suggested not only by Peirce's early, previously noted, uncertainty over whether the final object is dependent on thought in general but also by passages in some of Peirce's late writing in which he places the end of inquiry in an infinite future. Thus, although Peirce is clear about his conception of a convergence on a final, ordered universe and a perfected intelligibility, this convergence is not proposed as an actual future state, rather it is projected beyond any finite moment in time. Convergence, therefore, must evolve. Its terminus itself is an evolving, dynamical object. In order to develop this idea, it will be helpful to comment on the relation of Peirce's tychism to the point about the evolutionary condition of the dynamical object.

Peirce's view that chance or spontaneity is integral to the development of the universe includes the idea that Secondness as well as Firstness is never overcome; it should always be expected. Indeed, this point is essential to the classification of his own metaphysics as one of those that does not ignore or call for the rejection of any of his three categories – as does Hegelian idealism. If both Firstness, the category of possibility, and Secondness, the category of unintelligibility and resistance, are not overcome, but have an essential role in the cosmos in the growth of thirds, then the intelligibility of Thirdness is constrained and limited.

Reinforcement of the idea that resistance to closure of an evolving universe, and thus a resistance to the actualized ideal of complete knowledge, is clear also in Peirce's 1890s *Monist* articles. In these he attacks necessitarianism and attributes spontaneity to the lawfulness of the cosmos and to the law of the growth of laws, which is to insist on what he calls *the law of evolutionary love,* or *agape.*

Peirce's view that there is a residue-reality that escapes mind applies to all stages of the cosmos. Not only is there spontaneity and constraint in the present and at any actual, specified time in the future, but there is also an original "residue" in the very origin of the universe. Thus, the universe is neither explicitly nor implicitly founded on an intelligible source. As Peirce formulates the point, the actual universe originated from the definiteness of a "brute act" (2.203). (See also 6.192 and 6.200.) It is a kind of cosmic accident. Consequently, the origin could not be identified with mind or with what is mindlike in the sense of "mind" for objective idealism. The origin of the universe is out of absolute nothing (6.214–20), which at that original state has no order such that it can be considered intelligible. Thus, the cosmos does not follow from a matrix of necessary and sufficient conditions, or from an implicit set of laws that are worked out in history. This sort of origin would be one of the forms of necessitarianism that Peirce rejected. Nor is the universe fixed insofar as it has gained intelligibility. Peirce says, "In short, if we are going to regard the universe as a result of evolution at all, we must think that not merely the existing universe, that locus in the cosmos to which our reactions are limited, but the whole Platonic world, which in itself is equally real, is evolutionary in its origin, too" (6.200).

What we have seen about the origin of the cosmos has implications for its goal. If the cosmic accident with which the universe began is sustained under the categories of Firstness and Secondness throughout the course of evolution, would this spontaneity be extinguished if the final opinion were reached? An affirmative answer implies either of two alternatives. The first is that although inquiry would be terminated, there would be a static, independent object of thought in general. The second is that there is no such final, independent object, and the end of inquiry is a convergence in which mind – that is, perfect lawfulness – reigns exhaustively. In other words, the final opinion and its object are identical. In this latter case, the structure of the universe would be constituted as a final interpretant, or mindlike state – although, interestingly, an effete mindlike state – of being. Although, as already admitted, Peirce does refer in various places to the object of investigation as a system of stable regularities, which is thought- or interpretation-dependent, I think that neither alternative answers to the question of whether intelligibility-resistant conditions are present in the object of the final opinion fits Peirce's architectonic purposes. The first answer, that there is a static, independent object, seems prima facie unacceptable, because, far from being a terminus in a fully intelligible state, a static, independent final object would imply that the relation between opinion and object would be radically unintelligible. This, for Peirce, must follow because such a relation is a dyad. And if we were to suppose that mediation could be introduced to bring the terms of the dyad together, thought would be reestablished and would introduce further interpretation, contrary to the condition supposed that thought had reached its terminating conclusion.

What can be said, however, of the second answer, the answer that the final object is one with thought? I should like to mention two reasons for proposing that it is resisted by Peirce's overall architectonic. I propose the first reason only tentatively, because it is based on a passage in which Peirce may not have intended to offer a definite opinion of his own. The passage occurs in Peirce's review of Josiah Royce's *The World and the Individual*. He describes Royce's opposition to the view that the object of knowledge is no more than a would-be (8.103). After mentioning Royce's argument, he adds as commentary the following: "There is no escaping the admission that the ultimate end of inquiry . . . the mould to which we endeavor to shape our opinions, cannot itself be of the nature of an opinion. Could it be realized, it would rather be like an insistent image, not referring to anything else, and in that sense concrete" (8.104). In addition to observing Peirce's apparent rejection of the idea that the end of inquiry is an opinion, it is important to note that if it were an opinion, such an end would not be the sort contemplated by objective idealists, at least in terms of Peirce's conceptions of *image* and *insistent*. An image is an icon, and it is correlated with Firstness. And insistence falls under the category of Secondness.

As indicated, I am not certain that Peirce's comment in this context introduces his own position. But the interpretation that it does is reasonable on two grounds. First, the view that he mentions as an alternative to the view with which Royce disagrees is close to what Peirce does sometimes affirm in other places, namely, that "inquiry is directed toward the resultant of certain compulsions" (8.103). Second, Peirce does comment throughout the review, offering his own points of agreement or disagreement. Thus, it may be inferred that the comment added to the account of Royce's argument reflects Peirce's own view.

The second reason for regarding Peirce's architectonic purposes as resisting the conclusion that the final object is completely thought-dependent is that the final object is said to lie in the infinite future. It is perpetually approximated; it is something that only would be attainable if there were an assignable actual time at which all thought were to converge in the future. I take it that this conception of an infinitely distant finality is the other side of Peirce's tychism – which, it must be reiterated, is an integral part of his overall view of the universe. Tychism manifests the category of Secondness, as well as Firstness, and neither category is reducible to the other categories.

And tychism is sustained in light of the infinite distance between the present and what must be understood as only a possible terminus. The role of tychism in Peirce's philosophy will be considered further in connection with his view of evolution.

The third reason for denying the idealist interpretation of the object of the final opinion is linked to the second; but it bridges its conception of an infinite future with the events at times prior to that future. The bridge is Peirce's commitment to the reality of would-be's. I should like to suggest that this bridge links the view that construes the final opinion as a dynamic, infinitely effective actuality with a side that construes the final opinion as an ideal that regulates the course of inquiry. The latter is a proposal that has been made before, and by others. The former, however, has not, I believe, been formulated as I have formulated it. Nor has the notion of an ideal limit been bridged intelligibly with the notion of an inexhaustible actual reality. Nevertheless, the bridge is, I think, required by what Peirce says. I shall try to press this idea of the bridge further, although I certainly do not claim to resolve it fully.

We have considered the role of would-be's as real patterns in nature, and it was acknowledged that Peirce's insistence on the reality of generals did not necessarily contradict his commitment to metaphysical idealism. However, the issue now concerns the relation of would-be's to the final opinion and their role in the final object. The importance of would-be's for the object of the final opinion is overlooked by some of the most admirable interpreters of Peirce. Peter Skagestad, for instance, refers to Peirce's view of the final opinion as that on which investigators *will* ultimately agree.[19] Interestingly, however, Skagestad adds discussion that suggests agreement with my point about the need to understand the final opinion in terms of would-be's. He lends support for his view by quoting a passage in which Peirce proposes as a possible postulate the statement that any fact "must be such that it would ultimately present itself in experience or not." Peirce adds that if it will so present itself, then the postulate is unnecessary, "since we shall ultimately be entitled to use it as a premise." On the other hand, if any fact *never would* so present itself, then the postulate "is valid as far as possible experience goes" (6.41). Skagestad correctly, I think, then shows that on the whole, Peirce's statements provide a view of inquiry as "indefinitely prolonged."[20] The ideal limit remains unknown in any finite future, but it has "empirical meaning by extrapolation from the course of inquiry to date into the indefinite future."[21] My qualification of his account is that I think there is a differ-

[19]Skagestad, *The Road of Inquiry*, p. 166.
[20]Ibid., pp. 166–7.
[21]Ibid., p. 167.

ence between an infinite future and an indefinite future. An indefinite future is one that in principle may be reached. An infinite future is unreachable. One might be able to equate these two notions if one were to provide some construction of a notion of infinity that succeeded in closing the gap between eternity and temporal everlastingness. What I mean is that one would need a way of construing infinity so that it is at once atemporal and temporally imagined. If this could be accomplished, it would provide a basis for saying that what is infinitely extended is what is atemporally infinite. Even on this construal, however, the unreachability of the ideal limit of the final opinion would not be contradicted. Let us then return to Peirce's notion of the final opinion as requiring the conception of would-be's.

That would-be's are relevant to the final opinion is explicit. The last passage quoted from Peirce's account of Royce (8.104) itself refers to the ultimate end of inquiry as a possibility. Thus, he characterizes it as something that "could . . . be realized." Other passages also support the application of the idea of possibility, of a conditional completion of inquiry. For instance, in a defense of what Carus had called his "social theory of reality," Peirce insists that he "never anticipated that anybody would urge" that "the real is the idea in which the community ultimately settles down." He says that

> we cannot be quite sure that the community ever will settle down to an unalterable conclusion upon any given question. Even if they do so for the most part, we have no reason to think the unanimity will be quite complete . . . All that we are entitled to assume is in the form of a *hope* that such conclusion may be substantially reached concerning the particular questions with which our inquiries are busied. (6.610)

And he goes on to explain that the social theory of reality "inevitably leads to" tychism. The final opinion, then, may be understood as an ideal limit, but also as an object of hope, which implies envisaged (although not therefore actualized) actuality. Further, the object is subject to tychism, which is to say that inevitable actual departures from law conflict with what is hoped for, with final unanimity. I take this to imply that the aim of inquiry is an ideal limit, which is a possibility, although not a real or actualizable possibility and which also regulates an actual inexhaustible process of convergence.

Other explicit evidence of the relevance of generals or would-be's to the final opinion appears in a 1905 paper, "What Pragmatism Is." Peirce's comments here also lean toward the notion that the final opinion is both ideal and a condition that functions as an actuality. Explaining his conception of reality, Peirce says that "according to the adopted definition of 'real,' the state of things which will be believed in that ultimate opinion is real. But, for the most part, such opinions will be general" (5.430). Thus, the opinion does have an object; and this object is the referent, access to which depends on would-be's. The object of the end of inquiry is an object of inquiry that is a system rendered intelligible by virtue of its would-be's, its generals or thirds. The object, then, must be the embodiments of these, which are resistant instances of the would-be's. Further, even though the objects are intelligible as would-be's or generals, they are not exhausted. There are necessarily more referents that embody these generals. If would-be's are possibilities, or ideals not exhausted by their instances, then inquiry does not terminate in some perfected state of knowledge – knowledge about itself – that ceases to change. Reality is dynamic, because the object of the final opinion is dynamic, as are Peirce's generals and as is his dynamical object understood as the final object of interpretation.

What I have just said construes the object of the final opinion as an actual inexhaustible actuality. The final object, then, is understood as an actual end converged on by a universal community of investigators. This end, however, is not severed from the notion of a final end that is an ideal. It is so as a would-be. And it is so as an end that is ideal. The final object is an ideal limit that is approached without being reached. Thus, on the one hand, it is conceived as a final object that is a regulative ideal for inquiry and, on the other hand, this unreachable object is a dynamic or actualizing reality.

It is appropriate to suggest, from a different perspective, further support for the idea of the bridge between the final opinion as an ideal and as an inexhaustible actuality by considering briefly the notion of limits. The final opinion is a limiting point for the convergence of inquiry.[22] I should like to suggest two ways of understanding limits conceived very roughly in mathematical terms.[23] One kind of limit is determinate and is illustrated by the series, $1 + 1/2 + 1/4 + 1/8 + 1/16$ ... as it approaches 2. The end, or what may be referred to as that on which the series converges, is determinate. However, it is unreachable in principle by any series of decreasing finite fractions. Another illustration is found in the series, $1 + 1/3 - 1/5 + 1/7$ ... as it approaches pi/4. This series, like that of the first illustration, never attains equality with the determinate end, pi/4. These determinate ends remain unreachable.

The second way of understanding a limit is illustrated by an asymptotic line that approaches a point in the infinite distance. This point

[22]Willard Quine has criticized Peirce's notion of convergence on an ideal limit as an improper use of a mathematical notion for metaphysical purposes. A response to this criticism will be offered in the next chapter.

[23]The two ways of understanding limits were suggested to me by Emily Grosholz. My interpretation and use of these are my own extensions of her account, and anything misleading in what I say is not her responsibility.

as an end is not a determinate concept insofar as it is conceived in terms of infinity. It is not definable prior to its approximation. It is only determinate as a limit infinitely remote. The point approximated is never reached, and may then be regarded as receding. It is this second kind of limit that is ordinarily associated with Peirce's final opinion, and properly so because he himself refers to limits of approximations as limits approached asymptotically. However, what I have been pressing is the idea that he wanted both conceptions of limit as operative conditions for understanding how inquiry is founded, even though it includes deviations from a linear process aimed at a final end. The end is determinate but only ideally and without the envisagement of a state that will be perfectly known at some future time. It is like pi/4 in that if it *were* reached, something completely definite would be realized; but this is only an ideal that cannot be formulated and reached at any assignable time. Further, the series of steps toward the End itself may be pictured as like the series in the illustration insofar as negative fractions are analogous to departures from regularities, or instances of spontaneity, in nature. And, with respect to its nonactualizability, the pi/4 series is at the same time like the indefinite point that is only approximated asymptotically.

Let us return to this issue by seeing it in terms of epistemological and metaphysical idealism versus realism. It may be said that Peirce held an epistemological idealism with respect to the evolution of knowledge projected toward a convergence in the future. In turn, he held a metaphysical realism with respect to the status, origin, and destiny of the condition of knowledge, or the condition of the idea of a final object. This condition is what is real in his system, which, previously called a residue-reality, is more precisely understood as the condition that is manifest in a residue-resistance that falls under the category of Secondness. It is the condition of constraints that are not internal to the system within which inquiry takes place. The terminus of thought, as a regulative ideal, is, in objective idealists' terms, mind-like, insofar as it is a fully rational system, a system marked as essentially exhibitive of thought. Yet, as an ideal, it is not actualizable, and in that sense, it is an indeterminately final opinion. To reemphasize, not from the standpoint of an epistemology or logic of inquiry – rather, from the standpoint of phenomenology and the metaphysical speculation that follows from it – the other two categories are not overcome. Thus, Peirce is a metaphysical realist in the sense of realism presupposed at the beginning of this discussion. There is something real that is independent of thought in general, that is, with respect to thought as the intelligible mediating structuring of experience. What is independent of thought in general is the dynamism that compels the growth of law, or the evolution of thought.

To conclude this section, let me briefly summarize my reasons for proposing that Peirce leaned toward a metaphysical realism with respect to his envisaged architectonic. And let me then suggest a fundamental problem that this proposal raises and the direction that needs to be taken to respond to the problem. I have tried to show that there are at least as many passages in Peirce's writings that affirm some form of realism as there are passages in which he claims allegiance to idealism. In saying that matter is effete mind, he simply follows through with his conception that matter is rigid law, and this does not guarantee that he is an idealist. The discussions of perceptual judgment indicate that Peirce regarded percepts as having a form of externality or independence from mind. The role of the dynamical object also affects Peirce's view of percepts as well as an insistence on a condition that is interpretation-independent and thus mind-independent. Further, generals or would-be's are also realities and are crucial to Peirce's opposition to nominalism and his avowed commitment to scholastic realism. Peirce's conceptions of evolution and tychism suggest that the cosmos sustains an inevitable bit of Secondness or unintelligibility. And this increment of unintelligibility is projected into the infinite long run. Thus, the end of inquiry is an ideal, a regulative ideal justifying continued attempts to bring the results of inquiries together for a community of investigators. And the unintelligible increment manifest under the category of Secondness serves to ground the particular directions that inquiries take. Thus, the referent of this ideal, when understood from the standpoint of metaphysics, is dynamic. The ideal is itself a would-be, or system of generals, which, as operative in the cosmos, are dynamic. As such, they do not escape the constraints or compulsive conditioning of their referent, the dynamical object. Thus, rather than being interpreted as a metaphysical idealist and an epistemological realist, Peirce might well be thought of as an epistemological idealist and a metaphysical, evolutionary realist.

The fundamental problem that this interpretation of Peirce raises concerns what more can be said about the reality-residue that sustains the mind-independence on the part of the condition that constrains thought as it aims at convergence on an ideal finality. In an important respect, nothing more can be said, because to say it would be to shape it in terms of the thought that it resists. It may, however, be approached and brought into a more refined focus.

The first step in refining it is to concentrate on the object of the final opinion. In what way does it serve as the condition of the residue-resistance that sustains the indeterminacy of the opinion or the system of interpretation that would be final if it were reached? The opinion in question, as an actualizable, complete interpretation is not a real possibility. Rather than calling it the "final opinion," perhaps we should call it the "finalizing opinion." It is an ideal limit that is regulative, inspiring heuristically the continued pursuit of inquiry. Yet the residue-resistance is actualizable and indeed actualized from moment to moment in time. This residue-resistance exhibits the object that compels inquiry in one way or another.

In keeping with the extent to which the discussion has become increasingly speculative, let me propose another way of forming the picture of what Peirce may have in mind. One could find an analogy between the final opinion conceived as the dynamical object and Plato's account of the final goal of dialectical thinking. Whether the goal is pictured as The Good or as The One Itself, the analogy consists in relating these to Peirce's condition of extralinguistic and extraconceptual conditions for constraints on thought. Both Plato's and Peirce's conditions of knowledge function as normative conditions and effective compulsions and resistances relevant to our thinking. They are not themselves analyzable. Yet they are conceived as the necessary conditions of whatever is analyzable and knowable. Further, there is a kind of access we have to them insofar as we encounter their effects in constraints on our efforts. We have clues to their ways of affecting us through the ways we are pushed or resisted. No clue, however, provides certainty, because thinking is fallible and future constraints and propulsions may be signs of originative forces in reality that is dynamic.

In order to refine further the way this dynamic residue is related to the thought with which it interacts, we need to turn to what Peirce refers to as his *synechism*, which is the foundation of his pragmaticism and, I think, of his evolutionary realism. We shall find that synechism affirms the essential role of continuity and that his conception of continuity must depend on his analysis of infinitesimals. If continuity is constitutive of thought, as Peirce insists in his attribution of continuity to generals or would-be's, then the residue that may compel and sometimes redirect generals or thought – thereby serving as a condition of the evolution of law and even of Platonic Forms – must be located in the infinitesimals that inexhaustively fill continua. This proposal for an account of Peirce's synechism leads us to the next section of this chapter.

Spontaneity, Synechism, and Evolution: The Realism at the Foundation of Pragmaticism

One way to enter the topic of Peirce's synechism – a way that is integral to Peirce's speculative grounding for the distinct branches or sciences of philosophy – is through his account of evolution. At the basis of this account is his conception of spontaneity, which is a conception that raises problems for the view that continuity underlies all objects and events. As was suggested at the end of the preceding section, the reconciliation of spontaneity with continuity should tie together the various facets of the envisaged architectonic.

In a paper that, it seems to me, has not been given sufficient acknowledgment by Peirce scholars, "The Doctrine of Necessity Examined," Peirce offers a penetrating argument against the extreme form in which creativity in evolution may be denied (6.35–65). In developing his argument, Peirce's characterization of his own view suggests principles with which he constructs his conception of agapastic, cosmic evolution. I shall not review Peirce's argument in detail. It should be enough to highlight certain parts of the argument in order to show that Peirce did not introduce the idea of agape as an afterthought and that he saw agape as a principle necessary to any viable alternative to determinism.

The Attack on Necessitarianism

The argument is directed toward all forms of metaphysical determinism that conceive the universe as a whole to be proceeding according to rigid law. These laws are regularities that are reversible, that is, that permit deductions about the past and, by deductive predicting, the future. He describes such determinisms with reference to the formula:

The state of things existing at any time, together with certain immutable laws, completely determine the state of things at every other time (for a limitation to *future* time is indefensible). Thus, given the state of the universe in the original nebula, and given the laws of mechanics, a sufficiently powerful mind could deduce from these data the precise form of every curlicue of every letter I am now writing. (6.37)

Although Peirce does not make clear just how extensive is his conception of necessitarianism or what I have called *determinism*, his conception of necessitarianism is not limited to a determinism that affirms efficient causation and rejects or ignores final causation, or teleological determination. For what supports predictability is the principle that the data to be predicted can be deduced from knowledge of laws and circumstances. Thus, a sufficiently informed and powerful mind could refer to teleological causes or ends in order to predict by deducing what has happened and what will happen. This form of necessitarianism, I think, may be included in what Peirce calls "anancastic theory of evolution," or *anancasm*, when, in the last paper of the series of which the present one is second, he reviews three forms of theories of evolution. Anancasm assumes that evolution proceeds according to a logical development of ideas already established; thus, if this kind of logic is what Peirce in another place accuses Hegel of affirming – a "wooden" logic – then this theory belongs to the necessitarianism that Peirce attacks.

Peirce's argument against this view turns on two kinds of reasons: an attack on the assumptions that underlie the determinist position and an appeal to observation of what science encounters in applying its hypotheses to the world. In short, one of the key attacks on determinists' assumptions is the assertion that necessitarians postulate their principle on a hope that the postulate is true. A hope is not a proof. Most telling is his argument that the necessitarians' assumption commits them to the view that the whole system of laws and the particular consequences of them – including all the diversity and specificity of events and all the arbitrary variations of the laws and their variations – "were introduced in one dose, in the beginning, if there was a beginning, and that the variety and complication of nature has always been just as much as it is now" (6.57). The necessitarian thinks this presupposition is necessary if the universe is intelligible. However, Peirce counters that the universe is more intelligible on his own hypothesis, which holds that "diversification, the specification, has been continually taking place" (ibid.). This counter is tied to his positive reasons for affirming the hypothesis that chance or spontaneity is real or active in the universe.

There are two kinds of observations to which Peirce appeals. Both of these support his contention that his affirmation of spontaneity offers a more cogent explanatory hypotheses than does his opponent if one takes into account the observation of what goes on in the universe day by day. One kind of observation consists of noting the deviations from regularities, the lack of exactness, expected in experimental results. "Try to verify any law of nature, and you will find that the more precise your observations, the more certain they will be to show irregular departures from the law" (6.46). The other kind of observation consists of noting that there is everywhere growth and increasing complexity. In opposition to necessitarians, Peirce thinks that the spontaneity hypothesis has a kind of explanatory power of its own.

By thus admitting pure spontaneity or life as a character of the universe, acting always and everywhere though restrained within narrow bounds by law, producing infinitesimal departures from law continually, and great ones with infinite infrequency, I account for all the variety and diversity of the universe, in the only sense in which the really *sui generis* and new can be said to be accounted for. . . . variety can spring only from spontaneity. (6.59)

Mechanical necessity excludes the idea that newness can spring up here and there throughout time – as Peirce points out, any variety would have had to be fixed from the beginning of time. On the postulate of necessitarianism, irregularity in the course of time is unintelligible.

But my hypothesis of spontaneity does explain irregularity, in a certain sense; that is, it explains the general fact of irregularity, though not, of course, what each lawless event is to be. At the same time, by thus loosening the bond of necessity, it gives room for the influence of another kind of causation, such as seems to be operative in the mind in the formation of associations. (6.60)

This last reference to another kind of causation must be understood within the context of the whole essay and the subsequent papers in the series. The kind of causation, which seems operative in the formation of associations, is evident in generalization, in "the tendency to form habits" (ibid.). In the subsequent paper, Peirce discusses the law of mind, which concerns the spread of ideas as they influence and are influenced by ideas in their past and future. The relevance of this paper for Peirce's synechism or his insistence on continuity will be addressed later. Before turning to Peirce's explicit defense of synechism, however, the role of the attack on determinism in the development of his theory of evolution needs to be pursued.

The theory of evolution is called *agapasticism,* or the theory that growth and diversity are the outcomes of evolutionary love. Evolutionary love is also called *agape,* which, of course, is the stem for the term *agapasticism* and other variants. As will be shown in more detail in a moment, the term refers to an agency that serves as a source of spontaneity and that nourishes it for the sake of whatever it creates. Peirce's concentrated discussion of this view in the 1890s series of articles in the *Monist* appears in the last of the series. And the term *agape* is for the most part limited to this article. The earlier articles paved the way for it, however, and we can find anticipations of the principle of agape in the argument with the determinists. The conception of something in the universe that functions in the way Peirce describes agape, then, is not limited to this essay. It certainly is implicit in at least two of the articles in the series, as I shall show in what follows. Thus, in response to the objection that the place of agape in Peirce's philosophy is insignificant because he only mentions it by name in "Evolutionary Love" seems to me to be beside the point.[24] Let me add here that what is presumed to be the Christian religious origin of the term is also beside the point, because the characterization of agape and the conceptual advantages it has as a hypothesis for interpreting evolution can be offered without reference to Christianity. I think the

[24]This objection was made to me orally by Christian Kloesel and indirectly by Charles Hartshorne. Kloesel's remarks were made in connection with his reading of my paper, in "Eros and Agape in Creative Evolution: A Peircean Insight," *Process Studies* 4, no. 1 (Spring 1975), pp. 11–25. This paper develops for different purposes some of the points in the present discussion.

logic of Peirce's discussion of it is essentially neutral in this respect, although he does view agape in terms of a rhetoric that includes religious terminology at various moments in his discussion.

There are four points at which agape is suggested in "The Doctrine of Necessity Examined." The first and second have not been mentioned explicitly in my brief account of the highlights of Peirce's argument. However, they are evidently both consistent with and appropriate to his attack on determinism and his defense of the spontaneity hypothesis. The first and most explicit suggestion occurs when he says that there "probably in nature is 'some agency' by which complexity and diversity is increased" (6.58). It is important to notice that Peirce refers to some agency as a condition that is, or is related to, the referent for his term *chance*. This is not necessarily to equate spontaneity with an agency. It does show, however, that Peirce recognized a source or originating condition associated with irregularity. Thus, he makes clear that he thinks of chance neither negatively, as the absence of cause in a possible causal relation, nor as a passive occurrence. The idea of an instance of spontaneity as a manifestation of an agency indicates that chance or spontaneity is or at least may be inseparable from an originative condition that is in some sense responsible for its own action. It is an activity that is its own source. What kind of source it is is not pursued in the argument against the determinists. Instead, I am suggesting, the character of this source is pursued in the last paper on evolutionary love.

The second point at which agape is anticipated is found in Peirce's statement that his spontaneitist hypothesis "leaves room for another kind of causation such as seems to be operative in the mind" and such that "the uniformity of nature could have been brought about" (6.60). This statement clearly refers to a context in which spontaneity contributes to evolution. And it does so in the way mental action occurs when ideas evolve. Thus, again, the idea of a special kind of causal agency underlies Peirce's conception of chance.

The third anticipation occurs in the claim that his hypothesis inserts mind as a self-intelligible thing that is the place of "the fountain of existence" (6.61). It is significant, I think, that Peirce here says that mind as self-intelligible is the "place" of the fountain of existence, which is not to say that it is the fountain itself. Thus, more than the agency of mind functions in the origin of new intelligibility within evolution. That there is more than mind, or a finite mental agent, seems evident in Peirce's conception of agape as a unique causal source that can act only in context in which it transcends itself. I shall say more about this in a moment.

The fourth anticipation of agape is his proposal that his hypothesis makes room for a principle of the tendency to form habits, or for a kind of spontaneity that is to some degree regular (6.63). The last statement is important because it introduces the idea of lawfulness as inseparable from spontaneity, which is one of the conditions under which agape functions. These points must now be seen in the light of a consideration of Peirce's discussion in the article on evolutionary love.

Agape

The overall design of "Evolutionary Love" depends on a discussion of three kinds of theories of evolution: tychasticism, anancasticism, and agapasticism. It should be mentioned that Peirce describes three theories of evolution in the first article of the *Monist* series "The Architecture of Theories." These are: (1) the Darwinian theory, with which he associates that of Herbert Spencer, presumably because Peirce regards it as depending on mechanical principles, but which he also believes to be illogical so that, presumably, he does not give the Spencerian variation on Darwinian theory a status as one of *the* three theories of evolution; (2) the Lamarckian theory, which Peirce says supposes that there are insensible increments of growth in individuals because of effort and exercise; and (3) the theory of Clarence King, which interprets evolution in terms of environmental conditions and cataclysmic geological changes (6.13–17). The second and third types of theory do not correspond directly to the second and third in the later article. The difference in classification seems to be the result of a difference of purpose; in the earlier essay, he is not concerned with relating the theories reviewed to his own theory, but simply with describing several views of evolution that, he thinks, attempt the kind of explanation appropriate for "accounting for the laws of nature and for uniformity in general" (6.13).

In "Evolutionary Love," the first kind of theory discussed is represented mainly by the Darwinian view, which Peirce couples with developments in political science and physics (6.287–97). It views evolution as proceeding "heedlessly," by discontinuities appearing as mutations or chance variations with no reason whatsoever. Generalized, the idea is that chance, "fortuitous events," may result in law (6.297). Chance, however, for the tychistic conception of evolution is not linked with any direction or end. The struggle for existence results in the sustaining of some organisms and the decline and extinction of others. And Peirce sees this account as supporting the idea that greed is celebrated in the economic arena, which again supports an ethics of self-interest – "the Gospel of Greed" (6.294). In spite of Peirce's vigorous opposition to this view of how evolution occurs, it is a component (but only a component) in his own theory. As he says later, in 1898, "I object to having my metaphysical system as a whole called Tychism. For although tychism does enter it, it only enters as subsidiary to that which is really, as I regard it, the characteristic of my doctrine, namely that I chiefly insist upon continuity or Thirdness" (6.202).

The second type of theory of evolution, anancasticism, is deterministic. "Diametrically opposed to evolution by chance are those theories which attribute all progress to an inward necessary principle, or other form of necessity" (6.298). Peirce refers to the necessity appealed to as mechanical. He probably had in mind his earlier classification offered in "The Architecture of Theories," where he cites Herbert Spencer as holding a view according to which evolution is explained by mechanical principles. Thus, whether inner or external, the necessity works so that evolution proceeds through a succession of events from which the line of development cannot deviate. Nothing is due to chance. And, if we consider the earlier article, we see that on the mechanistic account, the law of the conservation of energy, which Peirce attributes to Spencer's view, "is equivalent to the proposition that all operations governed by mechanical laws are reversible; so that an immediate corollary from it is that growth is not explicable by those laws, even if they be not violated in the process of growth" (6.14). The irreversibility of evolutionary developments is central to Peirce's own theory.

The third type of evolution affirms the presence of a form of love that plays a role in development. Peirce introduces his account of this third theory by relating it to the view of Lamarck (6.299). He states that Lamarckians add to mechanical causes factors including effort directed toward ends — what he calls "energetic projaculation" by which "new elements of form are first created" (6.300). The new elements are then established and brought into harmony with their contexts by habit. He then adds that "this account of Lamarckian evolution coincides with the general description of the action of love," thus laying the basis for his own agapasticism. "Three modes of evolution have thus been brought before us: evolution by fortuitous variation, evolution by mechanical necessity, and evolution by creative love" (6.302). The third mode, agapasm — Peirce's name for the mode or process is *agapasm* — incorporates the other two. Evolution occurs through phases and with a propulsion toward perfection (a characteristic of anancasm), and its changes arise from unprecedented, unnecessitated variations (a characteristic of tychism). Agapasm is evolution that includes chance and necessity and something else: it is the synthesis of chance and necessity, which is not reducible to either or to both simply added together. Agapasm is a synthesis that adds an increment of sympathy or tendency toward an expanding continuity that is made possible by the introduction of an arbitrariness that supports "vital freedom which is the breath of the spirit of love" (6.305). Peirce's view is made somewhat clearer in his application of his brief account of agapasm to the "historical development of human thought":

The tychastic development of thought, then, will consist in slight departures from habitual ideas in different directions indifferently, quite purposeless and quite unconstrained whether by outward circumstances or by force of logic . . . The anancastic development of thought will consist of new ideas adopted without foreseeing whither they tend, but having a character determined by causes either external to the mind, . . . or internal to the mind as logical developments of ideas already accepted, such as generalizations. The agapastic development of thought is the adoption of certain mental tendencies, not altogether heedlessly, as in tychasm, nor quite blindly by the mere force of circumstances of logic, as in anancasm, but by an immediate attraction for the idea itself, whose nature is divined before the mind possesses it, by the power of sympathy, that is, by virtue of the continuity of mind. (6.307)

It is significant that Peirce understands anancasm to be a process in which development is necessary without being purposive – "The character which distinguishes it from agapasm is its purposelessness" (6.312). In contrast, "The agapastic development of thought should, if it exists, be distinguished by its purposive character, this purpose being the development of an idea" (6.315). A comment about this account of anancasm and its implications for a teleological understanding of evolution may help sharpen Peirce's own agapasticism.

Presumably, Peirce characterizes anancasm as purposeless because progression is inevitable, being necessitated from one step to the next. It seems, then, that according to my claim that anancasm covers teleology as well as mechanism, Peirce considers teleological processes to be purposeless. External circumstances compel development; internal conditions predestine development. And if my interpretation of anancasm and teleology is correct, it is understandable why Peirce reserves the conception of purposiveness for his own *developmental* teleology. "Developmental teleology," is referred to in the preceding, third, article in the series, "The Law of Mind." In anticipation of our consideration of that essay, we may note here that developmental teleology is the view that there are purposes that may evolve spontaneously. Applying his law of mind to human personality, Peirce says that a personality is "some kind of coordination or connection of ideas," which "has to be lived in time," and which may grow:

But the word coordination implies somewhat more than [momentary apprehension or self-consciousness]; it implies a teleological harmony in ideas, and in the case of personality this teleology is more than a mere purposive pursuit of a predeterminate end; it is a developmental teleology. . . . A general idea . . . is already determinative of acts in the future to an extent to which it is not now conscious. . . . Were the ends of a person already explicit, there would be no room for development or growth, for life. . . . The mere carrying out of predetermined purposes is mechanical. (6.156–7)

Given these remarks as a framework for Peirce's agapasm, it may be inferred that when he insists on the absence of purpose in anancasm and the inclusion of it in agapasm, he conceives of purpose as self-determining action.

Self-determining action is fundamental to evolutionary love. We can now see why he reaches for a condition that transcends determinism and heedless arbitrariness. Thus, if we return to the quasi-theological setting through which Peirce approaches his theory, we can see how the idea of agape serves as this condition. A condition that is permissive of future growth is needed, and this condition must not negate any tendency that may seem at odds with it. The directedness of the condition, then, may be characterizable – metaphorically or analogically – in terms of the notion of a god that loves its creatures with no prior expectations concerning what fulfills that love. It is an overflowing love, which is not to be understood as the kind of love represented by eros. Eros is dependent on striving for a perfection that lures an agency or a process that is driven toward that perfection. If evolution were understood as a manifestation of a condition characterizable as evolutionary love in the sense in which love is a form of eros, then evolution would be predestined by the end, the perfection, sought by eros. This would be a form of anancasm. And evolution would be "purposeless" – from the perspective of that which is in process. If evolution is open to creative change, change not flowing from some form of necessity, external or internal, then it must be conditioned by something that is open to what it does not determine and which may turn in a direction not already determinative of the condition itself. It must surrender its perfection for the sake of its creatures, giving them an independence that may conflict with that perfection and that may transmute the process into something quite different, even ugly.

Quoting Henry James, Sr., Peirce says, creative love "must be reserved only for what intrinsically is most bitterly hostile and negative to itself" (6.287). Yet there is an underlying optimism about the outcome, even if it has its ugly moments. A bit later, Peirce says, "Love, recognizing germs of loveliness in the hateful, gradually warms it into life, and makes it lovely" (6.289). Whether the optimism commits Peirce, after all, to a necessitarianism in the sense that harmony must win out in the long run, it seems clear that Peirce's figurative picture of agapasm offers the insight that whatever the condition of evolution is, it must be dynamic and self-determining. Only thus can spontaneity be a real ingredient in the universe – without being simply the absence of necessity, regularity, or order, or without being simply a condition of arbitrariness. Spontaneity, in evolution, is inseparable from, and contributes to, the growth of law.

Thus these two elements, at least, exist in nature, Spontaneity and Law. Now, to ask that Spontaneity should be explained is illogical, and indeed absurd. . . . But to explain a thing is to show how it may have been a result of something else. Law, then, ought to be explained as a result of Spontaneity. Now the only way to do that is to show in some way that law may have been a product of *growth*, of evolution. (MS 950.00010–11)

And this is what Peirce considers himself to have done insofar as agapasticism has the general explanatory power of giving us a figuratively expressed hypothesis that locates not only law but also its evolution. "But my hypothesis of spontaneity does explain irregularity, in a certain sense; that is, it explains the general fact of irregularity, though not, of course, what each lawless event is to be" (6.60). However, we still face the question of how this view of irregularity or departure from uniformity and thus from continuity can be reconciled with the other side of Peirce's metaphysics, synechism, or the doctrine that makes continuity essential to intelligibility.

Spontaneity and Continuity

Access Through "The Law of Mind" As suggested earlier, an entry into this topic can be gained through Peirce's third article in the *Monist* series, "The Law of Mind." I should like to use this essay as the frame of reference for proposing a way of understanding Peirce's conception of spontaneity and continuity. Although "The Law of Mind" preceded his account of evolutionary love, Peirce had already conceived of at least one essential ingredient of his theory of evolution. Not only is this evident in his previous article in which he argued for the role of chance rather than strict necessitarianism in evolution, but at the beginning of "The Law of Mind," he introduces the term *tychism*. And he adds that he had shown "that *tychism* must give birth to an evolutionary cosmology" (6.102). His intent in this article, however, is to focus on the other dimension of his speculative system: "In doing this, I shall for the time drop my tychism out of view, in order to allow a free and independent expansion of another conception signalized in my first *Monist* paper as one of the most indispensable to philosophy, though it was not there dwelt upon; I mean the idea of continuity" (6.103). Peirce's reference to the first article, "The Architecture of Theories," probably is specifically to his discussion of the law of habit, which concerns uniformities of phenomena that provide the generals. As we have seen, generals constitute the intelligible structure of the world, and they exemplify continuities. In any case, in "The Law of

Mind," Peirce explains what he means by synechism, which, as was pointed out earlier, is crucial to what he believes supports pragmaticism and is the most apt label for his metaphysics, with the proviso, of course, that we understand it in conjunction or in integration with his tychism, support for which is offered in the argument against necessitarians.

Synechism, Peirce says, is the "tendency to regard continuity, in the sense in which I shall define it, as an idea of prime importance in philosophy" (6.103).[25] The law of mind, the referent of the title of this article, then, is a specification of synechism. This can be seen in the necessary connection between it and the relation of one idea or mental phenomenon to another. This relation is continuity. I should like to focus on Peirce's conception of the continuity that threads its way through thought first by examining his analysis of the activity of consciousness through a series of intervals. I shall then summarize what I take to be Peirce's conclusion about the most adequate theory of continuity, at least at this stage of his career when he is explicitly concerned with continuity as a metaphysical notion. Later, we shall turn to some developments in his mathematical discussions of continuity that, I think, confirm what he says in the context of metaphysics in "The Law of Mind." Let me emphasize that the task at hand will be undertaken with benefit of only relatively scant mathematical considerations. However, even if more extended attention were given to such considerations, we would still face the need to apply the mathematical base for Peirce's theory of continuity by interpreting and attending to the translation from the technical language of mathematics into a descriptive language that is relevant to cosmology or a metaphysics of evolution. Of concern for our purposes is what Peirce says interpretively about the mathematical underpinning insofar as it can be understood as an account of the relation of chance to the uniformities that identify regularities – that is, of the role of spontaneity in synechism.[26]

---

[25] Peirce later (1902) defines *synechism* for Baldwin's *Dictionary of Philosophy and Psychology* in the same way. (See 6.169.).

[26] In case someone objects that Peirce's mathematics is outdated – the idea of infinitesimals, for instance, no longer viable, having been discarded in favor of the method of limits – I should emphasize two points. First, with respect to the favoring of the method of limits, Peirce was aware of this preference among mathematicians and explains why he refuses to dispense with the idea of infinitesimals. Interestingly, the conception of infinitesimals recently has been taken seriously again by some mathematicians. Nevertheless, his concern, it should be kept in mind, is not with pure mathematics but with the application of certain concepts, treated by mathematicians as well as other philosophers, to processes in the actual world. Second, my own concern is not with assessing Peirce's answers to issues in mathematics but with his view of evolution and what he considered fundamental in understanding both continuity and discontinuity.

In turning to Peirce's discussion of the law of mind and its exemplification in conscious experience we should remember that Peirce is not interested in limiting what he says about mental activity to individual or subjective expressions of mind. As has been argued earlier, his conception of mind is broader than the range of data limited to private or subjective conscious processes. The discussion of synechism in terms of mental activity, specifically, the law of mind, is a discussion of the fundamental structure of the cosmos. What, then, is that law?

"Logical analysis applied to mental phenomena shows that there is but one law of mind, namely, that ideas tend to spread continuously and to affect certain others which stand to them in a peculiar relation of affectibility" (6.104). As they spread, they lose intensity but gain in generality and in being "welded with other ideas." (We shall note later the use of the idea of welding in one of Peirce's mathematical definitions of *continuity*.) How do ideas spread? How can an idea be passed on from one moment to the next? How can ideas be distinct and at the same time be carried into the future and be effective for other ideas? Specifically, Peirce asks, "But what can it mean to say that ideas wholly past are thought of at all, any longer?" (6.106); "How can a past idea be present?" (6.109).

Peirce's answer is that we must be directly aware of ideas in the immediate past. If we were not, we would be cut off from them. For if one appeals to the conception of vicarious ideas in the present standing for past ideas, there still would be a gap between present and past, between the copy, which is in the present, and the original, which is in the past. Further, one's entire knowledge of the past could only be vicarious or a "delusion." We must, then, be directly aware of the past as it recedes, and this means that the past "can only be going, infinitesimally past, less past than any assignable date" (6.109). "We are . . . forced to say that we are immediately conscious through an infinitesimal interval of time" (6.110). Thus, we are led to a concentrated examination of the experience of being conscious through a flow of time that must be understood in terms of infinitesimal components.

We have seen that Peirce's conception of temporal continuity in conscious experience is anticipated in what he says about thought in his early cognition papers.[27] Perception and cognition in general arise in a continuum. This idea is crucial to Peirce's relatively early struggles with accounting for the basis of thought. It may be recalled that in "Questions Concerning Certain Faculties Claimed for Man" (5.213–63), Peirce proposed the image of an inverted triangle that is being

---

[27]The following review of Peirce's analysis of the consciousness of an interval of time is based on and for the most part follows part of a discussion offered in my "In and Out of Peirce's Percepts."

dipped into water. The example is used to show why he denies that there are first cognitions, or self-evident judgments, intuitions, supposedly serving as a foundation for knowledge.[28] The horizontal lines on the triangle appearing at the surface of the water represent cognitions, the most recent being the liveliest and being pictured by the longest line. Peirce contends that there is no limit to the number of lines that "can be assigned at finite distances below it and below one another." Thus, "it is not true that there must be a first" cognition. And "cognition arises by a *process* of beginning, as any other change comes to pass" (5.263). It is clear neither how one cognition is related to another (granted that there is no point at which there is necessarily another different, previous cognition) nor at what level a line on the triangle is a process that is precognitive rather than cognitive. In part, at least, the discussion in "The Law of Mind" provides Peirce's mature attack on the latter part of the question. And an understanding of cognitive processes can be advanced by attending to his analysis of conscious perception in his account of how past ideas can be effective in the present (6.107–11).

What is at issue is the connection between a past idea and what is immediately present to consciousness in its immediacy, that is, what is present to consciousness at the instant of a present moment. Peirce says that consciousness does not embrace a present idea in a finite interval of time. If it did, we could have no direct access to past ideas, for each idea would be contained within limits. He insists that "the present is connected with the past by a series of real infinitesimal steps, and through an infinitesimal interval" (6.109–11). During such an interval, "we directly perceive the temporal sequence of its beginning, middle, and end . . . in the way of an immediate feeling" (6.110–11). It should be emphasized that Peirce here analyzes the relations of ideas in continua found only in perceptual experience. Thus, he says: "In an infinitesimal interval we directly perceive the temporal sequence," and he refers to related intervals that are immediate perceptions embraced by "an immediate perception of the temporal sequence" (6.111). However, if continuity is prescinded from its role in the analysis of perception, we can consider Peirce's discussion to apply to higher-order experiences or to reality itself. In any case, it is obvious that the account depends on Peirce's conception of infinitesimals. I shall not try to discuss this difficult conception in detail but, at best, offer a few suggestions.[29] The series of suggestions concerns some

---

[28]Murray Murphey's account of the development of Peirce's thought provides a close examination of the way Peirce's thinking about continuity affected his attempts to characterize cognition in the early paper and in "The Law of Mind," *The Development of Peirce's Philosophy* (Cambridge, Mass.: Harvard University Press, 1961).

[29]The conclusions to be proposed about continuity as the foundation of synechism, will

of the features of Peirce's analysis of infinitesimal intervals of perceptual consciousness that are evident in the passages from which the
quotations have been taken. Let me quote Peirce at length, adding
commentary at various points.

In an infinitesimal interval we directly perceive the temporal sequence of [the
instants of] its beginning, middle, and end – not, of course, in the way of
recognition, for recognition is only of the past, but in the way of immediate
feeling. (6.111)

It should be kept in mind that what is being analyzed is what is conscious. Presumably, there may be a preconscious process from which
or within which intervals of conscious perception arise. Further, it
must be emphasized that the intervals are infinitesimal. Finally, I suggest that the directly perceived temporal sequence to which Peirce
refers functions with Firstness as its prescindable background.

"Now upon this interval follows another, whose beginning is the
middle of the former and whose middle is the end of the former."
This second interval continues immediate perception insofar as it is
more than pure Firstness. With the second interval, the intrusion of
Secondness seems to be assured, for difference is the basis for the
relation of the first to the second interval of consciousness.

"Here, we have an immediate perception of the temporal sequence,
of its beginning, middle, and end, or say of the second, third, and
fourth instants." An instant, as Peirce says a few lines later, is a point
of time, each point representing a beginning, a middle, or an end.
The second interval is a condition for the introduction of temporal
sequence. The conception of instants and sequences obviously is based
on prescinding from the interval, for the transition from one interval
to another is not a transition over discrete units. Thus, Peirce is ana-
lyzing conscious perception so that he specifies its (prescinded) conditions. However, I think he makes clear that these conditions can be
recognized, by means of inferences, once perception continues in accord with future conditions consisting of later instants. Further, as
time continues, there is an insistency that exceeds the pure presence
of the immediate feeling.

From these two immediate perceptions, we gain a mediate, or inferential,
perception of the relation of all four instants. This mediate perception is ob-

be based in larger part on the analysis of consciousness of the past as an instance of
the law of mind. In addition, I shall draw some of my conclusions in light of a closely
argued consideration of Peirce's mature view of continuity offered by N. A. Brian
Noble in "Peirce's Definitions of Continuity and the Concept of Possibility," *Transactions of the Charles S. Peirce Society* 25, no. 2 (Spring 1989), pp. 149–74. He relies in
part on Vincent G. Potter's and Paul B. Shield's "Peirce's Definitions of Continuity,"
Transactions of the Charles S. Peirce Society 13, no. 1 (Winter 1977), pp. 20–34, which
also has been helpful to me.

jectively [inferentially], or as to the object represented, spread over the four instants; but subjectively, or as itself the subject of duration, it is completely embraced in the second moment (6.111).

When Peirce explains how he uses the term *instant*, as a point in time, he also says that *moment* means "an infinitesimal duration," which, I believe must have the same meaning as *interval*. With the entrance of mediate perception, we have inference and the origin of generality as it occurs according to the third category, that is, with some degree of definiteness of direction, and this implies an element of interpretation, because generality, though retaining some degree of indeterminacy, has sufficient definiteness to prompt interpretation. I omit the passage in which the meanings of the terms *instant* and *moment* are given.

If it is objected that, upon the theory proposed, we must have more than a mediate perception of the succession of the four instants, I grant it; for the sum of the two infinitesimal intervals is itself infinitesimal, so that it is immediately perceived. It is immediately perceived in the whole interval, but only mediately perceived [as prescindable] in the last two-thirds of the interval. Now, let there be an indefinite succession of these inferential acts of comparative perception, and it is plain that the last moment will contain objectively [as the object represented] the whole series. (6.111)

The last moment yields a perceptual, inferential experience that is spread objectively and thus concerned with "the object represented," or the semeiotic immediate object. Peirce continues, saying that when there is "a continuous flow of inference through a finite time," the result "will be a mediate objective consciousness of the whole time in the last moment." He is proposing by this analysis an account of the relation of felt temporal flow and the cognitive interpretation of this. The cognitive, mediate experience requires attending to past feelings, and imposing definiteness on them so that they can be compared, and this must occur as an interpretive act. At the same time, the "objective consciousness" of feelings is of a series of feelings marked by instants that distinguish intervals to be compared. Thus, the result is an inferential attending or perceptual judgment of an inferred object – "the object as represented."

Peirce's analysis not only depends on prescinding the conception of instants definable as *beginning, middle,* and *end;* most important, it also depends on the conception of infinitesimals, which constitute a genuine continuum. Peirce does not want to segment the experience of forming perceptual judgments into actual, discrete parts – a point to be emphasized in a moment. Abductions, or instances of spontaneity, we have seen, threaten to be or depend on discrete markings, or limits, between one part of experience and a subsequent, sometimes even unprecedented, idea. And so do the instants or points in time and, in turn, the intervals themselves that consist of moments of conscious perception. Thus, Peirce says at the beginning that these moments are infinitesimal and therefore consciousness is continuous. We face, then, a difficult issue concerning Peirce's conception of infinitesimals, which is integral to his theory of continuity in the 1890s. The relevance of these to the issue is obvious in Peirce's decision to provide a relatively long discussion of continuity immediately following the analysis we have just considered.

Continuity and Infinitesimals It is generally recognized that the theory of continuity was modified during Peirce's career, and that the version of it held in his later thought, at least when he wrote "The Law of Mind," is based chiefly on the theories of Kant and Aristotle, with the inclusion of both a qualified acceptance and a criticism of Cantor.[30] Relying on discussions outside as well as within "The Law of Mind," I shall only make a suggestion about what I believe is a crucial part of the theory as it bears on the way infinitesimals (applied metaphysically) compose continua. I think that changes in his thinking about mathematical continuity after 1908, the beginning of what Potter and Shields identify as the final period of his definitions of continuity, a period subsequent to the analyses in "The Law of Mind," do not affect the substance of what is suggested in "The Law of Mind" about continua for Peirce's view of evolution. Nevertheless, some post-1908 comments about continuity will be mentioned.

In commenting in 1903 on his definition that is included in 1898 in the *Century Dictionary*, the major issue with which we are concerned is articulated perhaps more clearly than at any other point in Peirce's writings insofar as his formulation is amenable to common sense and does not depend exclusively on mathematical concepts. We find that Peirce is working through a conception of continuity with reference to its constitution – that is, with reference to what might compose continua. Brian Noble pinpoints the issue when, as I understand him, he says that Peirce's treatment of continuity focuses on whether the components of a continuum are real possibilities regarded as possible *individuals* or instead are sheer possibilities, that is, are may-be's. And his thesis is that they are not the former. Continua are generals and require Thirdness. May-be's, however, would be firsts rather than thirds, unless they are mediated. Thus, I take Noble to assume that conditions must mediate may-be's (instances of Firstness) in order that

---

[30]Vincent G. Potter, S.J., and Paul B. Shields identify this stage in Peirce's view of continuity as the "Kantistic Period, 1895–1908"; it is one of four periods, the fourth being the "Post-Cantorian Period, 1908–1911"; see their "Peirce's Definitions of Continuity." I assume that the Kantistic period is the most relevant for understanding Peirce's thought about evolution.

may-be's function as would-be's, or real generals. Such mediating conditions would require interpretants. It then might be proposed that interpretants somehow functions as infinitesimal links between sheer possibilities. Whether or not sense can be made of this, however, Noble does not consider the function of infinitesimals in continua. Are they may-be's in triadic relations? Are they may-be's that are incipient would-be's? I believe they are the latter.

In any case the issue concerns Peirce's idea that any analysis that refers to discrete parts implies discontinuity, which is to imply breaks in the continuum at each place where a part is marked (made discrete). At such a point, intelligibility, or what is cognitively available, breaks down. Peirce indicates that there is discontinuity necessitated by the marking of parts when he states what it is that he prefers in Kant's definition of continuity. He says that Kant's definition "implies that a line, for example, contains no points until the continuity is broken by marking the points" (6.168). And he adds, "In accordance with this it seems necessary to say that a continuum, where it *is* continuous and unbroken, contains no definite parts; that its parts are created in the act of defining them and the precise definition of them breaks the continuity" (ibid.). At the same time, he draws on Aristotle. He says that according to "Aristotelicity" a continuum has "every point that is a limit to an infinite series of points that belong to the system" (1.66). This same idea is made more extensively in "The Law of Mind," where he says, "The property of Aristotelicity may be roughly stated thus: a continuum contains the end point belonging to every endless series of points which it contains. An obvious corollary is that every continuum contains its limits" (6.123).[31] We should notice also that he observes further that every real number is in a sense a limit of the series of numbers that indefinitely approximate to it. "Consequently, it is implied that between any two points an innumerable series of points can be taken" (6.124). However, "incommensurable numbers suppose an infinitieth place of decimals. . . . Thus, continuity supposes infinitesimal quantities." And in "adding and multiplying them the continuity must not be broken up" (6.125). This last quotation reinforces what was noted earlier, that in an unbroken continuum there are no points that are marked, and that it is broken when marked by points. (See 1.168, quoted earlier.)

I think that Peirce's latest descriptions of how parts may compose continuity also confirm the "Kantistic" component of his view, which was developed before 1908. Potter and Shields believe the crucial point

[31]This conception, I think, overlaps one of Dedekinds postulates, also influential on Peirce, that any point within a continuum that occurs after and prior to either extremity is an extremity either for the continuum up to that point or for the continuum after that point.

of Peirce's analysis in the final period lies in his reference to "the mode of connection between the parts," which "contributes to the nature of the whole."[32]

It is the mode of connection that constitutes a continuum, which makes it what it is. And this is to say that the *kind* of parts connected is what is unbroken in the continuum, for connections are relations, and if these are intelligible relations, then they are mediated and constitute generals. Peirce makes this point in a moment of self-criticism in which he claims to have blundered in "The Law of Mind" (6.174). A continuum, then, has its character as a general, and quantitative or metrical considerations are not definitive of whether something is a continuum, because metrical identifications are discrete and individualizing. It is with this in mind that I would qualify Noble's interpretation, agreeing that a continuum is not composed of individuals but suggesting that it is not may-be's but rather would-be's (generals) that make up the components of a continuum. Further, as Potter and Shields point out, Peirce adds to the Kantistic focus of his definition of *kind* the conception of parts that must be small enough to have "a uniform mode of immediate connection."[33] And this, Peirce says, drives him to "introduce the idea of time," which leads to the notion of continuity and commits him to circularity in the definition. Yet, he adds, to say that time is continuous is a standard by which time is understood (4.624). He seems to consider a conception of continuity to be prior to a conception of time – a priority that, we have seen, is the basis of his analysis of conscious perception in "The Law of Mind." The priority, however, seems to me to be a function of prescinding experiential continua. Thus, if the conception of continuity is not bound up with metrical considerations, which spatializes a continuum, then it is bound up with time. Yet to understand what it is for something temporal to be a continuum, one must prescind or consider what is presupposed. And this leads to the notion of infinitesimals, which merge temporal units, or moments, with spatially entertained units, or points.

Continuity, Spontaneity, and Realism Let me expand briefly on the way these perspectives on continuity are connected with Peirce's realism in affirming the necessity of including generals or would-be's as constitutive of the intelligibility of the universe. The relevance of these further remarks for this chapter will be evident in Peirce's 1902 characterization of continuity as the basis of his synechism (6.169, 170). In connection with his remark that mind may mark points in a continuum, we should note that it is mind, or the act of defining the parts,

---

[32]Potter and Shields, "Peirce's Definitions of Continuity," p. 30.
[33]Ibid.

that is responsible for marking points on a continuum. And this function that mind may perform fits precisely the idea that spontaneity, which is the paradigmatic manifestation of mind, may intrude in the uniformities evident in generals or laws and contribute to their growth, contrary to necessitarianism. And this is reinforced by his speculations about the "logic of the universe," where he says that the universe evolves from highest order continuity, a world of Platonic Ideas – which themselves evolve (6.191–6). However, unbroken continua preclude new laws, or new continua; the evolution of new laws must be conditioned by breaks in continua.

It is important to emphasize that in its role in synechism, the idea of continuity is for Peirce a presupposition of the idea of explanation, or put negatively, and in terms already emphasized throughout this book, the idea of continuity is a principle "to avoid the hypothesis that this or that is inexplicable" (6.171). Discontinuities as markable points or instants in which the continuum of a general is broken, are, in themselves, not explained. Yet with respect to the continuity that they break, they are relatable to larger contexts that are constituted by what is explicable. These contexts consist of the continuity that is broken and the evolved, originated continuity that follows the instance of spontaneity. (Hookway's explanation of Peirce on continuity makes the principle of nonexplicability central.) There is an intimate relationship between the instant of discontinuity and its continuous context. This is possible, I think, because the continuum is conceived of as constituted by infinitesimals. However, it seems to follow from what he says about infinitesimals that if we regard a break in a continuum as emerging from an infinitesimal, then the moment of spontaneity can be distinguished from something ultimate, which for Peirce is something inexplicable. The question of whether an instance of spontaneity is an inexplicable, ultimate condition is not relevant. It is law that wants explanation, not spontaneity. Further, an infinitesimal is not an ultimate, because it is not discrete. It is instead infinitely relatable with respect to what it is as a component of a kind or character that qualifies its continuum. As Peirce says, "The word infinitesimal is simply the Latin form of Infinitieth" (6.125). I suggest, then, that an infinitieth that is adjacent to a mark is relatable to something *other* than the property that up to the time of its occurrence characterized the continuous series, giving it its identity as this continuum rather than another. A moment of chance or spontaneity, then, occurs as a reaction within a continuum at a point that had been an infinitesimal and which, up to that point, had been a sheer possibility and a potentiality. Putting this point in the context of Noble's conclusions, it may be said that the moment of spontaneity in a continuum would be the moment at which a may-be, a first, is differentiated and brought into connection so that the sheer possibility, Firstness, is articulated and a would-be, a general, a third, emerges.

One of the key perspectives that Peirce brings to the attempt to understand infinitesimals is that they should be regarded positively rather than negatively; that is, they should not be regarded as absences of characterizable increments of a series. In saying this, I have in mind Peirce's critique of both Kant and Cantor, the former, according to Peirce, defining a continuum in such a way as to permit gaps and the latter defining it so that it permits the correlation of its elements with a series of discrete, quantitative units.

A continuum is composed neither of gaps nor an innumerable number of discrete individuals. "In adding and multiplying them [infinitesimal quantities] the continuity must not be broken up" (6.125). At the same time, infinitesimals grouped in a continuum are to be regarded as having some character. In other words, an infinitesimal is not a component that has an identity other than that of all the infinitesimals in the continuum in which it participates. And that identity is "located" in the connection between infinitesimals. Thus, in 1897, in discussing continua, Peirce says that "although it is true that a line is nothing but a collection of points of a particular mode of multiplicity, yet in it the individual identities of the units are completely merged, so that not a single one of them can be identified, even approximately, unless it happen to be a topically singular point, that is either an extremity or a point of branching, in which case there is a defect of continuity at that point" (4.219). The idea of completely merging, it may be noted, suggests the notion of welding mentioned earlier. The conception of all infinitesimals in a given continuum as having the same character is also made in his discussion in 1900 of infinitesimals, after he takes into account Dedekind's definition of an infinite collection. The relevance of Dedekind's definition is that it raises the question of what a part is. In relating his remarks about infinity and continuity to Dedekind, Peirce considers the notion of a collection as composed of individuals, which he characterizes as indivisible. He then goes on to discuss the way we may understand collections and multitudes that compose their members. He explains that he conceives of continua as composed of infinitesimals. If a line is taken as an example, points may be thought of as determinable on it, but they are for him at infinitesimal distances, and the points themselves are not distinguishable by correspondence with collections of individuals thought of as individual quantities (3.563–8). If the points were individuals, they would be distinguishable in the only three ways in which individuals can be distinct from one another: "For individuals can only be distinct from one another in three ways: First, by acts of reaction, immediate or mediate, upon one another; second, by having *per se* different qualities; and third, by being in one-to-one correspondence to individuals that are distinct from one another in one of the two first ways." An infinitesimal does not have a character in itself. Yet it is potentially characterizable in some way other than by the character of the continuum. Again, in 1900, he says that whatever is not determinate and as such cut out from a continuum is a possibility for determination. "Now the points on a line not yet actually determined are mere potentialities, and, as such, cannot react upon one another actually; and, *per se* they are all exactly alike. . . . [T]he possibility of determining more than any given multitude of points, or, in other words, the fact that there is room for any multitude at every part of the line, makes it *continuous*" (3.568). And a bit earlier, 1898, Peirce refers to a continuum as a "potential aggregate of all the possibilities that are consistent with certain general conditions" (6.185). He refers to components of a continuum as individuals that are determinable, although not of a distinctive quality for each individual. They are distinguishable by virtue of relations into which they may enter (6.187–8).

Infinitesimals, then, are the conditions for determinations, which is an affirmation of what Peirce says even later, in 1902, in defining the term *synechism:* "A true continuum is something whose possibilities of determination no multitude of individuals can exhaust" (6.170). The continuity of the continuum, then, is not constituted by individuals. And there is always room for further determination. Now, given the earlier statement about how individuals may differ from one another, it seems that an infinitesimal is a possibility. It is a possibility for there to occur a determination that depends on a reaction marking a difference of relation or mode of connection and subsequently of quality that has intelligible character (a third over and above a first). As absolute, undifferentiated possibility, all components, all infinitesimals, that make up a continuum, retain the same character, that is, compose the same inner connections. And this character must be an instance of Firstness, which may be manifest in a first; that is, it may be an instance of Firstness such that it is some quality or qualitative aspect of a phenomenon. (It is also a degenerate third, because it is raised to interpretation with respect only to the identification of its character.) But as such and as the character of a continuum and thus of any infinitesimal belonging to the continuum, there is (as yet) no individuality that is assignable to any part of the continuum. Otherwise, the continuum would be broken. At the same time, each infinitesimal is the locus of tychistic possibility – of the spark for evolutionary development.

It may be helpful to apply this proposal about the discontinuities that may enter a continuum to the discussion in which Peirce appeals to continuity to develop his notion of the law of mind. The application focuses on Peirce's account of perception in "The Law of Mind." On the basis of his analysis of conscious perception, it may be inferred that in the succession of moments in an infinitesimal interval of perceptual consciousness, we have instances in which infinitesimal possibilities are initially brought into situations that are developing toward determination, and this progressive determination is the formation of a perceptual judgment. Possibility of determination of an initial experience becomes a potentiality in process of actualization. This growth, however, cannot be merely an increase in the intensity of the character of an experience that is an instance of perceptual consciousness. Perceptual consciousness includes perceptual judgment, which itself includes an increment of abduction or of creative growth in general, which is an outcome of spontaneity. Thus, perceptual consciousness is evolutionary and not merely subject to quantitative or mechanical change. Within the continuity of perceptual consciousness, there is a point of reaching an "extremity" or "a point of branching" – a "defect of continuity" (4.219). For differentiation enters as the passage moves from one interval to a second and in turn to a third. And it is in the transition from the second to the third ("mediate") interval of perceptual consciousness that the moment of interpretation is initiated. This is to be expected, for the introduction of interpretation is the introduction of judgment and thus of abduction, which marks the emergence of spontaneity. However, there is no break in the perceptual act as a whole, because there is no break within the continuity of the perceptual consciousness of the immediate present. Rather, the break or defect is at the point of branching, which is internal to the process of being perceptually conscious. It is my suggestion that the branching is introduced at the point of the transition between the second and third intervals. It is here that a direction or a tendency begins in contrast to the sheer brute pressure introduced at the moment of transition from the first to the second interval.

The upshot of the brief account of the role of continuity and infinitesimals in general as well as of the role of continuity in perception is that perception and process generally occur in continua that must include "defective" moments by virtue of branching. In perception, the so-called defect is inevitable if abduction is conditioned by spontaneity. Thus, out of pure Firstness that is present in the first interval, Secondness arises as the second interval contrasts with the first and opens perceptual consciousness to the pressures of the dynamical object. From this point, there is initiated an abductive branching that occurs with the third moment. The branching arises as the dynamical object ceases to pressure or simply press itself on consciousness and is given direction by an abductive leap toward generality. Generalized to the level of cosmology, this description of the relation of spontaneity to continuity suggests that spontaneity in the universe may occur at the branching, or junctures at which uniformities are transmuted into other uniformities. This unquestionably means that continuity is not exhaustive of the cosmos. Peirce does not claim that continuity is so exhaustive. He says rather that continuities are of prime importance; but so are instances of spontaneity. Both continuity and spontaneity are constitutive of the universe through the function of infinitesimals. These are the infinitieth possibilities that leave uniformities open to branching and the universe open to new laws.

Conclusion

As a conclusion to this chapter, it is appropriate to comment on the main theme of this book, the theme that has driven the discussion to my speculative suggestions about the unique kind of realism that undergirds Peirce's architectonic. In order to focus on this theme, I shall not attempt to review the discussions in the various chapters. Nor shall I attempt to summarize Peirce's philosophy as a whole. I have made no claim that the intent of the book is to present an exposition or critical account of Peirce's entire philosophy. It seems to me that such an undertaking would and should take several volumes. I have neglected many topics that fit into the network that Peirce has partially made explicit and that, in my opinion, he has suggested throughout his career as a single, unified view. For instance, I have not examined Peirce's classification of the sciences, although the hierarchical ordering of them has been brought to bear on some of the discussion of the priority of phenomenology and mathematics in philosophical thought. I have not treated Peirce's logic of abduction, except insofar as this conception of inference has entered what has been said about spontaneity in thought as expressed in human perception and inquiry as well as in the cosmos. I have not addressed, except in passing and indirectly, the issue of relating the idea of the final and an ultimate interpretant in semeiotic. Nor have I considered one of the ways Peirce views the end of inquiry, as concrete reasonableness and as conditioned by the summum bonum.[34] The list of omissions could go on – perhaps into the infinite future. However, I have tried to organize and emphasize what I think are the most crucial dimensions of Peirce's philosophy in providing a framework for

[34] I have dealt with some of these issues in articles that have not been mentioned in connection with the discussions of the various chapters of this book. The question of value, the summum bonum, and concrete reasonableness were treated in "Value and the Peircean Categories," *Transactions of the Charles S. Peirce Society* 15, no. 3 (Summer 1979), pp. 203–23.

his envisaged architectonic. And I have tried to lead progressively to what I think is the fundamental grounding of this architectonic, his synechism.

We might speculate about a hierarchical structure within which pragmaticism, semeiotic, phenomenology, evolutionary realism, and synechism take appropriate places. Such speculation would be dangerous. Peirce's architectonic is formed by a sufficiently interdependent arrangement of components that it is questionable whether it is proper to say that one component has priority over another. Yet he saw philosophy as structured by an order in which some parts build on other parts. Thus, it does seem to me that his phenomenology, insofar as it articulates the categories as the most pervasive structure of all phenomena and all that is real, actual, and possible, deserves a somewhat more general, if not more fundamental, role than any specific dimension of his thought – except, in a sense, his synechism. I say this because I think it is synechism that condenses the two poles of overarching tension and gives content to the form provided by the categories. Spontaneity in the face of uniformity in the continua that make up the universe furnishes the spark and stability that makes the universe dynamic and intelligible. From instances of spontaneity flow an evolutionary reality rendered amenable to the semeiotic grasp that intelligence may gain on the ways of the universe. These are the ingredients of the categories: spontaneity itself manifest in Firstness, effective through Secondness, and intelligible through the uniformities to which it contributes in instances of Thirdness.

With this in mind, and without attempting to suggest a hierarchical structure for the envisaged architectonic, I should like to reiterate the point that pragmaticism and semeiotic may be understood as dependent on synechism and its exhibition in evolutionary realism. Pragmaticism, it was indicated earlier, is Peirce's pragmatism cleared of arbitrariness and subjectivistic elements that may enter into one of the directions in which the maxim may be taken. Pragmaticism is a metaphysical realist basis for determining meaning through inquiry and in the long run; and ideally, it is the basis for determining truth. At the same time, it is the determination of meaning and, finally, truth as conceived in terms of semeiosis. Semeiotic should not be separated from pragmaticism – all thoughts are signs. And both pragmaticism and semeiotic presuppose the categories in the general structuring of what these "sciences" are about. However, pragmaticism and semeiotic would be themselves lacking in a basis – would be dangling components in an architectonic – if they were not tied to Peirce's evolutionary realism. In turn, the categories need the evolutionary realism as content for their formal function. This again directs us to what I think is the one fundamental dimension of Peirce's architectonic, the synechism. For it is in synechism that spontaneity and uniformity show themselves. Applied to pragmaticism, the synechistic conception of infinitesimals as potentialities for new continua (new laws) underlies the way spontaneity shows itself in the abductive or hypothetical innovations possible in inquiry, whereas the synechistic conception of continuity, as uniformity that contains infinitesimals, shows itself in the laws that hypotheses lead inquirers to discover and construct. As I tried to show, it is in infinitesimals that branchings of continua or uniformities (laws) originate. This is why, in inquiry, such branchings are at the core of hypothesis formation, or abductive leaps.

Applied to semeiotic, the conception of continuity as uniformity shows itself in symbols, or the mediating, interpretant signs that provide stable relations in an ongoing process. Applied to semeiotic, the synechistic conception of infinitesimals underlying spontaneity shows itself in the intrusions of iconic innovations and indexical compulsions that contribute to the breeding of new symbols. However, most important, I think, is the function infinitesimals have in semeiotic as the potential for breaks in the manifestation of the dynamical object, which intrudes itself through the compulsiveness encountered in instances of Secondness and in constraints on interpretation that come from conditions other than those the source of which lies in the sign interpreter. It seems to me, then, that the expression and evidence of a conditioning, compulsive source that is the function of the dynamical object can be understood in terms of the potential departures made actual in the points marked on a continuum or order or law – points that are the actualizations of infinitesimals. These suggestions are obviously highly speculative. I offer them as one picture of an architectonic that is incompletely articulated – perhaps inevitably so in an infinite long run.

Let me conclude with a comment about the need for further study. Are there many particular dynamical objects for each referent of a sign – for each object of a finite investigation? Or is there only one ultimate dynamical object, suggested in passages cited earlier – for instance, the "object of unlimited final study" (8.183)? The former notion of a plurality of dynamical objects seems called for by Peirce's accounts of Secondness and the determining function of objects of signs and in the "external" constraints that are present in finite situations. One could, of course, construe these as a plurality of manifestations of a single, ultimate dynamical object that functions as a telos in many ways. This possibility, however, does not seem to me to be consistent with the tychism in Peirce's conception of evolution. The compulsiveness of the dynamical object is multiple and open-ended. However, if there are many individual dynamical objects, then how are these related to the constraint of the ideal limit, which is that point

at which an ultimate dynamical object would exercise its ultimate constraints – *if* such a point *were* reached? This issue has appeared also
in considerations of whether Peirce's conception of convergence is
multiple as well as final. Are there finite contexts in which a convergence is a condition for settling belief? If so, would such a convergence be subject to reinterpretation (found to be mistaken or at least
incomplete and premature) if an ultimate convergence were reached
in the long run? The architectonic I have tried to characterize for
Peirce seems to affirm the last alternative, but with a fundamental
qualification. This qualification rests on Peirce's fallibilism, now applied to the foundations of his system. In other words, the idea of a
final convergence is an idea of an ideal limit. It is not metaphysically
actual. It is instead a possibility, and a possibility of a peculiar kind,
for it is a possibility whose actuality is its unactualizability. Spontaneity
is an essential ingredient in reality; thus, fallibilism is an essential ingredient in knowledge. Perfect regularity is excluded. And we should
expect convergences to be provisional – provisional to an unactualizable possibility, because it inevitably recedes into the infinite future.

5

Evolutionary Realism and the Linguistic Turn

The conception of Peirce's envisaged architectonic can be projected beyond the context of the late nineteenth and early twentieth centuries. The projection with which I am concerned springs from two architectonic conceptions dealt with in the earlier chapters: semeiotic and evolutionary realism. These conceptions may be applied to current interconnected controversies over the possibility of deciding between metaphysical antirealism and realism and between relativism and antirelativism in interpretation theory, which for Peirce falls under the domain of semeiotic.[1]

Our main responsibility will be to see how Peirce's philosophical outlook avoids some of the consequences of recent attacks on the possibility of affirming realism. These considerations, in turn, have a bearing on the question of whether interpretation (in art criticism as well as in theoretical investigation) has a grounding outside texts and theories.

In the following remarks I shall respond from a Peircean perspective to the challenge that metaphysical assumptions about reality or extralinguistic objects and systematic speculation about all actual and possible experience are nonsensical, futile, or at least outdated. Philosophies that have dominated Western thought until the early twentieth century – and, indeed, have persisted in some circles in this century – presuppose a metaphysical or epistemological realism or an objective idealism (whether they are set forth in terms of these labels or appear as integral to rationalisms, empiricisms, and philosophies that suppose that there are noumenal or extraexperiential conditions of thought). These views share the assumption that there is something sufficiently objective to serve as a foundation that warrants rational argument and possible conclusions about which single perspective on experience or the world is more intelligible than another. The challengers to philosophies committed to the rationality of such contro-

---

[1] I have, in another place, applied Peirce's semeiotic to the issue whether interpretation can be given objective grounding in the context of the way in which metaphors may have extralinguistic and extraconceptual referents. *Metaphor and Art: Interactionism and Reference in the Verbal and Nonverbal Arts* (Cambridge: Cambridge University Press, 1989), appendix.

versies reject the idea that there is "a more comprehensive outlook," "a metavocabulary," a "common space," or a "neutral scheme," or a "God's-Eye View" by which cultural, moral, and generally, philosophical, differences can be assessed and settled. Rorty, for instance, comments on historicists who are relativists about the conception of "such a thing as 'human nature.' " He contends that they presuppose "a more comprehensive philosophical outlook that would let us hold" opposing human desires "in a single vision." However: "There is no way in which philosophy, or any other theoretical discipline, will ever let us do that."[2]

The challengers to traditional philosophical views have made "the linguistic turn" and have adopted an epistemological relativism or some form of pragmatism (not pragmaticism), deconstrucitivism, or existential philosophy. They base their attack on the assumption that traditional philosophical orientations presuppose a neutral, comprehensive vision of reality that can be supported by criteria of truth or adequacy. Thus, they accuse traditional philosophies of attempting the hopeless task of reaching a state of thought that is about a world or an object that is independent of thinking in any finite context of inquiry. Concepts or language is to be matched or made increasingly adequate, depending on philosophical "school," to an objective, structured thought in general that transcends particular systems of thought, to noumenal conditions about which valuational or normative reasoning is possible (although to which understanding has no access), or to a structured reality that is independent of thought in general. From a Peircean perspective, this conception on which the attack is based is an overdetermination of one's expectations of confronting reality.

One assumption shared by the insulation views in their objections to the tradition is an antifoundationalism. What they oppose is a foundationalism that may be traced to Cartesianism, but which also extends to views that have inadvertently failed to escape the clutches of rationalists' foundationalisms – for instance, empiricisms that depend on assuming that sense-impressions are discrete sense-data on which knowledge is built. In any case, the shared antifoundationalism carries with it the goal of leaving behind both objective idealism and traditional (if not all forms of) realism.

The opposition to the metaphysics of the tradition takes a variety of forms, depending on the method and aim of the linguistic-conceptual insulation view. From the standpoint of semeiotic, antifoundationalism appears as antirepresentationalism. This form is defined by the objection that thoughts or signs are not representational

[2]Richard Rorty, *Contingency, Irony, and Solidarity* (Cambridge: Cambridge University Press, 1989), pp. xiii–xiv.

of an independent world – or are not texts needing grounding in what is extratextual. Signs of course do represent, but what they represent is more signs and only signs – never a part or an aspect of an independent reality. An interpretation of Peirce as a linguistic idealist could be accommodated to this form of antifoundationalism. The forms of the insulation view that can be characterized as antirealism assume an opposition to metaphysical commitment. This is the perspective from which I have characterized the general position of antifoundationalists – the position that rejects the idea that there is some independent world or reality that grounds theory and interpretation. The epistemological form denies that truth is decidable in terms of the correspondence of sentences or concepts with an independent reality. This form overlaps, or is interdependent with, the metaphysical viewpoint.

Our attention initially will be focused on the most radical antifoundationalist challenge that the hope of language-independent criteria is futile and that we should accept the limits and contingencies of our linguistic situations. These radical challenges appear in the way contemporary controversies converge on questions concerning whether philosophy can be sustained as an autonomous discipline. In place of traditional realism and idealism, the antifoundationalist, at least the more extreme kind, affirms radical contingencies, which are supposed to reign in both inquiry and in the world, which itself is known only as a linguistic construct. Language constructs texts that are not controlled or constrained by independent conditions or stable contexts to which the texts may be expected to be adequate. Such antitraditionalists' views conflict with the idea that truth is a legitimate aim of philosophy, for they reject the aim of understanding a reality or system of thought that is independent of language and concepts. For them, truth might be thought to be made, not found.

The more radical philosophers to be considered are Richard Rorty and Donald Davidson. In addition, brief attention must be given to Quine, who raises an explicit objection to Peirce. A slightly lengthier consideration will be given to some of Hilary Putnam's proposals for preserving what for him is a form of realism. His alternative to the contingency views is, I think, also an alternative to Peirce's realism, and it helps to show the uniqueness of the Peircean view. A response to these representatives of the rejection of metaphysics will indicate what seems to me to be at the heart of the various controversies, including those raised by metaphysically oriented antifoundationalists – Dewey, perhaps, and extreme process philosophers, particularly Europeans, such as Bergson – who want a metaphysics without the foundationalism of the tradition. Thus, if Peirce's evolutionary-semeiotic-realism can avoid the contingency-view conclusion, it also avoids other antifoundationalist challenges.

The Peircean response to the radical antifoundationalist or contingency view will be undertaken in four stages. The first will be a brief overview of the general challenge and a sketch of the Peircean response. The second stage will consist of an account of those aspects of Rorty's contingency view that bring out the fundamental issue. The third stage will treat the main points of Davidson's proposals about how to avoid what he sees as the traps of traditional "scheme–content dualisms." It will be suggested that Davidson's view is closer to Peirce's realism than may be immediately apparent. The fourth concern will be to see in what respect Putnam's view is responsive as an alternative to Peirce. His differences from Peirce will show most sharply what I believe is the proper Peircean response to the contingency view. In connection with one of the explicit rejections of at least part of Peirce's view found, in particular, in Rorty, it will be helpful also to consider an objection of Quine's to Peirce. The discussions within each stage will include some critical observations from a Peircean perspective. Finally, I shall summarize the respects in which a Peircean view of what is knowable, that is, his evolutionary realism, avoids the main objections that have been raised by the antifoundationalists and thus offers a way to reaffirm the aims of traditional philosophies without succumbing to the difficulties the challengers find in them.

Before pursuing these challenges and the response in somewhat more detail, it may be appropriate at the outset to mention a crucial point that may have occurred to the reader. Peirce's overall philosophical outlook in a sense is itself antifoundationalist. The previous chapters make this evident, for he rejected Cartesian, Kantian, and Hegelian affirmations of foundations that ground thinking on what has antecedent status – in the case of Hegel, this antecedent ground is implicit, for the Absolute turns out to be what is developed in accord with its internal logic. As we have seen, in place of such foundations, Peirce looked to the future, to a fallibilistically knowable foundation – an evolving ground that is foundational as an ideal limit. It is with the special character of this fallibilistic foundation in mind that I believe that the attacks on foundationalist thinking and on realisms miss the mark where Peirce is concerned. If Peirce's idea of evolutionary realism is accepted, then an extraconceptual, extralinguistic ground can be given for theory and interpretation that is not subject to the critiques of Davidson, Rorty, and Putnam, who agree in rejecting views that assume that there is some independent metaphysical ground.

An Overview of the Issue

This overview of the major issue and a Peircean response to it may be developed by consideration of why I think that the contingency theorist's rejection of realism assumes an "overdetermination" of the referent of language. The main reason for the opposition between a human world, the world according to conceptual and linguistic conditions, and a so-called nonhuman world of reality independent of concepts and language (an opposition referred to by Rorty as a seesaw) is that the tradition of philosophy, at least insofar as this tradition is committed to metaphysical realism, is portrayed as a quest for a structured world, "on the other side of language." Putnam, for instance, says, "Metaphysical realism presents itself as a powerful transcendental picture: a picture in which there is a fixed set of 'language-independent' objects . . . and a fixed relation between terms and their extensions."[3] This fixed world, this side, is said to be inaccessible because it cannot be known apart from our languages and perspectives. Thus, it is impossible to show how it makes an epistemic contribution to language, or to interpretation. In the sense that there is no "external" source for what is known and knowable, the intelligible world, this side of Rorty's seesaw, has no other source than human thought and action. The world that is intelligible is given its structure *as if* it were made or created by "us."

One approach to the issue raised by this picture is indicated by the question of whether the human world must be regarded as made in the sense of a pure creation ex nihilo. In human creating, discovery is inseparable from the generative act. Control is shared between creative actor and what is acted upon. The condition of discovery controls the activity as well as does the creator, and it is this discovery condition that is in question. In the present context, this discovery condition is that for which tools are made. And those who reject this as an independent condition think that the tradition has construed it as something that functions as an antecedently determined, complex system. However, such a fully determined condition is not necessary to account for the constraints that compel the creative discoverer. This is a point that is crucial to the Peircean view.

I propose that there is a way off Rorty's seesaw, because what language, or interpretation, is expected to be adequate to is neither a nonhuman structured reality nor the essential structure of something human that is projected as an absolute. In other words, the straightforward correspondence theory of truth that serves as the brunt of the criticism that prompts the seesaw figure is a straw person from the perspective of my interpretation of Peirce.

According to this suggestion, there is an extralinguistic condition, a condition that in principle functions as an objective correlate of sentences. This condition may be named "reality" and the relation of it

---

[3]Hilary Putnam, *Realism with a Human Face,* ed. James Conant (Cambridge, Mass.: Harvard University Press, 1990), p. 27.

to some system of thought named "truth." The world, however, is not constituted by "furniture," or by brute facts supposed to consist of relations among atomic elements. This sort of world is a straw person, because it needlessly invites the obvious objection that inquirers cannot "get outside" their languages or vocabularies in order to gain access to the presumed furniture. My point is that the referent of language, or the intended "world" to which some language is directed, need not be regarded as well formed. One need not climb outside language or a vocabulary. One rather encounters resistance to the vocabulary that is not reduced to more vocabulary. In explaining the "linguistic turn" in philosophy, C. G. Prado argues that the pre-Copernican seamen who found that they did not fall off the earth where its flat surface was supposed to end could have revised the way they were willing to talk and believe. And they could have continued to insist that the world is flat if they had "readjusted their beliefs to allow for odd events.";[4] It must be kept in mind, however, that the initial condition that supposedly prompted the seamen to change or adjust their ways of speaking was not itself a change in the language, or in belief. The initial condition that they encountered was expressed as a resistance to their accepted language and belief. It was a resistance to expectations. The initial condition of this resistance was not language, even if its interpretation takes place in inescapable language or vocabularies. The seamen would have found it increasingly difficult to stick by their adjusted beliefs as they gained more experience. Their adjustments would not have been arbitrary.

The constraints given with resistances (the surprises and discoveries) do not guarantee that specific sentences are true or false, although they do function negatively to prompt the abandonment or modification of what were regarded as "true," or as justifiable and acceptable. What such constraints do is prompt changes that bring about evolution in thinking and language. What justifies the kind of changes is continued growing agreement, or at least the expectation that if the changes seem to be anomalies, they will eventually be reconciled – in future situations in which networks of beliefs or sentences fit together.

This idea of convergence is not quite what some of its critics take it to be. For instance, C. G. Prado refers to the pragmatists who affirm convergence as foreseeing a consensus to which science will inevitably lead.[5] On his interpretation, it is assumed that convergence is actually headed toward a fixed point on a fixed path. However, another way to understand convergence, and one that seems to me to be suggested

[4]C. G. Prado, *The Limits of Pragmatism* (Atlantic Highlands, N.J.: Humanities Press International, 1987), p. 10.
[5]Ibid., p. 18.

by some of Peirce's remarks, at least after the 1890s, if not earlier, is to regard the terminus of convergence as an ideal limit the ontological status of which is a possibility that is inevitably open to spontaneity and change. The path, then, is not fixed. Nor is the possible final network of judgments (or propositions) – the final object of a community of inquirers absolutely determined. For such a network of judgments lies in an infinite future, and it is about a reality composed of would-be's, or open possibilities. Only an ideal thought for an ideal, infinite thinker could select and actualize these in a final state; but this state is an ideal limit and no actual mind can reach this state – it can only approach it asymptotically. Any conception of a fixed point is an ideal limit that serves heuristically to ensure a "reason" to continue inquiry. The notion of the future as infinite is critical.

One might regard Peirce's conception of the ideal limit as a terminus of an indefinite future, assuming that indefiniteness leaves open departure from regularity – spontaneity in accord with tychism. However, the conception of indefiniteness is a species of indeterminateness that is subject to determinateness or closure of growth in an unchanging terminus. As argued earlier, this could be construed as a type of objective idealism, which Peirce considers to be a metaphysical view that excludes his first two categories. Further, as also argued, if there were a state of definite, determinate knowledge at a limit in the future, it will need to have as its "final" object would-be's, generals that are possibilities, so that the knowledge would not be frozen. Departures from would-be's could still occur. The limit is ideal and functions heuristically; at the same time, insofar as it functions as an actuality, a concrete terminus to be hoped for, it is an actuality that inevitably recedes into the future.

It is clear that part of a Peircean response needs to be directed toward this issue of an ideal limit, which was discussed in the previous chapter. However, this conception of an ideal limit is not the only one that is relevant to the way Peirce's evolutionary realism responds to the antirealist's objections. The antifoundationalists considered here set their sights only on this first part of Peirce's evolutionary realism. They highlight Peirce's commitment to the final opinion, the convergence of thought on an ideal limit – found in the ideal of comprehensive agreement. They overlook the second component, which is most evident in the importance Peirce assigns to Secondness and the dynamical object. The dynamical object is the condition for local resistances and constraints and the eruptions of spontaneous divergences. That is, it is a function of tychism. Thus, the function of the dynamical object for Peirce may be seen as a counter not only to the complaint about convergence at an ideal limit but also about the claims that linguistic contingencies are constrained by intralinguistic conditions, there being no hope of finding extralinguistic conditions on interpretation and particular theory changes.

The kind of process I have just suggested exhibits the structure of developmental teleology. In such a teleology, each purpose is initiated by an evolutionary spark manifest as spontaneity. The structure of the object of knowledge is always subject to development, but development that is not preestablished by an antecedently structured teleology. The basis for this development lies in the relation between language and the referent of language – the referent of language as a whole and of specific instances of particular systems of the languages as they are historically situated.[6]

Rorty's Contingency View of Language

Richard Rorty's contingency view is, I think, an integration of the variety of forms of antifoundationalism, and a summary of his view will make reference to the terminology appropriate to them. It will be helpful to begin illustration of the radical antifoundationalists as represented by Richard Rorty with part of a discussion found in Constantine Kolenda's careful exposition of Rorty's position. Kolenda says that for Rorty "there is no direct access to any kind of given; it always must be articulated in some vocabulary." Kolenda's summary statement identifies the key point of the objection to the traditional foundationalist's assumption that drives the linguistic contingency view: inaccessibility to an independent condition. Inaccessibility is a theme that runs throughout the antifoundationalist objections to traditional or classical realism. It is the core of the antifoundationalists' rejection. Thus, in discussing his differences with Putnam, Rorty says that he does agree with Putnam's recommendation that "we drop the notion of a God's-eye point of view," which presupposes an independent world accessible to a supreme intelligence.[7] Rorty also says there is no way to get outside our language.[8] And in criticizing the idealist rejection of realism, he says: "What was needed, and what the idealists were unable to envisage, was a repudiation of the very idea of anything – mind or matter, self or world – having an intrinsic nature to be expressed or represented."[9] Rorty makes clear that he is not saying that there is no world or that the world is simply made. Rather, he is saying

---

[6]Using Peirce's terminology as it is found in his semeiotic, the referent here serves as two linked conditions of interpretation or theory: as the immediate object, or the object of the sign as the object is represented, and as the dynamical object, or the object of the sign as it functions as a resistant and constraining condition.

[7]Richard Rorty, *Objectivity, Relativism, and Truth* (Cambridge: Cambridge University Press, 1991), p. 27.

[8]*Philosophy and the Mirror of Nature* (Princeton: Princeton University Press, 1979), p. 178.

[9]Richard Rorty, *Contingency, Irony, and Solidarity*, p. 4.

that truth is made, because truth belongs to sentences and "Where there are no sentences there is no truth"; "sentences are elements of human languages," and "human languages are human creations."[10] "The world is out there, but descriptions of the world are not."[11]

What, then, does it mean to utter the words, "the world," and what does it mean to entertain the idea that there is a world "out there"? Within languages, one refers to groups of sentences that are accepted as true. With respect to whole languages, "the idea that the world decides which descriptions are true can no longer be given a clear sense."[12] Entire languages – systems of sentences based on different axioms and fundamental presuppositions, such as those that governed the differences between the systems of Ptolemy and Copernicus or Newton and Einstein – do not change arbitrarily, because these changes are constrained by their own "weight"; changes in habit are "gradually lost," and language users gradually acquire the "habits of using others."[13] The relation of languages to the world (that does not determine their truth) is not clear – as Rorty himself suggests – but what can be said about this relation is crucial to what will be proposed as the Peircean response.

As we have seen, Rorty refers to a "seesaw" between two grounds for the adequacy of language: Language is understood as a medium that stands between "the nature of the human species" and "the structure of nonhuman reality."[14] He then draws on Davidson's view of language as consisting of various vocabularies, which Rorty describes as tools that may be more or less efficient. Thus, he says that vocabularies

are not the result of successfully fitting together pieces of a puzzle. They are not discoveries of a reality behind the appearances, of an undistorted view of the whole picture with which to replace myopic views of its parts. The proper analogy is with the invention of new tools to take the place of old tools.[15]

At least two problems raised by Rorty's recommendations are especially relevant to a Peircean response. The first was suggested earlier when we noted that the relation between language and a world "out there" is not clear. One way of clarifying the relation is to envisage an ideal limit of investigation at which the world would be fully and clearly accessible. Thus, the ideal of the convergent agreement in the final opinion seems to project a relation of convergence of language and an objective world. Rorty mentions this idea but rejects it.

[10]Ibid., p. 5.
[11]Ibid.
[12]Ibid.
[13]Ibid., p. 6.
[14]Ibid., p. 11.
[15]Ibid., p. 12.

He makes this explicit in a discussion in which he explains how Davidson avoids skepticism without falling into either physicalism or idealism. He says that Peirce's conception of an ideal limit of inquiry is one
way to accomplish the same purpose. This would provide an objective
grounding for investigation – the hope of a comprehensive knowledge of the world at the ideal limit. Rorty objects to this resolution
because he thinks that the notion of the ideal limit is unclear. Drawing
on Michael Williams, he says:

> The Peircean redefinition, however, uses a term – "ideal" – which is just as
> fishy as "corresponds" [correspondence to an independent object or reality].
> To make it less fishy Peirce would have to answer the question "How would
> we know that we were at the end of inquiry, as opposed to merely having
> gotten tired or unimaginative?" . . . Peirce's idea of "the end of inquiry" might
> make sense if we could detect an asymptotic convergence in inquiry, but such
> convergence seems a local and short-term phenomenon.[16]

He might also have referred to a similar criticism made by Quine:

> But there is a lot wrong with Peirce's notion, besides its assumption of a final
> organon of scientific method and its appeal to an infinite process. There is a
> faulty use of numerical analogy in speaking of a limit of theories, since the
> notion of limit depends on that of "nearer than," which is defined for num-
> bers and not for theories. And . . . there is trouble in the imputation of
> uniqueness ("the ideal result"). . . . Scientific method is the way to truth, but
> it affords even in principle no unique definition of truth.[17]

The Peircean response to these objections to the notion of an ideal
limit will be suggested after we have considered the other problems
raised by Rorty's contingency view of language as well as the views of
Davidson and Putnam.

The second problem Rorty's view raises concerns the question of
what can be said about why some tools are more efficient than others.
Rorty would reject this question insofar as it is understood in terms
of the traditional philosophical demand for criteria for determining
whether we have the "right" language, whether the language correctly represents the world or is fitting. The question of efficiency
should not be understood as a question about truth or conditions used
to justify the use of one set of linguistic tools rather than another.
However, the question concerning the efficiency of tools has force
apart from the traditional interpretation of it. Efficiency or inefficiency is a function of a causal connection between the language and
something else that may be thought of as a world. On the linguistic-
insulation view, any such world would need to be understood only by

---

[16]*Objectivity, Relativism, and Truth*, p. 131. His acknowledgment of the influence of Michael Williams is to "Coherence, Justification and Truth," *Review of Metaphysics* 34
  (1980), pp. 243–72.
[17]Willard Van Orman Quine, *Word and Object* (Cambridge, Mass.: MIT Press), p. 23.

some vocabulary. Yet if this vocabulary is the language that is the tool, then language is simply self-controlling, and the efficiency of the tool or language as a whole must depend on itself. And if the control or constraint on efficiency or inefficiency of the tool is the world, the effectiveness of the world as a constraint seems to be simply some other language, and another tool makes the first tool efficient or inefficient. In that case, we have not been told why the second tool is efficient. And it seems odd to refer to a world or to any independent condition that makes a vocabulary efficient or inefficient if that world turns out to be simply another tool or vocabulary. Rorty seems after all to be a linguistic idealist with respect to epistemological considerations, although his intention is to regard these as irrelevant. I do not see how these considerations can be separated from the question of whether we can indeed reject metaphysical conditions and (philosophically) get by exclusively with epistemic or purely linguistic conditions.

A consequence of Rorty's view that relates to at least one aspect of Peirce's semeiotic concerns the role that metaphor may play in vocabulary changes. Metaphors, as Rorty recognizes, are the instruments for vocabulary changes. They do not conform to old criteria of the efficiency of a language. They are needed to create new languages when vocabularies clash or need revision.[18] Rorty appeals to Davidson's conception of metaphor to elaborate on his own understanding of how vocabularies undergo creative change. The issues raised in his account pinpoint the traditionalist's reason for requiring the notion that language is not simply a collection of utterances, but is a system of utterances that articulates meanings, meanings that may grow through metaphorical shifts in the use of language.

The issue of what accounts for changes can be seen in Rorty's view that linguistic tools are used "for purposes of getting along in the world." What are the conditions that constrain and propel language users to "get along"? As Kolenda puts it for Rorty, the answer is that "Better and worse descriptions depend on success in connecting with already successful descriptions. And success is determined by . . . predictability and control."[19] However, this answer leads to the question of what conditions are correlated with predictability and control? To say that the conditions are parts of the world does not answer the question, because there is no way of knowing the world unless "the

[18]This need for metaphor to accommodate the need for creative change was suggested and discussed in my *A Discourse on Novelty and Creation* The Hague: Martinus Nijhoff, 1975) and developed at length in my *Metaphor and Art* Albany: SUNY Press, 1984; originally published, (Cambridge: Cambridge University Press, 1989). My purposes and conclusions, of course, differ markedly from those of Rorty.
[19]Kolenda, *Rorty's Humanistic Pragmatism* (Tampa: University of Florida Press, 1990).

world" is simply the constraining force of more vocabulary. After all, the constraints found in the consequences of successful predictions could not be the specific language itself, which is what is affected by the conditions.

The counter that the constraints appear in additional instances of language seems to me to overlook the way constraints occur when language uses are resisted and these uses undergo change. The resistances we encounter when we act on our expectations show something other than our linguistic responses affecting or conditioning those responses. Our ways of speaking change not only in connection with changes in custom; they also are sometimes forced on us when we can find no way to say what we mean. As pointed out, Rorty anticipates this point, saying that we then resort to figurative language in attempts to give adequate expression to something not in available language. The "noises" (as he puts it) that we search for are surely not needed merely because we like fresh noises. New noises are needed to respond intelligibly – in part, successfully – to surprises or resistances in what is experienced.

On Davidson's view, which Rorty follows, metaphors are unusual uses of words, different "noises," that do not articulate meanings, but provoke linguistic responses not correlated with prior uses of words. This view of metaphor, however, seems to me to fall short of why metaphors are needed, that is, in order to respond to pressures that cannot be handled by available language, or when new uses for words are needed. The issue raised concerns whether what is "new" is whatever is simply different (which might be a nonsensical or bizarre use of words) or instead is relevant or appropriate so that the pressures are responded to effectively. Either any response is as relevant as any other or, if one metaphor is more relevant than another, then it cannot be so exclusively because of the very changes that are regarded as relevant. Changes occur in a context that includes the limits of language when language is evolving.

It seems to me that it is at just these points of strain on vocabularies that the function of an extralinguistic condition is appropriately hypothesized. This claim might be construed as landing us back on one side of the seesaw, the side of a God's-eye knowledge of independent reality. And this in turn might seem to belie the conception of genuine (irreducible) newness. However, this is only the case if we overdetermine the object that is wrongly thought to be represented on this side of the seesaw. It is here that the Peircean notion of a dynamical object – the category of Secondness that manifests resistances that constrain and serve to compel thought, and the conception of an evolving reality – provides a step toward resolving the issue from the standpoint of metaphysics. With this Peircean extralinguistic or, for him, extrasymbolic condition in hand, I think we can avoid the seesaw – at least the one that Rorty describes.

Davidson's View

Donald Davidson raises the question of whether he shares without qualification a common ground with Rorty. He says in one place that he is willing to consider the question of whether we cannot "get outside our beliefs and our language so as to find some test other than coherence" for truth and knowledge.[20] Davidson does not think Rorty is willing to raise the question. The answer, of course, is crucial, because Davidson himself certainly does repudiate traditional realism. If there is a test of beliefs and language, if there is a world in which a certain situation must obtain in order for a sentence to be true, then we may ask what this world is that must be what it is in a certain way. Does it differ at bottom from Peirce's world of evolutionary reality? For Davidson as well as Rorty, however, this question is unanswerable. In order to see this, we need to expand briefly on Davidson's conception of the world, at least as I understand it.

Davidson insists that true sentences are true by virtue of situations in the world. For instance, for the sentence, "Snow is white," the situation by virtue of which it is true is that of snow's being white. Furthermore, Davidson qualifiedly rejects a correspondence theory of truth – the theory that beliefs are true because they correspond to something real or that can be confronted and compared with thoughts or sentences. His qualification is that there is "correspondence without confrontation."[21] Thus, he does accept a qualified correspondence rather than unqualified coherence theory of truth: "We can accept objective truth conditions as the key to meaning, a realist view of truth, and we can insist that knowledge is of an objective world independent of our thought and language."[22] In his discussion of the coherence theory of truth, he argues that coherence alone is not what gives sentences truth value. Rather, what gives truth value is the cumulative mass of accepted beliefs that serve as backing for individual sentences when these are consistent with that mass of beliefs. However, Davidson does not want to say just what serves as criterial conditions of the mass of beliefs. If the sentence "Snow is white" is true if and only if snow is white, it is not appropriate to ask, Is snow *really* white? This

---

[20]"The Coherence Theory of Truth and Knowledge," in *Truth and Interpretation: Perspectives on the Philosophy of Donald Davidson*, ed. Ernest Lepore (Oxford: Basil Blackwell, 1986), p. 1.
[21]Ibid., p. 307.
[22]Ibid.

question can only be understood as asking whether the sentence "Snow is white" coheres with the bulk of our accepted beliefs as these are expressed in sentences.

We might think that empirical evidence is relevant here. In a sense, for Davidson, it is. He does view interpretation as constrained by evidence that consists of "circumstances under which speakers hold sentences of their language to be true."[23] What are these circumstances? An example suggests an answer. He points out that a speaker holds the sentence "Es schneit" if and only if "at time t it is snowing at that time and it is snowing near the speaker." Yet whether a sentence is true, whether it is snowing at time t in a certain place, is inevitably determined with reference to the circumstances of the speaker, which in turn must be determined by the beliefs and attitudes of the speaker and his or her community. Thus, the evidence found in circumstances consists finally of having certain attitudes. What grounds interpretations of events and objects is a pattern of widespread agreement according to which speakers agree that sentences about these things can be asserted.

Similarly, Davidson does not see a need to say why the world is a certain way so that we can say that the majority of our collective beliefs is true. Instead, he tells us that they do not hang independently or autonomously by their own bootstraps, not because they correspond to a confrontational world, but because they can be understood with reference to causes: physiological, cultural, psychological. "What we have shown is that it is absurd to look for a justifying ground for the totality of beliefs, something outside this totality which we can use to test or compare with our beliefs."[24] We are left with a different kind of answer to the problem: "to find a *reason* for supposing most of our beliefs are true that is not a form of *evidence*."[25] The reasons consist of identifying causes for beliefs. And we are left without any settlement of the question of grounding or justifying the majority of our beliefs. Correspondence without confrontation is correspondence with more beliefs, and these are assessable only in the sense of describing their causes. Like Rorty's vocabularies, they seem to be contingent with respect to criteria – although not contingent with respect to causes. Davidson, then, assumes that there can be truth that is to be expected when the majority or totality of our beliefs is considered, but this is not to define truth by describing independent criteria that it must meet. This assumption about truth is based on the idea that truth is a primitive notion, as Rorty points out for Davidson. Thus, it is mean-

[23]*Inquiries into Truth & Interpretation*, p. 152.
[24]Ibid., p. 314.
[25]Ibid.

ingless to try to find "a basis of knowledge outside the scope of our beliefs." [26]

There is another question that arises, even if we abandon the idea of a belief-independent criterial condition. It is not clear what is to be included in the scope of beliefs that we cannot escape. Does it include what would be believed under unknown circumstances? Does it include what ought to be believed by an informed community? Does it include the instinctual beliefs that are often ingredients in common sense – and which are not always consistent with informed beliefs? Does it include future beliefs? If we distinguish these kinds of belief – once we refer to the scope (as a whole) of our beliefs, or the majority of our beliefs – it seems that we assume a perspective taken from outside the scope. This perspective can hardly be intended as a minority opinion – which it is, after all, given both "our" current opinions and our tradition of Western civilization. If, however, it is intended as true, then truth here is more than coherence with the majority of beliefs. Is it a God's-eye perspective?

Whatever may be said in answer to such questions, there is a sense, I think, in which Davidson commits himself to an answer to the criteriological question. His world functions in the way Peirce's does if we understand the world as independent from systems of signs and as a condition consisting in what for Peirce is the dynamical object. [27] One reason that Peirce's notion of a dynamical object is not immediately seen to be crucial to the considerations we encounter in interpreting the Davidsonian position is, I think, the status a dynamical object has as a term introduced in semeiotic. Using the notion to indicate an aspect of Peirce's evolutionary realism is to take it beyond a purely semeiotic function. The most general way of putting this is to say that it must bear the responsibility of moving, so to speak, from epistemology to ontology.

In any case, the Peircean way of understanding Davidson's "world" means that there is not, as Davidson makes clear for himself, a confrontation between beliefs and a world or an independent reality – "If meanings are given by objective truth conditions there is a question how we can know that the conditions are satisfied, for this would appear to require a confrontation between what we believe and real-

---

[26]"A Coherence Theory of Truth and Knowledge," p. 310.

[27]The possibility that Davidson's view is like Peirce's with respect to the functioning of dynamical objects or of the world was at least in part confirmed by some suggestions made by Christopher Hookway in a recent discussion I had with him about his response to this chapter. However, one needs to extrapolate from Davidson's view and engage in ontological proposals in order to find this common ground. One cannot affirm epistemological commitments and reject ontological consequences that may be added to these commitments.

ity; and the idea of such a confrontation is absurd."[28] For the world or an independent reality is not confronted as a structured system of objects represented by beliefs – which is the kind of confrontation that Davidson seems to believe absurd – but instead as a growing system of resistant and compelling possibilities. These are not confronted, if confrontation means being in a position of comparison between two realms. In other words, Davidson's world, which he is willing to affirm, is, I think, Peirce's dynamical object understood in the way I have suggested in the earlier chapters of this book. Davidson's picture of this condition, of course, is indirect and elusive. The "world" is whatever it is that can be referred to through a shaded window of sentences and beliefs. Beliefs about what? Whatever it is that the majority of our beliefs is about. We avoid confrontation because we have closed the shade. It should be noted that there is for Peirce a kind of confrontation. What is confronted – and this is where the Peircean view departs from Davidson's as well as Rorty's and provides a certain advantage that gives new meaning to traditional forms of realism – are resistances and constraints that are given directly in immediate experience.

Putnam's Realism

It should be emphasized that consideration of Hilary Putnam's views will be confined to those ideas that enjoin or challenge Peircean realism, as were the discussions of Rorty's and Davidson's views. This point is important here because the restriction is particularly appropriate for Putnam. His ideas have undergone changes – in his discussions and critiques of the views of others as well as in his own philosophical perspective. I shall not try to pin down what may be a statement about his overall philosophical position (which includes moral and social issues); however, attention will be given to what in the past few years has been a key to this position: his internal or pragmatic realism.

At first glance, Putnam's view seems to agree with the Peircean resistance to the spectator view of knowledge insofar as this is a reflection of Cartesian foundationalism. Further, Putnam agrees with Davidson, Rorty (and Quine and Goodman) in their pragmatic stance, namely, the rejection of a spectator view of metaphysics, or the idea that there is a God's-eye or neutral version of the world against which various versions of *the* world can or ought to be tested. Thus, he calls his view pragmatic as well as internal realism.[29] Further, as James

---

[28]Ibid.
[29]Hilary Putnam, *The Many Faces of Realism* (LaSalle, Ill. Open Court, 1987), pp. 20–21.

Conant says, Putnam has come to be increasingly accepting of Kant. And Putnam explicitly acknowledges that his "indebtedness to Kant is very large."[30] As has been pointed out in previous chapters, Peirce also acknowledges a debt to Kant. This does not mean, of course, that either Putnam or Peirce intend to affirm things-in-themselves. It does mean that they regard understanding as limited to the perspectives by which interpretation distinguishes ("cuts up") the world that is the object of interest. For Putnam, however, if there were one world, there could be more than one version of it. And there is no independent condition that makes one version more correct than another. Putnam's view is that "Internal realism is, at bottom, just the insistence that realism is *not* incompatible with conceptual relativity."[31] Thus, his view commits him to finding a "picture that enables us to make sense of the phenomena from within our world and our practice, rather than seek a God's-Eye View."[32] This "internal" stipulation, I think, is a version of Kantianism and allies him with one aspect of Peirce's semeiotic.

Putnam's internal realism can be seen in light of his treatment of the ideas of truth and reference. "That truth *is* a property – and a property which, unlike justification, or probability on present evidence, depends on more than the present memory and experience of the speaker – is the one insight of 'realism' that we should not jettison."[33] Putnam believes that *truth* can be attributed to theories, although he prefers to use the term *right* in place of *truth,* and he thinks that rightness or goodness belongs properly to "representations, various languages, various theories," when these are considered from specific perspectives, points of view, or contexts of assumptions about basic concepts that rule interpretations. Being right, however, is not a notion that applies to correspondence between descriptions and facts independent of theory and language. And being true is not a notion that intelligibly applies to absolute conditions: "Talk of there being 'absolute space-time points,' or sets 'really existing,' or 'not really existing,' I reject."[34]

With respect to reference, Putnam does accept the notion that terms refer to objects. In his account of reference in "Meaning, Other People, and the World," he seems to recognize (relatively) fixed objects.[35] Among these are referents of terms or expression such as *water* and *cat.* Further, these objects have constitutions: Water is H_2O or – on

---

[30]James Conant, in his introduction to Putnam's *Realism with a Human Face*, pp. xvii–xiv. Putnam's words are found on p. 3.
[31]Ibid., p. 17.
[32]*Representation and Reality* (Cambridge, Mass.: MIT Press, 1988), p. 109.
[33]*Realism with a Human Face*, p. 32.
[34]Ibid., p. 41.
[35]*Representation and Reality*, pp. 19–41.

Twin Earth, which is another possible place in which the term *water* refers to substances that have different chemical constituents – XYZ, and cats are constituted by a certain biological structure (different on Twin Earth). Thus, we should notice that Putnam contends that a factor in reference is the substance referred to – "the reference of the term 'water' is partly fixed by the substance itself."[36] Even though what is called water on the two earths behaves for practical purposes in the same way, and even though the Twin Earth and Earth dwellers have the same mental representations of the two substances, the reference of water on Twin Earth was and is different from the reference of water on Earth, because the substances are different. What is crucial in this criterion for being water is the behavior of the sample within its environment, which is a criterion that is independent of the mental representations of those who use terms to refer to samples. "*Meaning is interactional. The environment itself plays a role in determining what a speaker's words, or a community's words, refer to* [italics in original]."[37]

This account suggests a question about the independence of the environment and the objects in the environment in Putnam's position. It is clear that Putnam endorses a realist world of objects. However, these belong to his world regarded from a realist point of view where the term *realism* is spelled with a small *r*. This is a commonsense realism, not a metaphysical realism, spelled with a capital *R*. The difference between objects in these two senses of realism is in part evident in Putnam's view that the objects are not claimed to exist independently, in a world existing apart from humans. The difference is also evident when we see how the objects are fixed and what it is to claim that some statements about them are true. As we have seen, truth is not correspondence. Yet it is a property of interpretation. If water samples and cats do not exist independently of the uses and contexts of terms to refer to them, then truth or rightness of instances of referring or of interpretation in general depend on conceptual choices.

It seems to me that this point and Putnam's internal realism can be better understood if we turn to the disquotational account of truth according to which a statement is true if it affirms what is the case. For example, "snow is white" is true if and only if snow is white. That is, the statement in disquotational form is the affirmation of the sentence that initially appears within quotation marks in order to indicate that it is being mentioned rather than used. This tells us what it is for a statement to count as true, but it does not tell us whether what is affirmed is the case. We need other information for that, and there

---

[36]Ibid., p. 30.
[37]Ibid., p. 36.

seems to be no access to such information except through statements that interpret what statements mean. However, Putnam does not accept this disquotational account of truth as complete or as having rightly indicated what it is for a statement (or version) to be true. He points out that the term *truth* is sometimes used to say more than is said by simply affirming the statement that is thought to be true.[38] At the same time, he refuses to fall back on a conception of truth that requires that it be understood only by means of the "conceptual apparatus of the exact sciences."[39] Instead, he recommends that we understand truth as what is *"warrantable* on the basis of experience and intelligence for creatures with 'a rational and a sensible nature.' "[40] We can, then, still ask, Is there anything in or about the objects — about samples of water or cats (or snow) – that is not caught up in the conceptual perspectives that are presupposed by referring acts? The answer for Putnam, as far as I can determine, is no. This presumably is required by internal realism.

How, then, does Putnam's view differ (if it does) from the contingency view of Rorty and the pragmatic exhaustiveness of Davidson? We might find something granted to be independent from conceptual perspectives in Putnam's notion of *fact*. He says that no truth is *absolutely* conventional, for no truth is "free of every element of fact."[41] However, when we ask, What are facts? Are they somehow constitutive of metaphysical Reality? we find once more a renunciation of such a condition. "We can and should insist that some facts are there to be discovered. But this is something to be said when one has adopted a way of speaking, a language, a 'conceptual scheme.' To talk of 'facts' without specifying the language to be used is to talk of nothing."[42] What, then, are facts? The answer is that the determination of what is fact is a matter of degree. There are no "raw" facts. Further, there is no single conception of fact. Thus, in place of cultural relativism of the kind Putnam sees in Rorty's view, we have rather a convention relativism, by which I mean a kind of conceptual relativism, according to which no account of the condition of resistance to convention outside the conceptual assumptions is given. I am not sure, then, whether Putnam recognizes that there is any sort of constraint other than that within and dependent on conceptual perspective.

There is, however, one interesting point at which he suggests that he acknowledges a fundamental perspective or version of the world. After rejecting the idea of an "Archimedean point" by which one could

---

[38]Ibid., p. 68.
[39]Ibid., p. 70.
[40]*Realism with a Human Face*, p. 41.
[41]Ibid., p. 113.
[42]Ibid., p. 114.

know about what kind of objects exist in the world, he comments on the way two (or more) versions of the world are referred to: "It is possible to see how it can be that what is in one sense the 'same' world (*the two versions are deeply related*) . . . [my italics]."[43] What is this "deep relation"? Could this deep relation be a future or ideal final perspective, like Peirce's final opinion? I suppose that this is a question that Putnam would put aside − does, in fact, put aside if his aims in the place just cited are the same as those in another place when he says that he will avoid "deep" (metaphysical) issues that are associated with any philosophical view.[44] In any case, the deep relation must be consistent with a rigorously applied picture of internal realism. In this case, it could be a condition to which we have access only through some version (picture) − for Davidson, this would be through sentences we are willing to affirm by virtue of their coherence with the majority of beliefs held in our community. Or it might be a presupposed version of reality to be discovered or to be acknowledged explicitly in the future. However, there is a third option: For Davidson, it might be a condition that *functions as Peirce's dynamical object does.*

This option, I think, implies some additional account of internal realism. Without some such addition, I find it difficult to distinguish Putnam's view from Rorty's. We would need to suppose that the terms *relative to* and *internal to* make no sense at this level of building a picture of versions of the world. Philosophical argument falls by the wayside and we cannot expect to settle the issue with argument, as Rorty himself declares for his own contingency view at the beginning of *Contingency, Irony, and Solidarity.* Internal realism would then be one vocabulary along with others. Perhaps this is what Putnam has in mind in his modest claims that he only proposes a picture. Yet he does argue for this picture, and presumably he considers it more right at least than metaphysical realism, and for reasons not confined to its helping us to get along better in our culture, or to its being a more efficient tool. It must be a picture that has "idealized rational acceptability."[45]

In any case, it seems to me that if Putnam does recognize a constraint that is not exclusively internal to the controls of language and conceptual choices, then at this point his internal realism is a step toward Peirce's evolutionary realism. The internal reality Putnam affirms would be a reality for Peirce that is caught up in systems of immediate objects. If there is some extraperspectival constraint, then in Peircean terms reality consists in one of its functions in a dynamical object. This consequence, I think, raises again the point that the re-

[43]*The Many Faces of Realism*, p. 20.
[44]*Representation and Reality*, pp. 57−8.
[45]*Realism with a Human Face*, p. 41.

cent challenges to metaphysical realism have an overdetermined conception of what a metaphysical realism must affirm about reality. Before returning to further consideration of this point, however, let us pursue the issue of whether an internal realism may acknowledge something like Peirce's dynamical object. The issue can be raised in the form of a different question.

If versions of a world – not an independent, furnitured world – are relative to conceptual perspectives, to what are these conceptual perspectives relative? If reality is internal, it must be internal to versions of it that are controlled by concepts that are assumed by the use of the key terms that are used in the version – for instance, *space, point, mass,* and *object,* To what in turn are these conceptual assumptions external? What is *external?* The answer for Putnam must be that these conceptual choices are relative to more conceptual choices, which constitute what is external. To expect a single condition to which they are reducible implies an expectation of an answer that "makes sense *independently of our choice of concepts.*"[46] Thus, they are internal to themselves. How, then, can they share deeper relations? There seems to be another, deeper internal relation of one version to another version (although presumably nonneutral) that obtains within a larger context of externally related actual and possible conceptual choices. So Putnam's antimetaphysical realism resists all attempts to get outside what is internally warrantable. Let us then turn to the Peircean way outside.

I shall try to show how there are two ways outside: One is teleological and involves the notion of the ideal limit to inquiry in the long run – in the final opinion – and the other way is immediate and localized in instances of inquiry. The second way is overlooked or dismissed without comment, as far as I can determine. Special attention needs to be given to the first way, because it introduces the conception on which the antimetaphysical realists focus as if it were the only way Peirce's evolutionary realism is an alternative to their views. It is this conception that they subject to criticism. Moreover, the notion of the ideal limit of inquiry is one function of the dynamical object, which is the semeiotic dimension of the Peircean response. It will be helpful to begin with this point.

The Peircean Picture

The Dynamical Object as an "External" World

It should be emphasized that what has been said about the elusiveness of anything that constrains a version of the world – or, for Davidson,

---

[46]*The Many Faces of Realism,* p. 20.

the majority of beliefs in a culture, or what I have taken to be interpretations from the standpoint of a Peircean semeiotic – other than
additional versions, beliefs, or interpretations is not to say that we or
language or culture make the world. The world for Putnam, and I
take it for Davidson, is not a product. Nevertheless, we can only affirm our interests and values, our versions, our beliefs, our interpretations. A Peircean view, on the other hand, countenances affirming
something about the world insofar as it is an extrasemeiotic constraining condition (insofar as it is a dynamical object).

Peirce's world as independent of the worlds of immediate objects is
the dynamical object. However, the notion of the dynamical object has
two roles. One is teleological, as the dynamic end on which investigation or thought in general converges. Here it is the ideal limit referred to earlier. It also plays a role in Secondness, which is not teleological, although it can serve teleology when it enters agapastic
evolution. Its role in Secondness is to serve as a condition of local
resistances that propel thinking one way or another away from the
resistance, in some positive, constraining direction. What I am describing for Peirce is, of course, an account that is figurative, and, as
such, it clearly exemplifies what it is to be a picture of the world –
another picture that is an alternative to the metaphysical realists as
well as the antimetaphysical realists. It is one alternative to the view
that Putnam admits is his own picture and, I think, to what Davidson
and Rorty picture in accounting for language and their (pictured)
worlds. Let us return to the issue of whether it makes sense to entertain the idea of an ideal limit to investigation.

The Ideal Limit and Convergence

We have seen Rorty's objection to the ideal limit.[47] In that context, I
suggested that Rorty could have added a comment about Quine's criticism of this notion. This criticism should be noted before we expand
on a possible Peircean response to any rejection of his use of the notion in connection with the idea of final convergence. Quine's objection that the analogy is faulty assumes that the notion of an ideal limit
presumably is confined to mathematical notions. Aside from the issue
whether, if it was intended by Peirce to be only a mathematical notion,
it cannot be used intelligibly in an analogy, it should be observed that
there is reason to suppose that Peirce did not confine the notion to
mathematical status. The idea of *limit* in mathematics, or at least one
such idea, refers to something that cannot be reached. Therefore, it

---

[47]The crucial passage was quoted in Rorty's *Objectivity, Relativism, and Truth,* p. 131, n.
  12. All references in the following discussion of his objection to are found on this
  page. The entire discussion of Peirce in Rorty occurs on pp. 129–32.

should be unnecessary to qualify the term with the notion of its being ideal. In light of Peirce's qualification of the idea of limit with the adjective "ideal," it is plausible to conclude that he intended more than a mathematical notion. Of course, the notion still raises questions. Quine refers to a crucial one, namely the puzzling character of the infinite long run. The notion, as has been indicated and as will be further pointed out in the context of this discussion, is integral to Peirce's tychism. At some point, then, a decision must be made about where we are most intellectually satisfied about where we leave unresolved puzzles. Unresolved puzzles can be identified in any view that reaches toward the limits of what can be said in discursive language. Deciding where to leave them is one of the fundamental tasks of philosophy. In any case, without further development of Quine's criticism, it is difficult to respond to his criticism.

It is obvious that neither Davidson's nor Putnam's views are open to the notion of a definition of truth in terms of a final opinion at an ideal limit. The recommendation that sentences, beliefs, versions of the world, and so forth, be assessed in terms of the majority of beliefs held at a certain time or in terms of coherence with sets of conceptual presuppositions is of course in agreement with one side of Peirce's conception of truth. This is Peirce's view that inquiry is meaningful in terms of a community. One determines beliefs with respect to their agreement among themselves in a communal context. In such contexts, there can be convergences within limited particular communities at particular times (local convergences). However, the notion of a final convergence that would give a complete, systematic description and an explanation of all that there is to be described and explained is what is questioned, as we would expect, because it is a notion assumed to be affirmed by metaphysical realism. The final opinion at the end of inquiry is, for the antimetaphysicians, an external condition.

I assume that Davidson and Putnam would agree with Rorty's confession that he finds the notion of an ideal limit unclear or as he says, "fishy." He believes it is fishy because Peirce does not make clear how we would know that we were at the end of inquiry, or that the opinion reached corresponds to reality. It is interesting that Rorty adopts – and I think rightly – the realist interpretation of the final opinion here. For he might have demanded that knowing that inquiries are at an end is not concerned with whether one's opinion corresponds to reality but instead is concerned with whether one's opinion is a complex, internally coherent whole. On this idealist interpretation, one would know that the opinion is final if one could be aware of all components of the whole, their connections within the system, and their stability or freedom from intrusion. In any case, what is needed, Rorty says, is that "we could detect an asymptotic convergence in inquiry." He thinks such convergence "seems a local and short-term phenomenon." I should like to set forth two interdependent responses to this critique, assuming that these responses cover what I think are the kinds of objections that both Davidson and Putnam would raise along with Rorty. The first concerns the objections raised to the notion of an ideal end. The second concerns the idea of convergence.

I do not see how to counter the point that it is not clear (that it is "fishy") how we could know that we were at the end of inquiry, if the "we" refers to finite inquirers at any assignable time. Although Rorty does not explain his use of the term *know* in this context, presumably, the term has some relation to a reflexive state in which knowing is a state of believing (free of error) and being aware of the believing (free of error). Given this interpretation, it does seem that no *individual* and no finite loci of intelligence would be certain of being in a state of finality with respect to the totality of beliefs, or the opinion that is final. Only a supreme intelligence could be (or come to?) such a state, if such a state is attainable. We are back to the notion of a God's-eye view. For Peirce, such a supreme intelligence would be a supreme community in which individuals are submerged and resistances, Secondnesses, no longer function. I take this community to be at least one of the ideas Peirce has in mind when he writes of God. God would be the final intelligence.

One point concerning Peirce's view seems clear, however. The notion of the final opinion is an ideal, and it is not proposed as a state that ever will in fact be attained. If one objects that as long as it is unattainable, it is to that extent unintelligible. This extent of unintelligibility, however, is consistent with Peirce's tychism, which is a component of his conception of evolution. Moreover, it can be countered that the open-textured aspect of the notion of the final opinion is no more unintelligible in principle than is the notion of a general when we recognize that generals are open-textured with respect to their instances – no multitude of individuals can exhaust them. In any case, the unattainability of the final opinion has two sides. First, as an ideal, it is not proposed as an actual state. It is a regulative, normative notion that gives reason for continuing inquiry when our momentary fixed system of beliefs meets with resistance. At such moments, further investigation is appropriate. Why? Because future convergence and settlement of doubt is expected; otherwise we would stop short and concede that we must learn to live with this particular challenge to belief. A temporary convergence of agreement, as temporary, would be followed by disruption or challenge, some resistance recalcitrant to the agreement, and further inquiry would be invoked with the hope of convergence of agreement in the future. If it makes sense to try to reestablish harmony in our beliefs and harmony in the relation of those to our environment at any finite moment when resistance arises, it makes sense to suppose that such efforts should be undertaken in the future, even though this is a future that has no foreseeable end – except ideally if some state with no resistance *were* reached. This is implied, I think, by the idea of asymptotic progress toward an end in the infinite future. Asymptotic movement is toward a receding terminus, an idea to be mentioned again later. The persistence of our pursuit of finite goals in which agreement and convergence are sought inevitably implies more such goals, unless we believe that at some point a radical unresolvable bit of Secondness must prevent this. I do not think Peirce would regard such a belief as long-lasting. Not only would it counter our demands for rationality, but sooner or later it would be caught up in a larger system of regularities as inquiry advanced. This side of the final goal on the Peircean view suggests that to imply more goals is to imply goals without end, an infinite future of goals all envisaged under the umbrella of an ultimate goal. In this respect, Secondness, as a category, is everlasting; it is an ingredient to be encountered into the infinite future. This persistence of Secondness, however, is not the persistence of any particular instance of Secondness. And a final goal, as we have seen in the earlier chapters, is something never to be reached at a finite time. It lies in an infinite future. Yet it is *recommended* that the goal be pursued, because this mobilizes the intellect at any particular moment at which it is challenged.

What I have just suggested concerns the aspect of the final opinion in which it serves as an ideal that lures inquiry and is not an actual state that one should expect to reach. In making this point, however, another side of the notion of unattainability emerges. This other side is that an ideal limit as a determinate object of thought that is not itself receding but that is not reached because the series of steps that approach it include negative increments as well as positive increments (as $pi/4 = 1 - \frac{1}{3} + \frac{1}{5} - \frac{1}{7} + \ldots$).

As Mary Hesse has suggested, even though there are radical revolutions in science such that divergences seem more fundamental than convergences, natural science also seems to be pragmatically progressive. Predictability in local contexts of applied theories is not overturned and excluded from the whole of science, that is, from the interconnections of different particular branches of the sciences. Progress is possible, although this possibility does not require convergence of the conceptual framework toward a fixed, universal, final truth. There is always room for further conceptual revolutions.[48] This conception

---

[48]See, for instance, *Revolutions and Reconstructions in the Philosophy of Science* (Blooming-

of an end never to be reached, however, seems to be more than a purely regulative ideal; it is a hope that *cannot* be reached because of the contingencies of our encounters with phenomena, or data. And I think this way of looking at the final opinion is consistent with Peirce's intentions.

Peirce did propose the final goal as something more than a would-be, an unactualizable ideal. He saw it as a hope. Hope is more than a purely intellectual conception of possibility. This suggests that there is an actual, concrete state to be expected. However, this expectation is thwarted by the prospect of an infinite future. The Ultimate Would-be does not lose its status as a would-be – that is, its instances are never exhausted. Its ideality and its role in actuality as it takes its bite on the life of the inquirer are merged.

It seems to me that this picture makes sense. I must confess, however, that it does so by introducing difficult conceptions that in various forms have been puzzling to philosophy since its inception. These are the ideas of *infinite* and *counterfactuality,* the latter being crucial to the idea of would-bes. The antimetaphysicians might well have had these in mind in not considering Peirce in more detail as an alternative. Nevertheless, the counterfactual notion, puzzling or not, can hardly be avoided in any view, antimetaphysical as well as metaphysical. And Putnam himself suggests that he at least does not throw out counterfactual notions completely when he is willing to resist rejecting the meaningfulness of some objects that are not reducible to individuals. This is to assume an openness to the would-be of a general.

The second response to be proposed concerns the idea of convergence, which is the substance of the notion of an ideal end. Rorty asks for evidence (something "detectable") for asymptotic convergence of inquiry. In the same sentence in which he raises this question, he adds that "such convergence seems a local and short-term phenomenon." There are local convergences, and Rorty seems to grant this. He does not see this as evidence of long-term, asymtotic convergence, however. In other words, short-term convergence is not evidence of final convergence. It is not clear, however, why short-term or local, asymtotic convergent agreements are not evidence for long-term, infinite asymtotic convergence. For if these local convergences are asymptotic, they are candidates for being evidence; they are something "detectable" concerning asymptotic convergence at least somewhere in inquiry. If Rorty believes they are not evidence, surely this is not because he believes that local convergences are perfectly closed, reached, and finally terminated. The point of contact would then cease to re-

ton: Indiana University Press, 1980), esp. p. 158, and Michael A. Arbib and Mary B. Hesse, *The Construction of Reality* (Cambridge: Cambridge University Press, 1986), pp. 147–70.

cede, and the convergence would not be asymtotic. An asymptotic progress in agreement would occur only up to that point of contact, but this would be nonasymtotic, if being asymtotic is to advance toward an end that is out of reach in principle. On the other hand, if local convergences are asymtotic, then even local convergent agreement is not perfectly realized. And this leaves open the prospect of continued progress into the future.

It is possible, although unlikely, that Rorty believes that local convergences are irregularities in the steady development of theoretical interpretations – agreements intrude or disrupt overall growth in science. Thus, they would not count as evidence for long-run asymtotic progress. However, this would not be sufficient to preclude continued approximation toward a receding goal. Peirce thought of the progress of inquiry as subject to disruption, as his tychism makes clear.

Suppose, then, that Rorty does not deny that local convergences can be asymptotic. Why do local convergences not serve as at least a partial detection of asymptotic convergence in inquiry? The reason Rorty does not recognize this, I suppose, is that he does not regard finite asymptotic convergence as evidence that asymptotic convergence is infinitely continued. Perhaps, then, it is the puzzling notion of infinity that gives us trouble. There may be another reason that he does not recognize the long-term convergence. Scientific revolutions of major proportions, such as the revolution in which the Einsteinian world view might be thought to replace the Newtonian, show us that science may have as many divergences within it as it has progressive agreement. Whether Einstein's world "replaces" Newton's is moot. It may incorporate Newton's, giving it a place for a special range of calculations. However, I shall not attempt to tackle this issue. Suffice it to say that the idea of long-range, overarching converging agreement is not a dead conception among scientists and philosophers of science. The issue is alive. And surely there is something properly called *progress* in science, which implies approximation to goals, even though these may change and be replaced by different goals, just as different theories replace (without necessarily demolishing) old theories. (Even if one says that such progress is only technological and not conceptual, it is not conclusive that technological convergence of agreement does not incorporate some underlying concepts that suggest fundamental conceptions are headed somewhere, even if it is not evident now just where they are headed.)

It is interesting that in a footnote Rorty appeals to the possibility of conceptual scientific revolutions as a way of rejecting the detection of asymptotic convergence.[49] Peirce would be the last to deny that there

---

[49]*Objectivity, Relativism, and Truth*, p. 131, n. 12.

are such revolutions. Rorty must recognize this, for he adds to his note: "To insure against the indefinite proliferation of such revolutions in the future one would need something like Peirce's 'metaphysics of evolutionary love.' " This is exactly what "one" does have if we are taking into account Peirce's overall view. And along with this goes the evolutionary conception of tychism, of spontaneity as a constituent of the world, of the *dynamical* object, of irregularity in the midst of regularities, of departures from law (concepts however fundamental) – of agapastic evolution. However, what is even more significant for Rorty's criticism of asymptotic convergence is that it overlooks the way Peirce's agency of agape is driven by an openness to the infinite presence of disharmony in the universe – to the injection of secondness, spontaneity, which is never overcome (as Peirce thought it was for Hegel). Thus, instead of insuring against the indefinite proliferation of revolutions in the future, the notion of evolutionary love opens up the future to continued revolutions. It does this, however, while holding up the ideal of perfection as a final goal that is not actually final – that is perhaps better called *a finalizing goal.*

We noted at the beginning of the consideration of the Peircean picture as an alternative to Putnam's and antimetaphysicalism in general that there are two ways outside the insulation of internal realism, or more generally outside the insulation of linguistic contexts. The discussion has focused primarily on the notion of the final opinion or ideal limit of inquiry as one of the ways out. The second way has been suggested within this discussion. It arises in connection with a condition associated with local convergences. As was suggested earlier, the condition is that which is present in instances of Secondness, of resistance in individualizing circumstances, in moments of spontaneity and departure from law. Let us turn to this second way out in the Peircean picture.

Local Extralinguistic Constraints

The key to the role of local extralinguistic constraints is Peirce's idea of Secondness. According to this category of experience, there are moments of resistance that present themselves as at least partially independent of symbolic signs, or the intelligible systems of mediated signs – a system of interpretation. In the sense of not being reducible to this system, these resistances are extrahuman. This is not to say that instances of resistance are not relevant to human beings. Obviously they are. One need not appeal to the inhuman or nonhuman – that is, conditions "cut off" from human conditions – in being a metaphysical realist, at least in Peirce's sense of realism.

In this connection, it should be kept in mind that Peirce led the way in pointing to the context-bound and theory-laden character of beliefs, specifically in his account of the interpretive elements in perceptual judgment. Yet the contexts of interpretive schemes that affect thought are not fixed schemes. They shift. This is the evolutionary dimension of his realism as it applies to the semeiotic. The shifts that occur are not "made" by the shifting system itself. If they were, there would be no intelligible *change* in the shifts. There would be no growth. One condition of growth is the dynamical object as it is experienced in Secondness. This is an extrasymbolic, and in that sense, extralinguistic element in interpretation. It is in the Secondness of semeiosis that brute reaction functions in indexicality.

I take it that the antimetaphysical realist would not deny the presence of resistance as a phenomenally given item in experience. Opposition arises when it is proposed that at least some of these instances are more than purely human conditions, conditions that are extrahuman and thus extralinguistic. It might be proposed that the resistances encountered might be instinctual drives, unconscious motives, accepted beliefs so deeply ingrained in those who encounter them that they seem to be external to the deliberative, rational agent. If this is the reason given for denying that there are extrahuman conditions that affect interpretation or inquiry – vocabularies and linguistic habits found in the weighty mass of the majority of accepted beliefs – then it is appropriate to keep in mind that we have a theory, not a piece of evidence. This is not to say that evidence is wholly independent of theory, but is to call attention to the point that what is immediately experienced, that is, what prompts the claim that unconscious beliefs and so forth are responsible for what is experienced, is the resistance, the compulsion that is encountered in spite of one's will. Whether the condition of the resistance encountered is unconscious belief or an extrahuman dynamical object is hypothesized in terms of one's picture of the world. The unconscious-belief hypothesis is a denial of the dynamical object that is based on a different picture of the world or of the general character of human experience. It is a theory that is not incompatible with a strong component in Peirce, who does affirm the powerful role of instinctual beliefs and habits, many of which one is not aware. However, he also affirms the role of the compulsive act of nature on human thought. Nature has its own rules, and departures from rules, which are its own in the sense that what we react to is not limited to what is confined to human habit. If this were not so, spontaneity would not be a general feature of things in conjunction with continuity. The gaps between continuities are not limited to the gaps within human behavior.

This point about spontaneity might be interpreted as subjective, as moments when there are departures from belief-habits at the conscious level. If this is proposed as an alternative to the dynamical object hypothesis, beliefs are supposedly subjective, which must be to view them as mental events located, although not necessarily also unshared, in private consciousness. However, unless this interpretation adds further interpretation concerning what conditions the departures, it is only a claim that spontaneity is arbitrary deviation, and this alone does not imply subjectivity, for it says nothing about the resistance and constraints that are introduced spontaneously; it says nothing about the condition of the departures.

If instead it is said that the departures are eruptions of unconscious beliefs, beliefs not known to be elements of one's system of conscious beliefs, then the proposal may be assuming an underlying metaphysical idealism in which implications necessitate departures in an ongoing evolution toward an absolute. If the proposal does not assume this, then it must assume that unconscious unnecessitated beliefs erupt arbitrarily. The resistance encountered would be an arbitrary deviant belief. Its constraints and contribution to a change in the system would be an accident. For these alternatives that suppose underlying system or arbitrariness, the question arises as to what is different about the unconscious belief condition from the condition referred to as dynamical object. Why call the condition of spontaneity, of brute resistances as well, unconscious belief rather than an extrahuman, dynamical object? And here, I think, what decides the answer depends on a total picture of the world.

In Peirce's picture, one does not need to view the unexpected resistances that lead to a change in theory as themselves implicit theory. Or, from the standpoint of commonsense, experience, one does not need to view the pressures of the pavement on my feet as resistances of my belief. Closer to commonsense, one can view those pressures as extrasubjective things that contribute to what I form as my system of beliefs. Beyond commonsense, however, I do not need to conclude that the pressures I feel are prestructured, determinate objects that make up the so-called furniture of the world. With Peirce, I need only suppose that there is a dynamic condition imposing itself for me and the human community to interpret, adding to the picture structures for these resistances in terms of the ways the resistances constrain our interpretations as we build out the system of signs by which the dynamical conditions of our interpretations are interpreted. This picture simply seems more in accord with both commonsense and science than does the subjectivistic proposal that only more beliefs constrain us.

The advantage of this picture over the antimetaphysical realists pictures is that it cuts between the idea of an overdetermined independent world for a systematized, complete God's-eye viewing and an immersion within a view that admits nothing that has a status independent of human interpretation. Peirce's picture provides in principle a place for a condition that is not insulated within and subject to the contingencies of conceptual or vocabulary choices. It addresses the "deeper" issues directly. That is, it enjoins metaphysical hypothesizing that has endured since Thales in Western civilization, proposing a metaphysical realism that is not subject to the objections that hinge on seeing metaphysical realism as requiring a God's-eye view that is determinate and systematic. It acknowledges the contingencies of interpretation, but it finds a place for these, not stopping short of such acknowledgment in fear of not being human, picturing a world that is exhaustively human. Peirce's picture recognizes what is vital to those who have taken the linguistic turn and those who have become more Kantian than Kant. It affirms the need to turn away from a spectator view, but without abandoning something valuable in that view: the acknowledgment of constraints on our communal and individual habits, constraints that "we" do not make. It seems to me that this affirmation at least has a higher heuristic value than the other views.

Conclusion

One question that the Peircean response raises concerns whether there is any practical difference between the linguistic and conceptual insulation views and Peirce's picture. Putting aside the role of convergence on an ideal limit in the infinite future, and concentrating on bounded time intervals when local convergences may occur, it may be said that there is no difference between the Peircean and the antimetaphysical realist pictures with respect to what we do when we accept (or reject) a set of beliefs or one version or vocabulary rather than another. However, I think there is one difference; it lies in the Peircean picture of conditions for the pressures, the resistances, that are not exhausted by the formal or internal constraints of the system but are manifest in reactions falling under the category of Secondness. The antirealist view also admits resistances, but these are not the products of something other than what is pressured. Thus, if one reacts through the eyes of the Peircean picture, one is motivated and prompted differently. The picture one holds affects one's disposition to react. And one's disposition to react has practical consequences that include determination or will to resolve the conflict by looking in different ways, using metaphors that are headed somewhere and are not mere noises.

It is true that the sources in the Peircean picture are inscrutable. We can no more make the source intelligible in itself in the case of Secondness than we can in the case of the anti–God's-eye view. For the antirealist picture, however, the source proposed is also inscrutable, for the initiation of change through constraint is contingent and contingency itself is the source. Neither contingency, chance, nor any condition related to it, is itself understood as intelligible. There is nothing except the result of the contingent constraint that can be intelligible. The contingent shift just happens. The picture stops with it. What is beyond the picture remains unaddressed; and I submit that this restriction – that makes the point in the picture at which one is restrained from taking another step – is as inscrutable as Peirce's sources. Admittedly, whatever is claimed to be responsible on the constraints for the Peircean view also can be found intelligible only in its guise as an outcome of linguistic, conceptual interpretation. Nevertheless, the pressures of the constraint in the Peircean picture manifest themselves differently, even if they are not intelligible in the way they manifest themselves. This difference in ways of manifestation is a human way. It resides in a way available to one who discovers constraints that occur spontaneously, or at least as extraneous to what is expected, and that springs forth for one who uses the eyes provided by the Peircean picture. Thus, the constraints that are pressed out of brute resistance are heuristically colored. They are not recognized as merely contingent but rather as contingencies that occur as expressions of a dynamic condition that is integral to the larger picture in which there is evolutionary love.

Further, the Peircean picture offers a hypothesis to account for what is left unanswered for the antirealist, as long as the antirealist holds back from the "deeper" issues. The hypothesis suggests why some linguistic and conceptual changes become intelligible. This is the point of Peirce's claim that his hypothesis of spontaneity is an explanation in a broad sense. The occurrence of metaphors as instruments of language growth are not mere noises that *happen* to promote new intelligible linguistic and conceptual growth. They are not nonsense utterances that *happen* to succeed in persuading language users to change their ways. They are contributors – the sources of which are a dynamic (hypothetical) extralinguistic world.

If philosophy has the task of deciding where one finds puzzles most acceptably located, as I believe it does, then the decision I am recommending concerns where the puzzles should be located. If it is acceptable to "have pictures in philosophy," as Putnam thinks it is, then I am proposing that the Peircean picture is "better," because it fits more closely with at least what is heuristically effective and with what is phenomenally given, that is, what appears as external, compulsive resistance in experience. This is to say that evolutionary realism is a picture that is a uniquely human way of looking toward the extrahuman.

Index